Lecture Notes in Educational Technology

Series Editors

Ronghuai Huang, Smart Learning Institute, Beijing Normal University, Beijing, China

Kinshuk, College of Information, University of North Texas, Denton, TX, USA

Mohamed Jemni, University of Tunis, Tunis, Tunisia

Nian-Shing Chen, National Yunlin University of Science and Technology, Douliu, Taiwan

J. Michael Spector, University of North Texas, Denton, TX, USA

The series Lecture Notes in Educational Technology (LNET), has established itself as a medium for the publication of new developments in the research and practice of educational policy, pedagogy, learning science, learning environment, learning resources etc. in information and knowledge age, – quickly, informally, and at a high level.

Abstracted/Indexed in:

Scopus, Web of Science Book Citation Index

More information about this series at http://www.springer.com/series/11777

Daniel Burgos
Editor

Radical Solutions and Open Science

An Open Approach to Boost Higher Education

Editor
Daniel Burgos
Research Institute for Innovation &
Technology in Education (UNIR iTED)
Universidad Internacional de La Rioja
(UNIR)
Logroño, La Rioja, Spain

ISSN 2196-4963 ISSN 2196-4971 (electronic)
Lecture Notes in Educational Technology
ISBN 978-981-15-4275-6 ISBN 978-981-15-4276-3 (eBook)
https://doi.org/10.1007/978-981-15-4276-3

© The Editor(s) (if applicable) and The Author(s) 2020. This book is an open access publication.
Open Access This book is licensed under the terms of the Creative Commons Attribution 4.0 International License (http://creativecommons.org/licenses/by/4.0/), which permits use, sharing, adaptation, distribution and reproduction in any medium or format, as long as you give appropriate credit to the original author(s) and the source, provide a link to the Creative Commons license and indicate if changes were made.
The images or other third party material in this book are included in the book's Creative Commons license, unless indicated otherwise in a credit line to the material. If material is not included in the book's Creative Commons license and your intended use is not permitted by statutory regulation or exceeds the permitted use, you will need to obtain permission directly from the copyright holder.
The use of general descriptive names, registered names, trademarks, service marks, etc. in this publication does not imply, even in the absence of a specific statement, that such names are exempt from the relevant protective laws and regulations and therefore free for general use.
The publisher, the authors and the editors are safe to assume that the advice and information in this book are believed to be true and accurate at the date of publication. Neither the publisher nor the authors or the editors give a warranty, expressed or implied, with respect to the material contained herein or for any errors or omissions that may have been made. The publisher remains neutral with regard to jurisdictional claims in published maps and institutional affiliations.

This Springer imprint is published by the registered company Springer Nature Singapore Pte Ltd.
The registered company address is: 152 Beach Road, #21-01/04 Gateway East, Singapore 189721, Singapore

Foreword by Rory McGreal

Open science is a new concept arising out of the exponential growth in access to abundant scientific knowledge via the Internet and the World Wide Web in particular. This book is about openness and radical change. Daniel Burgos, the Editor, has a well-respected track record in supporting openness, and so is well positioned to ensure the relevance of the contributions in this volume.

It is often said that the only people who are desirous of change are wet babies. So, for educators living in this rapidly changing twenty-first century, acceptance of the realities of change may come with difficulty. In this book, the writers are not only desirous of change, but are also active proponents of openness, trusting that it will radically disrupt the established order in education, much to the chagrin of comfortable traditionalist instructors.

Such rapid change in education has not always been the case. The roots of science and science education are planted in the reality of knowledge scarcity rather than openness. When Hero of Alexandria, a mathematician, physicist and engineer, worked in the great library in the first century, other scientists and students could not access his knowledge without meeting directly with him in a room in the library (possibly the first classroom). His works later became available on scrolls, which were laboriously and expensively reproduced. They could then be distributed to other centres in a very limited way.

This limited access to knowledge was improved somewhat with the printing press and other developments, but real openness has only become possible now with the cornucopia of accessible knowledge available online to anyone anywhere who has an Internet connexion. Today, anyone with a mobile phone can access the Internet at a reasonable price in most countries. More than 90% of the world's population reside in communities with mobile access and most people have access to a mobile device. Of course there are limitations of language, culture and prior education; nevertheless, this represents an explosion in scientific openness.

Open Science is now supported by many if not most governments. Today researchers who receive grants from government agencies must place their papers online and have them accessible to the public. This has disrupted the educational publishing industry which has for long been highly profitable because they were the only gateway to knowledge and so charged institutions and individuals heavily for the privilege. These commercial publishers are guilty of 'openwashing' or claiming to support openness in order to maintain their closed commercial practices. They are deliberately closing off access to knowledge in order to create a false scarcity.

This collection of chapters on openness introduces the reader to relevant views on openness and its affordances for disruption of the academy and society. Chapter themes include investigations ranging from ethical issues in learning analytics to open educational resources, to prosumerism and its effect on disabled learners, as well as issues related to intellectual property rights. The challenges to openness as presented by the authors are disturbing, whilst at the same time intriguing. The authors are approaching the problems associated with openness suggesting possible solutions to support the transition to more open educational access. Open science is rapidly becoming the norm opening up access to knowledge, despite the efforts of commercial interests hoping to forestall it. The chapters in this volume point the way to preserve and expand openness with up-to-date research that points the reader in a positive direction.

Prof. Rory McGreal
Co-Editor IRRODL

UNESCO/ICDE Chair in OER
Athabasca University, Canada
e-mail: rory@athabascau.ca

Foreword by Colin de la Higuera

Openness: Why Quality Matters

The very recent decision by the general assembly of the UNESCO to recommend the use of open educational resources (OER) is great news and will certainly contribute to a better understanding of these questions and to their adoption by more and more countries. It should encourage players at all levels to build and share courseware, distribute and redistribute OER.

Of course, open educational resources represent just one aspect of open knowledge. Open source, open access and open data all contribute to the same ideals. But, because of the specific nature of education, of the huge numbers involved, this is an important move. We should keep in mind that it is estimated that about 258 million children and youth are out of school today: all what allows a better distribution of knowledge is the right approach.

Yet if we can see many positive signs, many problems are still to be tackled. These are, of course, being looked into by NGOs, Universities, researchers and activists. Let us mention the cost model to be better thought out: is it necessary to remind that *open* doesn't mean *free* and that the costs should be met in such a way as not to create new barriers?

But, in my view, the most complex issue may be the one of handling quality questions.

1. This may not appear at first to be that essential, but it is. When discussing the matter of replacing traditional textbooks by access to open educational resources with local and national authorities, it is the elephant in the room! 'Who will control the quality?' is the question raised, or—worse—not raised but underlying all the decisions which are going to be taken on the matter. There have, of course, been occasions whether a severe blunder or even an unacceptable pseudo-scientific fact has crept into a textbook published by some well-known publishers, but the general feeling is that these are rare and, since there is a publisher, an origin can be found, responsibilities can be taken, errors can be traced and the problem can be dealt with. And, most importantly, the

responsibility of the authorities is not questioned. And understandably—in my opinion—they need to be reassured when it comes to OER.

2. A quality slip is something authorities are fearful of. And when actively promoting the use of OER we should have our answers ready. Here are some possible answers:

   A. We can argue that the type of control proposed in the context of traditional publishing doesn't really exist. The editorial boards are made up mostly by people who all have some form of hidden (or not hidden) bias.
   B. We can argue that quality control can't be done because quality is essentially a subjective matter and that from an open point of view we should not reject an open textbook just because we don't like it. Perhaps this OER suits someone else. Furthermore, one goal of open education is to empower teachers and students, so we should really work on giving each the tools to better decide by himself. This position is either naive or irresponsible. In both cases, it will not make the problems disappear.
   C. We can address the problem, in all its complexity. We should address it with researchers. Easy solutions exist: a resource which is good is necessarily of quality, ergo all we have to do is measure popularity.

   Instead of popularity, we could measure engagement. If we can see that the material is being used, this is a sign of quality: we can certainly do this with videos which are usually streamed.

And, essentially, we should keep in mind the crucial question of **serendipity**. A system in which quality is the unique judge may backfire: as there will be a close connexion between quality of a resource and quality of the institution, interesting OER may find it difficult to get proposed, read and consumed. Serendipity is necessary for openness. The whole idea is to empower the creators of new resources. And if this means that the resource, in an open world may be invisible to others, is not 'given its chance', then the open education movement will have to deal with a new problem.

So the quality question is far from being solved and no simple path exists. This should stimulate the interest of researchers from many fields to come up with solutions which will aim at preserving all the benefits of open educational practices.

In this volume put together by Daniel Burgos, Unesco Chair at UNIR, a variety of questions are scrutinised and even when answers are given, the inevitable—and highly desirable—result of research is that you end up with more questions than when you started. So let me just add the quality question to this increasing set and wish that the reader finds in these texts the inspiring ideas she may be seeking.

Prof. Dr. Colin de la Higuera
Chair in Technologies for the Training
of Teachers by Open
Educational Resources
University of Nantes, France
e-mail: cdlh@univ-nantes.fr

Introduction

Radical Solutions & Open Science: An Open Approach To Boost Higher Education is the 2nd Book in a Trilogy of texts that presents radical, innovative solutions for recurring issues in higher education. Every book is focused on a key major field, and each chapter presents a thorough state-of-the-art exploration in a specific topic. The aim of the Trilogy is to provide useful and timely assistance to university professors, researchers, policymakers and students to understand current and potential future challenges in higher education.

This second book has a focus on open science as a powerful tool to advance our thinking and practice in learning and teaching and research. It provides an opportunity for the reader to take time to think deeply about the concepts of openness and how they are applied more broadly. Specifically, the impact across numerous areas such as policy, accreditation, ethics, certification, content, research, data, technology and access to cite just a few.

Several well-known authors in the field were asked to contribute to this book and their work has undergone peer scrutiny to assure the reader of the value and quality of the chapters presented here.

Chapter 1 by Weller debates the meaning of openness and whether there is any crossover in definitions and practices. Chapter 2 by Stracke has focussed on open science. Presenting an overview of how open science can be represented across three science dimensions of research design, processes and publications. Chapter 3 is presented by Griffiths who has a focus on ethics and our use of data in our higher education institutions. A great debate around the erosion of what institutions might call 'ethical waivers' for educational improvement. But, the chapter questions whether this partial erosion is, in fact, ethical.

The focus of Chap. 4 by Affouneh comes from Palestine and takes an important angle on the basic human right for access to ducation. Whilst Amiel et al., in Chap. 5, debates the political consequences of receiving funding of open educational resources, imploring the reader to question how neutral or apolitical funding is or else a warning about misalignment or—worse—suffering the consequences.

Burgos, in Chap. 6, has a focus on research impact and the ways in which researchers go beyond the typical development of patents, products, etc. and that papers, conferences and presentations must also count in how we understand the ways in which we communicate about their work.

Cullen, in Chap. 7, has an interesting take on prosumerism and asks whether it is turning higher education institutions into 'McBusinesses'. Pursuing the argument through the lens of whether it works for accessibility and disability this is a timely read when exponents are seeking greater control of learning by students.

Educator competencies are highlighted in Chap. 8 of the book with Nascimbeni discussing plenty of detail about six competences areas that the contemporary educator requires to thrive in educational environments: personal data management, capacity to leverage the open web, ability to engage in intercultural digital dialogues, critical view on media and capacity to deal with digital ethical issues and with accessibility issues.

Chapter 9 is of my favourites and if you have been struggling with getting your MOOCs into the curriculum for all sorts of good reasons then this discussion by Cha and So will be of interest to you. A handy framework also looks at credit recognition and online learning that leads to three types of MOOC-integrated learning experiences: Type I—formal MOOC learning, Type II—formal blended MOOC learning and Type III—non-formal/informal MOOC learning.

Chapter 10 by Ramírez-Montoya is a wonderful case study of a collaborative with multidisciplinary teams of energy, production and educational innovation, who designed and implemented 12 MOOCs through the MexicoX and EdX platforms. Operating at scale more than 2,00,000 learners were involved and a huge army of educators, administrators and researchers reaping benefits for social communities, government, business and decision-makers who are likely to be interested in learning environments and open educational practices.

Chapter 11 by Hamza provides an interesting case study of the University of Bahrain and how the University is transforming to address the global, regional and national challenges it is facing today. Readers will find the key pillars and the key performance indicators of the Transformation Plan 2016–2021 very relevant to their own contexts in a changing technological society where our learners require new models of learning and teaching and research must show greater societal impact.

All up, this 2nd Book in the Trilogy will provide food for thought across several areas that are extremely relevant in the twenty-first century. They are representative of different cultural countries as well and provide a global perspective that we can all learn from. In a complicated world with increasing individualism and global issues such as sustainability, ageing, health and climate change amongst many others this time will be a good read for many educators and beyond.

Prof. Belinda Tynan
Deputy Vice Chancellor (Education) &
Vice President (2016-contuning)
Royal Melbourne Institute of Technology, Australia
Immediate Past President International
Council of Open and Distance Education (ICDE, 2017–2019)
email: dvce@rmit.edu.au

Book 2: Editorial

About Open Science and Open Education

Daniel Burgos
daniel.burgos@unir.net
Research Institute for Innovation & Technology in Education (UNIR iTED), Universidad Internacional de La Rioja (UNIR), Spain (http://ited.unir.net)

There is a key difference between Open, Universal and Free. In 2017, the OUF (which stands for those three concepts) system was officially presented at the 27th ICDE World Conference on online learning in Toronto, Canada, to a large community of open education believers (Burgos, 2017). Until then, there was a broad misunderstanding between the concepts 'open' and 'free'. I assume that most of the misconceptions came from the wrong identification of 'free' as a gratis thing, with no cost. Maybe I am wrong. The fact, however, is that many scholars, students and stakeholders working on open education overlapped both concepts: whatever is open is always free and vice versa. In addition, in the kick-off meeting of the Erasmus+ Capacity Building project OpenMed (in 2016, Rome, Italy), there was an initial debate between what the boundaries of open education were. We agreed that something (a resource, for instance) could be open, but not accessible to everyone, and still be granted as an open educational resource (OER) (Stracke et al., 2019). Lastly, the concept of open education has evolved considerably (Walberg & Thomas, 1971), especially from 2015 (Hilton, 2019). As long as the movement is getting broader and deeper, the nuances play a role. We have moved from just OERs to open educational practices (OEP) and, lately, to open science. There is large agreement about a number of pillars that support open education, resources being just one of them. We could name content, methodology, data, research results, policies, licensing, technology, access and more to come. This larger umbrella evolves the previous concept of OER, and the previous one of learning object (LO) (Polsani, 2003), or even unit of learning (UoL) (Burgos et al., 2007), to a new scenario, where every stakeholder is taken into account, and content is no longer the only input to deal with.

Open Science is Way Beyond Content

A number of aspects came to move the discussion to a slightly more advanced level. On one side, teachers show their interest in open education and how to integrate resources and methodologies into the daily life (Chen & Bryer, 2012; Gramatakos & Lavau, 2019). They realise that the combination of formal, non-formal and informal learning into one harmonised backbone provides a richer and more complex soil to deploy effective educational methodologies, learning strategies and tools. On the other hand, technology awareness makes that very technology invisible, so that the teacher, the researcher or the student can focus on what matters most, with technology being just a simple tool. In addition, other stakeholders, like content providers or policymakers, can play a key role in the open scenario, since they complement and foster the concept and practical applications of an open, universal and/or free product or service to the society.

Meaning of Openness

Openness is not just a theoretical approach or word-based powerful speech, but a practical and active project that requires specific actions in motion, as a polysemy. Part of these actions comes along with logistics, politics, management, finance and many other aspects of the same Rubik's Cube so that the project is successfully implemented (Transgeniclearning.com, 2017).

In doing so, we also must be cautious with what we promise. Usually, these declarations hold goodwill but lack a twist of realism. If we commit to open up 50% of the resources at university X by 2020 or 2030 (the last magical number in every official document, anywhere), we must be sure to reach that threshold by then.

That figure should mean an engagement that drives the specific steps to get there. We cannot spread around self-given and unrealistic figures, placed far away on purpose so that events can modify the route or the promise along the way, and nobody is held accountable (Huston, 2019).

This community of openness is usually accused of being idealistic and impractical, producing a lot of words but little usefulness (Contact Nord, 2012). If we incorporate criteria and actions beyond the words, like the ones afore-listed, and we draw a realistic and verifiable plan, like the ones afore-proposed, we could break the glass ceiling between 'foolish goodwill' and the 'too realistic to take "open" seriously'. Meeting at the middle point would make both sides part of the same project, since there is a balance to find, possible, and at hand reach, to enrich all for the best of education.

From Commitment to Action. From Action to Accountability

Out of this historical moment, with so many people working in good conscience to open up education, and in the spirit of UN SDG 4, we need to be specific (United Nations, 2012; Unterhalter, 2019). We, the educational community, the society, need to move from commitment to action (like the motto of the 2nd OER World Congress, 2017, in Ljubljana, Slovenia) as well as from action to accountability. We need to be effective, to provide resources and services, but also to apply metrics and be smart. We need to move from a feeling of goodwill to a calculated project management-based action plan involving milestones, resources committed, impact factors, key performance indicators, dissemination metrics, scalability and, above all, sustainability. A good conscience goes to sleep when a real problem comes to the table, or a family issue, or the lack of funding, or the increasing need to multi-task on the job. So, we cannot guarantee a long-term action if there is not a business model and a strategic plan behind all those remarkable efforts (Downes, 2007; Kalman, 2014; Daniel et al., 2015). It is our duty not just as visionaries and good people, but also practical stakeholders of the educational game. We need to get into accountable actions, leaving behind promises in good faith and embracing a well-equipped master plan in motion. This is the key to success. And, as educators, it is our duty.

References

Burgos, D. (2017). Into the open: A transgenic evolution of the educational system, at 27th ICDE World Conference on online learning, in Toronto. Canada. Retrieved December 23, 2019, from http://onlinelearning2017.ca/en/abstracts-and-presentations/.

Burgos, D., Tattersall, C., & Koper, R. (2007). How to represent adaptation in eLearning with IMS learning design. *Interactive Learning Environments, 15*(2), 161–170.

Chen, B., & Bryer, T. (2012). Investigating instructional strategies for using social media in formal and informal learning. *The International Review of Research in Open and Distributed Learning, 13*(1), 87–104.

Contact Nord. (2012). How really relevant and practical are open educational resources? A case for a little humility about the potential. Retrieved January 18, 2020, from https://teachonline.ca/trends-directions/beyond-open-educational-resources/how-open-and-free-content-transform-post.

Daniel, J., Cano, E. V., & Cervera, M. G. (2015). The future of MOOCs: Adaptive learning or business model?. *International Journal of Educational Technology in Higher Education, 12*(1), 64–73.

Downes, S. (2007). Models for sustainable open educational resources. *Interdisciplinary Journal of E-Learning and Learning Objects, 3*(1), 29–44.

Gramatakos, A. L., & Lavau, S. (2019). Informal learning for sustainability in higher education institutions. *International Journal of Sustainability in Higher Education, 20*(2), 378–392.

Hilton, J. (2019). Open educational resources, student efficacy, and user perceptions: A synthesis of research published between 2015 and 2018. *Educational Technology Research and Development*, 1–24.

Huston, J. (2019). Reinventing the mission: The vital role of academic support in the higher education accountability era. *Voices of Reform: Educational Research to Inform and Reform, 2* (1), 87–95.

Kalman, Y. M. (2014). A race to the bottom: MOOCs and higher education business models. *Open Learning: The Journal of Open, Distance and e-Learning, 29*(1), 5–14.

Polsani, P. R. (2003). Use and abuse of reusable learning objects. *Journal of Digital information, 3* (4).

Stracke, C., Downes, S., Conole, G., Nascimbeni, F. & Burgos, D. (2019). Are MOOCs open educational resources? A literature review on history, definitions and typologies of OER and MOOCs. Open Praxis, vol. 11 issue 4, October–December 2019, pp. 1–11 (ISSN 2304-070X). https://doi.org/10.5944/openpraxis.11.4.1010.

Transgeniclearning. (2017) Transgeniclearning.com, retrieved December 23, 2019, from http://transgeniclearning.com.

United Nations. (2012). United Nations, Sustainable Development Goal number 4, Education. Retrieved January the 17, 2020, from https://www.un.org/sustainabledevelopment/education/.

Unterhalter, E. (2019). The many meanings of quality education: Politics of targets and indicators in SDG 4. *Global Policy, 10*, 39–51.

Walberg, H. J., & Thomas, S. C. (1971). Characteristics of open education: Toward an Operational Definition.

About This Book

This book looks into a number of topics related to open science—from ethical and privacy issues to specific application cases in higher education; from the role of a user at university level to the integration of online technology in knowledge transfer and from the integration of resources into formal environments to diversity. The compilation of chapters provides a diverse view into a number of challenges and common concerns amongst the community members, with a clear drive to encourage discussion and foster an open approach to this very concept that is always polysemic depending on the context, the culture, the target and the stakeholders involved.

Open science is a powerful tool to boost higher education. The most frequent use of OER has led to a broader approach to the concept of openness. Resources are not enough since they require a full context to support an effective implementation. Open science addresses access, technology, data, research results, licensing, accreditation, certification, policy and, of course, content. The smart combination of these factors will provide the higher education system with a strong platform to integrate formal, non-formal and informal education. The teacher, the student and the educational manager will strengthen their competences and resources for a better understanding and performance of the learning and the teaching processes. This book brings together all these key topics through a selected set of blind peer-reviewed chapters written by expert players in the field—experts who present the current state of the art and the forthcoming steps towards a useful and effective implementation.

Contents

1 **Open and Free Access to Education for All** 1
   Martin Weller

2 **Open Science and Radical Solutions for Diversity, Equity and Quality in Research: A Literature Review of Different Research Schools, Philosophies and Frameworks and Their Potential Impact on Science and Education** 17
   Christian M. Stracke

3 **The Ethical Issues of Learning Analytics in Their Historical Context** 39
   Dai Griffiths

4 **A Hidden Dream: Open Educational Resources** 57
   Saida Affouneh and Zuheir N. Khlaif

5 **Who Benefits from the Public Good? How OER Is Contributing to the Private Appropriation of the Educational Commons** 69
   Tel Amiel, Ewout ter Haar, Miguel Said Vieira, and Tiago Chagas Soares

6 **Online Technology in Knowledge Transfer** 91
   Daniel Burgos

7 **Prosumerism in Higher Education—Does It Meet the Disability Test?** 105
   Joe Cullen

8 **Empowering University Educators for Contemporary Open and Networked Teaching** 123
   Fabio Nascimbeni

9 **Integration of Formal, Non-formal and Informal Learning Through MOOCs** 135
   Hyunjin Cha and Hyo-Jeong So

10	MOOCs and OER: Developments and Contributions for Open Education and Open Science............................ 159
	Maria-Soledad Ramirez-Montoya
11	The Response of Higher Education Institutions to Global, Regional, and National Challenges 177
	Riyad Y. Hamzah

About the Editor

Prof. Dr. Daniel Burgos works as a Full Professor of Technologies for Education & Communication and Vice-Rector for International Research (UNIR Research, http://research.unir.net), at Universidad Internacional de La Rioja (UNIR, http://www.unir.net), a young 100% online university with over 40.000 students, 1.500 lecturers, 300 researchers, and premises in Spain, Colombia, México, Ecuador, Perú, Paraguay, Bolivia, Argentina and USA. In addition, he holds the UNESCO Chair on eLearning and the ICDE Chair in Open Educational Resources. He also works as Director of the Research Institute for Innovation & Technology in Education (UNIR iTED, http://ited.unir.net). Previously, he worked as Director of Education Sector and Head of eLearning & User Experience Lab in the Research & Innovation Department of the large enterprise Atos (http://www.atos.net), since 2007, and as Assistant Professor at the Open University of the Netherlands, before that (Welten Institute, http://www.ou.nl/web/welten-institute/). In 1996, he founded the first postgraduate online school on multimedia training and user interaction (ESAC), with over 6.000 students, worldwide.

His interests are mainly focused on Educational Technology & Innovation: Adaptive/Personalised and Informal eLearning, Open Science & Education, Learning Analytics, Social Networks, eGames and eLearning Specifications. He has published over 140 scientific papers, 4 European patents, 14 authored books and 21 edited books or special issues on indexed journals. He is or has been involved in +55 European and Worldwide R&D projects, with a practical implementation approach.

In addition, he is a Professor at An-Najah National University (Palestine), an Adjunct Professor at Universidad Nacional de Colombia (UNAL, Colombia), a Visiting Professor at Coventry University (United Kingdom) and Universidad de las Fuerzas Armadas (ESPE, Ecuador). He has been Chair (2016, 2018) and Vice-Chair (2015, 2017) of the international jury for the UNESCO King Hamad Bin Isa Al Khalifa Prize for the Use of ICTs in Education. He is a Consultant for United Nations Economic Commission for Europe (UNECE), European Commission, European Parliament, Russian Academy of Science and Ministries of Education in over a dozen countries. He is an IEEE Senior Member. He holds degrees in Communication (PhD), Computer Science (Dr. Ing), Education (PhD), Anthropology (PhD), Business Administration (DBA) and Artificial Intelligence (MIT, postgraduate).

Chapter 1
Open and Free Access to Education for All

Martin Weller

Abstract Open education has evolved over time and now has different interpretations. Three main versions of open education are considered, namely open universities, open educational resources (OER) and MOOCs. These all aim to increase access to education, but have different approaches for realising this aim. The open education landscape is explored using a citation analysis method, to reveal that there is little cross-fertilisation between the distinct areas. In order to address this, a conceptual model is proposed, and the result of a global survey used to analyse the manner in which different institutions are exploiting aspects of openness to increase access. The author concludes that the diverse interpretations of open education can be seen as a benefit, if it allows institutions to assemble approaches for increased access that are tailored to their context.

Keywords OER · MOOCs · Open University · Distance learning · Open education · Open access

1.1 Introduction

In considering open access to education, it is necessary to review different aspects and interpretations of open education, and to then bring these strands together. This involves different approaches and perspectives in open education including open universities, open educational resources (OER), open textbooks and MOOCs. The historical starting point for the current open education movement is a difficult one to pinpoint, as the answer will vary, depending on the interpretation of open education. This highlights that what we mean by open education is not easily defined. It is probably best viewed not as a single entity but rather as a collection of approaches, intersecting principles and ideas. This section will draw out these principles and ideas, by focusing on the roots of open education. I would suggest that there are three key strands that lead to the current set of open education core concepts: open universities, OER and MOOCs.

M. Weller (✉)
The Open University, Milton Keynes, UK
e-mail: martin.weller@open.ac.uk

© The Author(s) 2020
D. Burgos (ed.), *Radical Solutions and Open Science*, Lecture Notes in Educational Technology, https://doi.org/10.1007/978-981-15-4276-3_1

1.1.1 Open Universities

Open access to education can be dated back to the founding of UNISA in South Africa in 1946, which pioneered a distance education model to open up education to those who could not attend traditional institutions. With the foundation of the open university in the UK (OU) in 1969 this model was expanded, and the open entry aspect made central. Open approaches to education can be traced prior to these two institutions, for example, through public lectures and movements associated with the industrial revolution, such as the Workers Educational Association (WEA) which was founded in 1903 to improve the education of the working class. However, it is the establishment of the OU and its model which was widely emulated worldwide that provides a reasonable starting point for consideration. Originally proposed as a 'wireless university' in 1926, the idea gained support in the early 1960s, and became a Labour Party manifesto commitment in 1966.[1] It was established in 1969 with the mission statement that it is 'open to people, places, methods and ideas'. The aim of the OU was to open up education to people who were otherwise excluded because they either lacked the qualifications to enter higher education, or their lifestyle and commitments meant they could not commit to full-time education. The university's approach was aimed at removing these barriers.

The need to expand access to higher education to those who could not access the conventional model became something many governments recognised, and the reputation of the OU for high-quality teaching material and a highly valued learning experience made the approach respectable. Tait (2018) notes that this model was replicated globally, with around 60 Open Universities being established, 'with the largest number being found in Asia, followed by the regions of Europe and Africa'. Notably, the model was not adopted in some large countries such as Russia and the US.

Cormier (2013) suggests the following types of open were important in the OU model:

- Open = accessible, 'supported open learning', interactive, dialogue. Accessibility was key.
- Open = equal opportunity, unrestricted by barriers or impediments to education and educational resources.
- Open = transparency, sharing educational aims and objectives with students, disclosing marking schemes and offering exam and tutorial advice.
- Open = open entry, most important, no requirement for entrance qualifications. All that was needed were ambition and the will/motivation to learn.

In this interpretation, open education was part-time, distance, supported and open access. Significantly, there is no particular stress on cost, so financially free access to education is not emphasised in this interpretation. Education was to be paid for by the respective government, and open universities were closely allied to whatever form of widening participation they wished to adopt. The emphasis was often on *affordable*

---

[1] http://www.open.ac.uk/about/main/the-ou-explained/history-the-ou.

education, but prior to the advent of the internet, the other forms of openness were seen as more significant. It was with the advent of open source software that 'open' and 'free' began to be linked or used synonymously.

1.1.2 Open Educational Resources (OER)

In 2001, the OER movement began in earnest when MIT announced its Open CourseWare initiative. MIT's goal was to make all the learning materials used by their 1800 courses available via the internet, where the resources could be used and repurposed as desired by others, without charge. The William and Flora Hewlett Foundation, who funded the MIT project, define OERs as:

> teaching, learning, and research resources that reside in the public domain or have been released under an intellectual property license that permits their free use and re-purposing by others. Open educational resources include full courses, course materials, modules, textbooks, streaming videos, tests, software, and any other tools, materials, or techniques used to support access to knowledge (Hewlett Foundation n.d.).

Note that free cost is now a key component, but also central to this definition is the stress on the license that permits free use and repurposing. In order to satisfy the definition, it is not enough to simply be free as in cost, it has to be reusable also. There are other definitions of OERs available (see Creative Commons, 2013a for a comparison of these) but even if they do not explicitly mandate an open license, they all emphasise the right to reuse content.

Lane (2009) notes that openness as interpreted by the OER movement centres around the freedoms offered by the associated open licenses:

- freedom from paying any money to access and use the content for specified purposes,
- freedom to copy and make many more copies,
- freedom to take away and reuse without asking prior permission,
- freedom to make derivative works (but not necessarily freedom to make profits from them).

This list varies from the one above, being focused on content rather than access to the educational system. In this conceptualisation, the OER movement perhaps owed more to the open source community in terms of influence than it did open universities. It grew out of the growth of the internet and digital technology in the mid-1990s, which caused many educators to examine different models of content creation and sharing. The precursor to OER was Learning Objects, which specifically borrowed from software development ideas of object-oriented code, to enhance reuse. But even though it borrowed little from the OU model, open access to education was a key driver for the OER movement.

For example, a JISC review of the various OER programmes in the UK identified five major motivations (McGill, Falconer, Dempster, Littlejohn, & Beetham, 2013):

- building reputation of individuals or institutions or communities
- improving efficiency, cost and quality of production
- opening access to knowledge
- enhancing pedagogy and the students' learning experience
- building technological momentum.

As the authors point out, these motivations are not exclusive and often overlap, and one of them explicitly relates to open access. Similarly, the Hewlett Foundation (2013) state five motivations for why they fund the OER field, the last of which again relates to open access:

- radically reduce costs
- deliver greater learning efficiency
- promote continuous improvement of instruction and personalised learning
- encourage translation and localisation of content
- offer equal access to knowledge for all.

This range of motivations is perhaps not surprising. Universities, including open universities, are themselves complex institutions that fulfil a variety of roles, including education, research, centres of innovation (Etzkowitz, Webster, Gebhardt, & Terra, 2000), public engagement, agents of social change (Brennan, King, & Lebeau, 2004), curation and preservation of knowledge and the presence of an independent, trusted voice. So, it should not be a surprise that open education should similarly have myriad roles and purposes.

1.1.3 MOOCs

The third main strand to explore for open access to education is the MOOC phenomenon. Collins dictionary defines a MOOC as 'a free online course that many people can study'. The nature of delivery and free cost are the main components in this definition. MOOCs had some relation to the OER movement, as early MOOC pioneers such as David Wiley and Stephen Downes had also been influential in the OER movement. However, it was with the deployment of MOOCs by Stanford Professor Sebastian Thrun on an Artificial Intelligence course, which attracted around 100,000 learners and subsequent interest from venture capitalists that MOOCs really came to public attention. The New York Times declared 2012 to be 'the year of the MOOC' (Pappano, 2012) and this had little to do with either of the previous two movements addressed previously. MOOCs were free to access, but they generally did not come adopt an open licence so their content did not boast the freedoms set out above for OER. Learners were largely unsupported, and so MOOCs did not adopt the Supported Open Learning model of the OU, which places an emphasis on the support of part-time tutors.

Several problems began to emerge with MOOCs after the initial enthusiasm, which saw a reining back on some of the ambitions. The key ones were:

- Low completion rate—with around only 10% of registered students completing, completion rates have been problematic for MOOCs (Jordan, 2014).
- Learner demographics—most successful MOOC learners were usually already well educated (Christensen et al., 2013), and this finding undermined claims of MOOCs democratising learning.
- Sustainability—as the MOOC production model became industrialised they required high-quality media outputs, and so their costs increased considerably, particularly when staff time, marketing and support were factored in Hollands and Tirthali (2014). Finding sustainable business models that justified this expenditure has proven problematic.

These issues saw a change in tone around MOOCs, with MOOC provider Coursera (2013) announcing that they were going to 'explore MOOC-based learning on campus'. This resembles conventional blended learning, or e-learning, but with a new platform. Similarly, Georgia Tech announced they were offering a masters-level MOOC which was not free (costing $7000), once again conflating online learning with MOOCs, and Thrun's company Udacity 'pivoted' to focus on corporate training.

Once the initial hyperbole had died away, more practical applications of MOOCs began to emerge. Although the demographics and completion rates remain an issue, millions of people gained access to education through them, finding this way of learning enjoyable and useful, often in areas that are very meaningful to individual's lives. For example, Farrow, Ward, Klekociuk, & Vickers (2017) report on over 11,000 participants in a MOOC on understanding dementia. There are also examples of their use in formal education to expand the curriculum, for example, the Delft University of Technology offers a 'Virtual Exchange Programme' whereby its campus based students can take MOOCs with other accredited providers, and receive credit at Delft (Pickard, 2018). It can also be argued that MOOCs raised the profile of open access to education within conventional universities, particularly in an online format. Even if MOOCs themselves are only open in terms of enrolment, and not in terms of licencing, their presence has created a dialogue around access to education in a digital age.

1.2 Mapping Open Education

These three strands all have in common a motivation to increase access to education, often for learners who are otherwise disadvantaged and denied access to traditional higher education for a variety of reasons. However, it tends to be the case that practitioners in each of these areas sees their view of 'open education' as the dominant or even sole form of open education. This has implications for how open approaches to education develop, for instance, Wiley (2013), Wiley and Hilton III (2018) who is concerned with the OER movement, defines open pedagogy as the 'set of teaching and learning practices only possible in the context of the affordances of open educational resources as enabled by the 5Rs' and talks of OER enabled pedagogies.

This posits open pedagogy as a function of OER, but the concepts and practices associated with open pedagogy have a longer history than OER. Peter and Deimann (2013) highlight open education practices stretching back to the Middle Ages with the founding of universities which 'contained in them the idea of openness, albeit by no means comprehensive. This period highlights 'open' as learner driven, resting on a growing curiosity and increasing awareness of educational opportunities' (p. 9). Any phrasing of open access education that highlights one form of open education, necessarily does so at the expense of another.

There is then a strong tendency to be self-referential in each of the strands mentioned, with little reference to other forms of open education. A preliminary systematic search (Rolfe, 2016) for 'open education' across a number of databases, retrieved over two hundred articles and revealed that there was an initial peak in the period 1970–74, with articles relating to the founding of the OU and similar approaches. The next significant peak in publications is found in 2010–15 as MOOCs, open textbooks and OER gain traction (Fig. 1.1).

Using a citation analysis method, the landscape of research in open education could be constructed (Weller, Jordan, DeVries, & Rolfe, 2018). This method proceeded by gaining an initial sample of 20 documents on the basis of literature database searches for items which referred specifically the history or definition of openness [('open education', 'open learning', openness) AND (history, definition)]. The references of these articles were then extracted, and the papers which were cited by at least two of the original sample items were then added to the sample to include their references in the next iteration. Although this process could be repeated indefinitely, four iterations were carried out as meaningful clusters had emerged at this point. At this point, the network included 5,217 references from a total of 172 publications. Using the social network analysis tool Gephi, a network of citations could then be

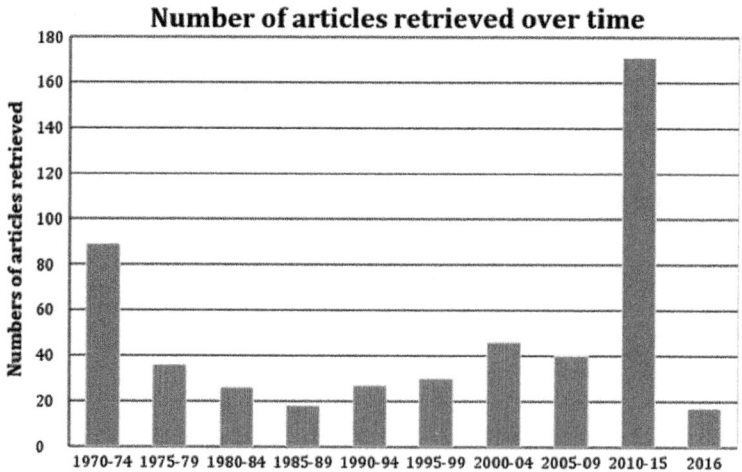

Fig. 1.1 Frequency of published articles on open education over time

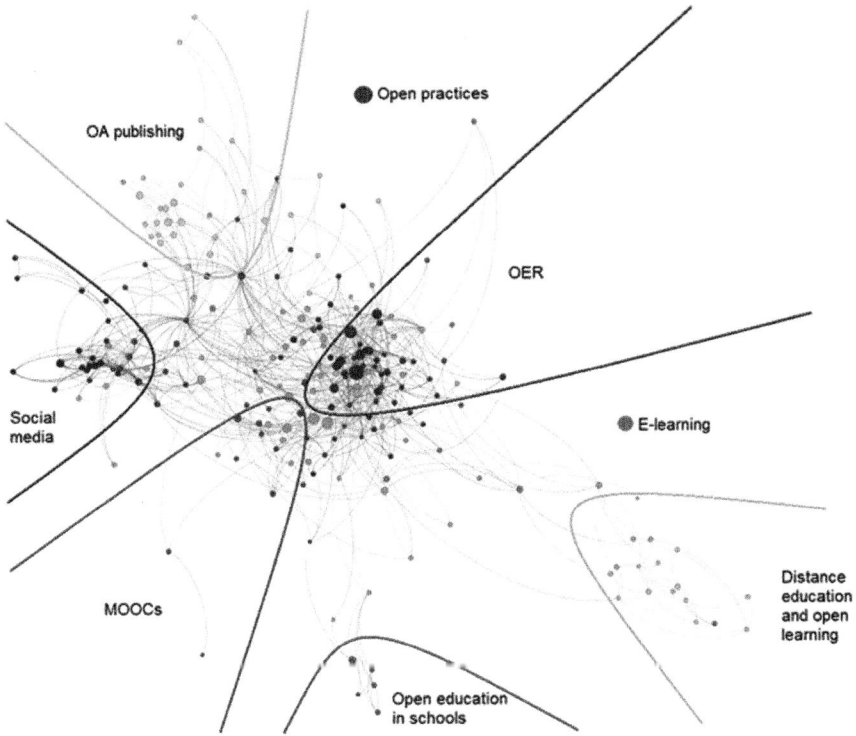

Fig. 1.2 Citation network of open education articles

plotted. Clusters within this could be identified, and appropriate labels imposed. The resulting network is shown in Fig. 1.2.

From this network, eight distinct areas within open education emerged: Distance education, e-learning, open education in schools, OER, MOOCs, Open Access publishing, Social media and open practices. All of these areas have elements of opening up access to educational practice as a core motivation or principle.

What the network demonstrates is that there is indeed little cross-referencing between these areas. Articles on MOOCs, for instance, do not tend to reference ones in OER, and vice versa, and neither reference open and distance education research and so on. In some areas, this might be understandable, for example, many articles on open access publishing are from an information science, librarianship perspective, and similarly the work on social media emerged from a communications focus and evolved into consideration of academic use of such tools. Given the similarity in aims and issues faced by distance education, MOOCs and OERs, the absence of much overlap between them is surprising, however.

Perhaps the area of most interest is that of open practices, or open educational practice (OEP), which acts as a bridge or glue between many of the other clusters, located as it is at the intersection of social media, open access publishing and OER. It

Table 1.1 The primary drivers for different areas of open education

Area of open education	Primary driver
Open, distance education	Removal of barriers to higher education
E-learning	Delivery of education and support online
Open education in schools	Physical spaces, inclusion
OER	Reuse, access to teaching content
MOOCs	Free access to content
Social media	Sharing of ideas
OA publishing	Reuse, access to research content
OEP	Sharing of process and content

is, however, also a term that has multiple interpretations, with Cronin and MacLaren (2018) identifying four distinct strands of OEP definition. This generality, or ambiguity, means that it encompasses both the research and teaching remits of higher education, and thus does not form a distinct cluster. In terms of opening access to education, OEP can be viewed then as motivated by both a desire to remove barriers to education, and also to open up the *process* of education, by sharing data, content and blurring boundaries between academic institutions and the general public.

The eight areas identified in Fig. 1.2 can be summarised as foregrounding different aspects of open access. For example, for open learning, the key component is the removal of barriers to participation in higher education, whereas, for OER, it is the ability to reuse and access content that is of primary importance, while MOOCs highlight the free cost of study. These primary drivers for each of the eight areas are summarised in Table 1.1

What Table 1.1 highlights is that open access to education comes in many different forms, and with differing intentions. No one interpretation is 'correct' but rather their suitability will vary depending on the aims of the institution, educator and learner. However, this multiplicity of definitions, intentions and outcomes can be detrimental to the open movement as it makes the term 'open' so broad as to be meaningless. What is required therefore is a conceptual model to combine these approaches in manner that is meaningful for higher education institutions.

1.3 A Model for Openness

Orr, Weller and Farrow (2019) propose such a model, combining open, online, flexible and technology-enhanced (OOFAT) aspects of education. The model needed to provide sufficient structure to provide a meaningful analysis, while being broad enough to capture the range of open approaches we have seen. In order to accomplish this, the conceptual model abstracts higher education to core functions.

Building on Agarwal (2016) who classifies these functions as: clocks, content and credentials, so higher education can be thought of as comprising how it is delivered ('clocks'), what is delivered ('content') and how achievement is made recognisable to third parties ('credentials'). With a slight reformulation for clarity and conciseness, the basic conceptual model used in this research was based on the following three central processes:

- Content—consisting of subject knowledge, support and guidance and learning analytics, which together make up the entirety of all didactical process.
- Delivery—consisting of the qualities of place, pace and timing of delivery of the content, and format so as to include online, blended and face to face.
- Recognition—consisting of both assessment and credentialisation, which are formal processes leading to recognition of learning achievements. Assessment is a phase of evaluation at certain times in a learning process, while credentials are awarded on completion of formal learning units. In both cases, these evaluative processes entail a formal endorsement of learning and lead to recognition of achievement of the learner by third parties.

With these basic components, the impact of technology to open up the process can then be examined. Two dimensions were used for each of the three core processes, which both speak of new types of openness and flexibility made possible through digitalisation.

- Organisational flexibility: The quality of flexibility is a question of 'what' and 'how' and relies on digital technology to reduce the need for physical presence; from static to dynamic and changing due to specific circumstances. So, each of the three central processes (content, delivery, recognition and their sub-processes) can also be described by the extent to which they are delivered in a flexible manner, harnessing digital technology, that is, through online and technology-enhanced learning environments. This opens up access by reducing the barriers to participation in a strictly face–to-face, time constrained model, as seen with traditional and online open universities.
- Procedural openness: The quality of openness is a 'who' question and relies on how the principle of openness is integrated (in various ways) into the core processes (content, delivery, recognition and their sub-processes); from closed group to more open network. More open processes mean less limitations on who has access to and who delivers or controls content, delivery, assessment and recognition. This opens up access in different ways, for example, by allowing free access to content (as with OER), or more open forms of assessment such as digital badges.

This conceptual model is represented in Fig. 1.3. It comprises the three central processes of higher education provision at its corners and has the two qualities of flexibility and openness.

Using a 5-point Likert scale for how universities perceive themselves on each these dimensions, allows a visual representation, as shown in Fig. 1.4. A global survey of 150 institutions across 36 countries was then conducted to gather their representations

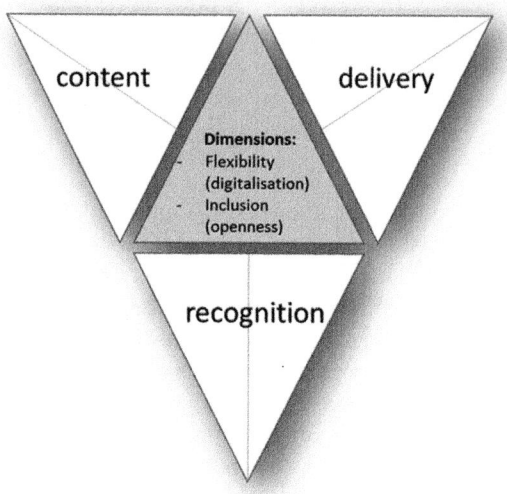

Fig. 1.3 The OOFAT conceptual model

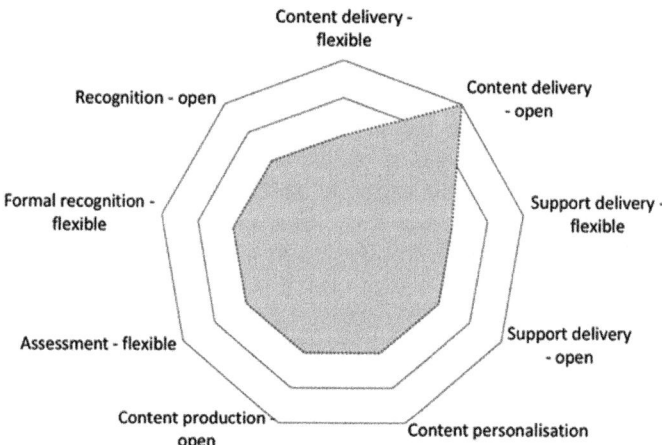

Fig. 1.4 Dimensions of the OOFAT model of Korea National Open University

on this model. Analysis of these different representations reveals some core patterns, which can be then be mapped to approaches to opening up access to education.

Six such patterns emerged from the data:

- OOFAT at the centre
- OOFAT for organisational flexibility
- OOFAT for a specific purpose

1 Open and Free Access to Education for All 11

- Content-focused OOFAT model
- Access-focused OOFAT model
- OOFAT for multiple projects

Each of these can be seen as a different, and equally valid, approach to opening access to education. To take each in turn:

OOFAT at the centre—This model can be visualised as a perfect, or near perfect, nonagon (with a scoring of 3 or higher on each dimension), suggesting that OOFAT is not implemented for one specific purpose, or market, but as an integral part of the institution's overall mission. For such institutions, openness is an integral part of every practice, for example, having open enrolment, free access to content, open forms of assessment. An example is the OER University, which is a network of institutions offering free online courses for students worldwide with OERu partners providing accreditation and content. The OERu has a mission statement of 'Towards more affordable education for all students worldwide'. This can be seen as combining both the approach of the traditional open universities and the open license philosophy of the OER movement, and free course approach of MOOCs.

OOFAT for organisational flexibility—many OOFAT visualisations emphasised the flexibility dimension of the three components. An example is the College of the Canyons (COC), which is a public two-year community college in the US. In terms of content, it is currently shifting from in-house content production to decentralised OER content production and reuse. For delivery, students can choose between various schedule formats (16, 12, 8 or 5 week terms, on campus, online, hybrid, etc.). Within these classes, the majority of students can choose time and place of assessments, and enrolment is open entry. This approach uses flexibility to open up access to education.

OOFAT for a specific purpose—regardless of the values given to other dimensions, many providers had at least one clear peak, where flexibility and/or openness was being implemented for a very specific function or market. This may be the result of a particular project or a specific strategy to target one aspect of delivery. For example, the Universitas Terbuka (UT) is Indonesia's 45th state university and employs an open and distance learning system to widen access to higher education to all Indonesian citizens, including those who live in remote islands. Only recently (since 2017), has the university begun to provide digital learning materials and it now gives free internet access via Wi-Fi to students. Opening access here was being focused for a particular audience.

Content-focused OOFAT model—in contrast to the flexibility model which emphasises the flexibility dimension across all aspects of the OOFAT model, other providers concentrate on the component of content specifically. An example is the National Open University of Nigeria (NOUN) which is a federal open and distance learning institution located in Abuja. NOUN encourages its staff to utilise OERs in their lessons and create OER for publication and reuse. With a focus mainly on adult learners, support is also flexible and offered when needed in a traditional distance educational model. This combines aspects then of the traditional open education model and OER to make increase access.

Access-focused OOFAT model—some providers are utilising digital technologies with the primary intention of increasing access to content or education for specific sets of learners. An example is the Odisha State Open University (OSOU), a distance learning state university located in Sambalpur, Odisha, India. They have a distance education approach, but are particularly exploring the use of other dimensions in terms of improving access. For example, content is free for all but, for certification a nominal fee is charged from eligible learners, adopting some of the MOOC model to increasing access. Faculty and part-time counsellors provide learning support at dedicated study centres. Academic counsellors also evaluate the learners. The system is open and flexible for learners to self-pace their learning path in terms of study time.

OOFAT for multiple projects—lastly, some OOFAT visualisations revealed multiple peaks, which were related to very different initiatives within the institution, suggesting experimentation with different dimensions of higher education provision, before the possible future development of a unified strategy. An example is Thompson Rivers University (TRU) in Kamloops, British Columbia, Canada, which has a large online, open education programme. A highly innovative university, it deploys a wide range of technologies at small scale. For instance, students may choose their own assignments or projects in many instances and frequent use is made of blogging platforms for assessment. Open textbooks are an increasing part of content development. Their delivery is often available without a start date and requires up to 30 weeks to complete.

These all represent different flavours of open education, using technology and a mixture of the three main approaches of MOOCs, open universities and OER to meet the needs of their specific contexts.

1.4 Discussion and Conclusion

Open practice has an obvious relationship with higher education. As Wiley and Green (2012) put it, 'Education is, first and foremost, an enterprise of sharing. In fact, sharing is the sole means by which education is effected'. Openness can then be argued to be central to the process of higher education, but through the practical limitations of funding and physical space, a 'closed' model has developed. This has come to be seen as the norm, or a natural state for higher education. The barriers to participation in traditional education are many: cost, time, physical presence, work or family commitments and entry requirements. In addition, cultural factors may conspire to exclude particular groups from participation, including women, certain ethnic groups and students from poorer backgrounds with no family experience of higher education.

Open access to education seeks to explicitly address these barriers and encourage participation in education through a variety of means. The traditional OU approach explicitly targets some of these barriers, as we have seen by the removal of entry requirements, part-time study and distance-based model. OER-based approaches are perhaps more indirect, for example, open textbooks can reduce the cost of textbooks for those in formal education (e.g. Wiley, Levi Hilton III, Ellington, & Hall, 2012), or study of OER provides learners with an opportunity to build up confidence in a subject, leading to participation in formal education (Weller, Jordan, DeVries, & Rolfe, 2015). MOOCs allow free access to whole courses, but often with the possibility to purchase a certificate of completion. This helps open education to those who may not want to enter formal education, or who already have undergraduate qualifications and seek to update skills or engage in leisure learning.

As the mapping exercise has shown there is little cross-fertilisation between these areas. However, as the work on the OOFAT model illustrates, higher education institutes are themselves combining these three approaches and more in order to realise open access to education. This is often complex, nuanced and tailored to the needs and context of the particular institution. The evolving nature of what constitutes 'open education' has meant that it is now a wide encompassing term, which can be to its detriment. As we have seen with open educational practice, it is a term lacking a clear definition which makes it difficult to identify benefits, or impacts. However, the diversity of opinion as to what constitutes open education can also be framed as a benefit. At the core of each approach is a desire to increase access to some aspect of education. The institutions surveyed in the OOFAT work are viewing these different flavours of openness as something akin to a component box, from which they can select the elements they require and combine these into different configurations which suit their needs.

References

Agarwal, A. (2016). Where higher education is headed in the 21st century: Unbundling the clock, curriculum and credential. Retrieved from https://blogs.timesofindia.indiatimes.com/toi-edit-page/where-higher-education-is-headed-in-the-21st-century-unbundling-the-clock-curriculum-and-credential/.
Brennan, J., King, R., & Lebeau, Y. (2004). The role of universities in the transformation of societies. *Centre for Higher Education Research and Information*. http://www.open.ac.uk/cheri/documents/transf-final-report.pdf.
Christensen, G., Steinmetz, A., Alcorn, B., Bennett, A., Woods, D., & Emanuel, E. (2013). The MOOC phenomenon: Who takes massive open online courses and why? *SSRN*. http://papers.ssrn.com/sol3/papers.cfm?abstract_id=2350964.
Cormier, D. (2013). What do you mean… open? http://davecormier.com/edblog/2013/04/12/what-do-you-mean-open/.
Coursera. (2013). 10 US State University systems and public institutions join coursera to explore MOOC-based learning and collaboration on campus. Coursera Blog from http://blog.coursera.org/post/51696469860/10-us-state-university-systems-and-public-institutions.
Creative Commons. (2013a). What is OER? http://wiki.creativecommons.org/What_is_OER%3F.
Cronin, C., & MacLaren, I. (2018). Conceptualising OEP: A review of theoretical and empirical literature in Open Educational Practices. *Open Praxis, 10*(2), 127–143. https://doi.org/10.5944/openpraxis.10.2.825.
Etzkowitz, H., Webster, A., Gebhardt, C., & Terra, B. R. C. (2000). The future of the university and the university of the future: Evolution of ivory tower to entrepreneurial paradigm. *Research Policy, 29*(2), 313–330.

Farrow, M., Ward, D. D., Klekociuk, S. Z., & Vickers, J. C. (2017). Building capacity for dementia risk reduction: The preventing dementia MOOC. *Alzheimer's & Dementia: The Journal of the Alzheimer's Association, 13*(7), P871–P872.

Hollands, F. M., & Tirthali, D. (2014). MOOCs: Expectations and reality. *Center for Benefit-Cost Studies of Education, Teachers College, Columbia University, 138*.

Jordan, K. (2014). Initial trends in enrolment and completion of massive open online courses. *The International Review of Research in Open and Distributed Learning, 15*(1).

Lane, A. (2009). The impact of openness on bridging educational digital divides. *The International Review of Research in Open and Distributed Learning, 10*(5).

McGill, L., Falconer, I., Dempster, J.A., Littlejohn, A., & Beetham, H. (2013). Journeys to open educational practice: UKOER/SCORE review final report. JISC from https://oersynth.pbworks.com/w/page/60338879/HEFCE-OER-Review-Final-Report.

Orr, D., Weller, M., & Farrow, R. (2019). How is digitalisation affecting the flexibility and openness of higher education provision? Results of a global survey using a new conceptual model. *Journal of Interactive Media in Education, 2019*(1).

Pappano, L. (2012). The year of the MOOC. *New York Times*, Nov 2, 2012, from http://www.nytimes.com/2012/11/04/education/edlife/massive-open-online-courses-are-multiplying-at-a-rapid-pace.html?.

Peter, S., & Deimann, M. (2013). On the role of openness in education: A historical reconstruction. *Open Praxis, 5*(1), 7–14. https://doi.org/10.5944/openpraxis.5.1.23).

Pickard, L. (2018). TU Delft students can earn credit for MOOCs from other universities class central. https://www.class-central.com/report/delft-virtual-exchange-program/.

Rolfe, V. (2016). *Open, but not for criticism? #opened16* (p. 2016). USA: Richmond Virginia.

Tait, A. (2018). Open Universities: The next phase. *Asian Association of Open Universities Journal, 13*(1), 13–23.

Weller, M., de los Arcos, B., Farrow, R., Pitt, B., & McAndrew, P. (2015). The impact of OER on teaching and learning practice. *Open Praxis, 7*(4), 351–361.

Weller, M., Jordan, K., DeVries, I., & Rolfe, V. (2018). Mapping the open education landscape: citation network analysis of historical open and distance education research. *Open Praxis, 10*(2), 109–126.

Wiley, D. (2013). What is open pedagogy? https://opencontent.org/blog/archives/2975.

Wiley, D., & Green, C. (2012). Why openness in education? In D. Oblinger (ed.), *Game changers: Education and information technologies*, pp. 81–89. Educause.

Wiley, D., & Hilton III, J. L. (2018). Defining OER-enabled pedagogy. *The International Review of Research in Open and Distributed Learning, 19*(4). https://doi.org/10.19173/irrodl.v19i4.3601.

Wiley, D., Levi Hilton III, J., Ellington, S., & Hall, T. (2012). A preliminary examination of the cost savings and learning impacts of using open textbooks in middle and high school science classes. *The International Review of Research in Open and Distance Learning, 13*(3) http://www.irrodl.org/index.php/irrodl/article/view/1153/2256.

William and Flora Hewlett Foundation. (2013). White paper: Open educational resources—breaking the lockbox on education. http://www.hewlett.org/library/hewlett-foundation-publication/white-paper-open-educational-resources.

Open Access This chapter is licensed under the terms of the Creative Commons Attribution 4.0 International License (http://creativecommons.org/licenses/by/4.0/), which permits use, sharing, adaptation, distribution and reproduction in any medium or format, as long as you give appropriate credit to the original author(s) and the source, provide a link to the Creative Commons license and indicate if changes were made.

The images or other third party material in this chapter are included in the chapter's Creative Commons license, unless indicated otherwise in a credit line to the material. If material is not included in the chapter's Creative Commons license and your intended use is not permitted by statutory regulation or exceeds the permitted use, you will need to obtain permission directly from the copyright holder.

Chapter 2
Open Science and Radical Solutions for Diversity, Equity and Quality in Research: A Literature Review of Different Research Schools, Philosophies and Frameworks and Their Potential Impact on Science and Education

Christian M. Stracke

Abstract Open Science is a phenomenon that can be traced back to the Middle Ages. In the end of the twentieth century and the beginning of the twenty-first century, Open Science is strongly growing due to the worldwide internet and related new technologies, tools and communication channels. Two core objectives (reliability and trust) and three main characteristics (transparency, openness and reproducibility) of Open Science can be identified but it is still too early for a broad definition of this growing movement. Its growth is happening in many disciplines and in diverse facets. This article presents an overview of how Open Science is introduced and established in all three science dimensions of research design, processes and publications. For the future, the benefits are analysed that Open Science is offering, as well as the challenges that it is facing. It can be concluded that it is desirable that all researchers collaborate in Open Science. Open Science can improve the different science disciplines, research practices and science in general. In that way, Open Science can contribute to overcome the post-truth age through increasing objective and subjective credibility of science and research. And in the long-term perspective, Open Science can improve the whole research, education, as well as our society.

C. M. Stracke (✉)
Open University of the Netherlands, Heerlen, The Netherlands
e-mail: christian.stracke@ou.nl

Korean National Open University, Seoul, South Korea

East China Normal University, Shanghai, China

© The Author(s) 2020
D. Burgos (ed.), *Radical Solutions and Open Science*, Lecture Notes in Educational Technology, https://doi.org/10.1007/978-981-15-4276-3_2

2.1 Introduction

Open Science is claimed as radical social innovation (David, 2004a) and as a disruptive movement for Higher Education (Vicente-Saez & Martinez-Fuentes, 2018). However, what is Open Science and how can it be used to radically change and improve research, education and our society? This overview article provides an introduction to the history of Open Science followed by an analysis of the current state-of-the-art of Open Science and its characteristics.

2.2 History of Open Science

Open Science is a combination of objective and subjective goals to improve research and science in general. David underlines that Open Science is "a fragile cultural legacy of Western Europe's history" (David, 2004a, 571) when he analyses the history of Open Science back to its appearance during the late sixteenth and early seventeenth centuries and the court patronage system of the late Renaissance Europe (David, 1998, 2004a, 2007). In the 17th century, the shift towards Open Science was visible in public life and first science periodicals were published (Kronick, 1976). The first science association was established: the Royal Society of London for Improving of Natural Knowledge, founded in 1660 with a strong focus on openness and including women indicating this shift, too (Willinsky, 2005). The basis for this appearance of Open Science was a change in the opportunities, needs and demands by western European feudalism and the fragmented and competing noble patrons (David, 1998, 2004a, 2007). The increasing importance of mathematics for many disciplines and the spread of printing were main factors for the Renaissance and the scientific revolution. Scientists were no longer interested in keeping the secrets of the nature in small circles (like the alchemy continued to do) but to publish their scientific news: According to the analysis of David (1998, 2004a, 2007), the "common agency contracting in substitutes" (David 2004a, 582) by the noble patrons as the political authorities led to the competition among the scientists. Innovations in technologies remained hidden to obtain economical or military advantages so that only new scientific results could be published and presented. Noble patrons engaged scientists to gain reputation and scientists were interested to present their results in public to achieve better contracts as most of them could not live from one single contract. That constituted also the major progress that fragmented Western Europe could gain in comparison with bigger monolithic politic systems such as the Heavenly Empire of China with similar conditions but failing to introduce this successful concept of Open Science (David, 1998, 2004a, 2007).

Science, in general, was evolving and increasing, also in the number of disciplines leading to specialized research, scientific communities and theories in the twentieth century. How changes in science and scientific theories are taking place is under controversial debate with three main representatives: Popper (1959) believes in the progressive and cumulative increase of scientific knowledge, while Kuhn (1962) postulates potential paradigm shifts in addition, whereas Feyerabend (1978) neglects progressive and cumulative increase of scientific knowledge, as well as the existence of universal methodological rules. In consequence, many science studies were undertaken with different labels and schools of thoughts to analyse the past and future of science. That includes the attempt to create a new discipline called the sociology of science (David, 1998, 2004a, 2007). It is often based on the sociology of science norms from "the Republic of Science" by Merton (1996, 1973) that can be summarized by the four core aspects: communism, universalism, disinterestedness and organized scepticism (also abbreviated as CUDO). Other scientists have revised them: Macfarlane and Cheng (2008) added originality and shortened organized scepticism to scepticism leading to the abbreviation CUDOS whereas Ziman (1994, 2000) has additionally changed communism to communalism. In general, the ambiguity between science as a subject for research and science as a methodology used in the research is causing confusion, at least in English leading to a variety of competing classification systems (e.g., science vs. technology studies or formal vs. natural vs. social sciences).

In the modern science of the twentieth century, Open Science is closely connected with the emergence of open source and open access according to Willinsky (2005). In the 1960s and 1970s, freedom dominated the academic world and science and any software developed by scientists and engineers in academic, as well as in corporate laboratories was freely shared, modified and re-used (von Hippel, 2005; Markoff, 2005). But only a few years later, the commercialization of Higher Education began with a large impact, among others on the publication and access to research results, too (Bok, 2003).

The open source movement started when Stallmann resigned his professorship and left MIT due to its decision for licensing any newly developed computer code leading to restrictions (Stallmann, 2005). He founded the Free Software Foundation and formed the GNU General Public License that quickly was and still is used broadly to release software as free products and code to be re-used by others. The confusion that free software means (as the GNU GPL still allows to charge for distribution or support of free software) led to the definition of the new term open source coined by Peterson in the year 1998 (according to the Oxford English Dictionary, cited by Willinsky, 2005).

Next to the commercialization of Higher Education (Czarnitzki, Grimpe & Pellens, 2015; Shibayama, 2015), new general copyright rules and laws were developed and approved inside and outside of the academic world and science (David, 2004b). They are mainly intended to protect intellectual property rights (IPR) and in particular economic interests of business and corporates. A major impact of them is the complete turnaround of the default: Before their approval, everybody could share and re-use any publication without a copyright statement. After their approval, everybody can share and re-use only publications with an explicit open license that allows sharing and re-usage. That led to confusion among researchers, as well as educators and all citizens and to several manifestos, that were initiated and published (Budapest Open Access Initiative, 2002; Berlin Declaration, 2003; Bethesda

Statement, 2003). Furthermore, Creative Commons were established as an association to develop global open licenses for different purposes. Currently, six licenses are defined based upon four conditions: 1. Attribution ("by"), 2. ShareAlike ("sa"), 3. NonCommercial ("nc") and 4. NoDerivates ("nd").

A more narrow understanding of Open Science reallocates its origin in the emergence of the term "Science 2.0" during the first years of this century, more precisely in the later 2000s (Mirowski, 2018). In this perspective, Open Science is a re-branding of Science 2.0 by *The New York Times* (Lin, 2012) and the British *Royal Society* (2012) in the year 2012. As a consequence, there was the appearance of many popular publications, white papers and policy documents, as well as of several institutions and initiatives promoting Open Science, mainly in Northern America including a television series ("The Crowd and the Cloud", broadcasted by the channel PBS in the year 2017 and funded by the American National Science Foundation) dedicated to the "Open Science Price" (Mirowski, 2018).

2.3 Current State-of-the-Art of Open Science

This section will provide an overview of the current state-of-the-art of Open Science. The Digital Age fosters new ways of communication and knowledge sharing that are changing social processes and societies including science disciplines and institutions (Peters & Roberts, 2012; Stracke, 2018a, b, 2017a, b, c).

Open Science is considered as a paradigm change that is challenging traditional research to improve accuracy, trust and transparency through openness standards facilitating replications (Makel & Plucker, 2017). It leads to a change of behaviours in the publications, as well as in the research itself, what Vazire (2018) considers as a credibility revolution.

2.3.1 Definition of Open Science

Open Science is a broad field with many divergent perspectives from different stakeholders and thus, several definitions of Open Science exist (Vicente-Saez & Martinez-Fuentes, 2018). Several stakeholder groups are not aware of this situation and the lack of a common understanding and of a formal definition is identified (Arabito & Pitrelli, 2015; European Commission, 2015; Kraker, Leony, Reinhardt & Beham, 2011; OECD, 2015). Many movements of Open Science appeared in the last decades and can be differentiated in several ways (Borgman, 2007). Fecher and Friesike (2014) tried to distinguish five schools of thoughts (democratic, pragmatic, infrastructure, public and measurement) but these schools are overlapping and cannot be differentiated clearly. Thus, I agree with the summary by Fecher and Friesike: "The assumed coherence in regard to Open Science still lacks empirical research" (Fecher & Friesike, 2014, 36) and adds that the classification of Open Science requires deeper analysis, too.

Based on their literature review, Vicente-Saez and Martinez-Fuentes (2018) have clustered the collected studies into four categories to characterize Open Science: transparent, accessible, shared and collaborative-developed. The integration of the four characteristics leads Vicente-Saez and Martinez-Fuentes to the definition: "Open Science is transparent and accessible knowledge that is shared and developed through collaborative networks" (Vicente-Saez & Martinez-Fuentes, 2018, 434). However, it remains questionable whether the sole focus on knowledge is covering a broad range of perspectives. Therefore, it is maybe more promising to address the multiple objectives of Open Science and to cover them through a broad definition for a common and clear understanding shared by all stakeholder groups. And I believe that it is still too early for such a global definition of Open Science in this "turbulent yet exciting time of transition" (Arabito & Pitrelli, 2015, 2) and it could maybe even be impossible given the diverse perspectives (like it is the case with the term Open Education, see Stracke (2019) and below).

In addition, the English language, in particular, and their terms and common understandings are causing problems for Open Science and its definition based on knowledge. First, the term knowledge has specific connotations and at least two understandings in the English language as singularity as pointed out by Fecher and Friesike (2014): There is a distinction "between knowledge creation that is concerned with the rules of the natural world (science) and knowledge creation that is concerned with the human condition (humanities)" (Fecher & Friesike, 2014, 4). Second, the term science is not covering all scientific subjects and disciplines: It was contrasted with humanities for a long time until Kagan was coining the new term *three cultures* adding social sciences next to sciences and humanities (Kagan, 2009; Sidler, 2014). This new distinction into three scientific sections makes it even more challenging to use the term Open Science. Furthermore, I have already discussed above which problems the term science is causing for the classification of disciplines. Thus, I will continue using Open Science as an umbrella term embracing and referring to all scientific subjects and disciplines, as well as different objectives and purposes that can be objective (such as better formal reliability) and subjective (more trust in research). A broad, and therefore, vague working definition could be (and will be used in the following): Open Science is a combination of objective and subjective goals and means to improve science in the diverse subjects and disciplines and as a whole.

2.3.2 Objectives and Characteristics of Open Science

There are two major objectives of Open Science: first, higher *reliability* of the research findings and second, greater *trust* in scientific research, both objectives with the intention to overcome the fake news from the post-truth age (Cook, Lloyd, Mellor, Nosek

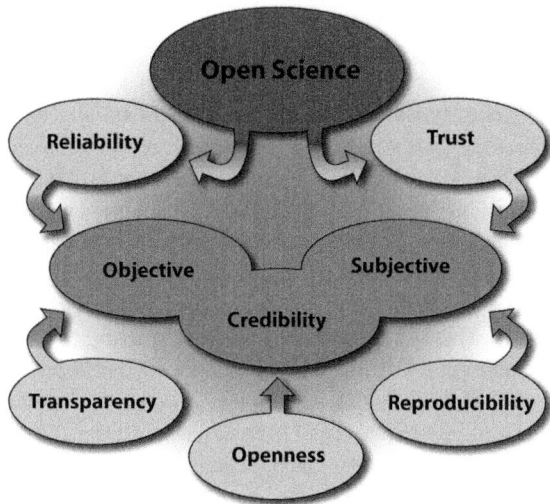

Fig. 2.1 The two objectives of Open Science: reliability and trust

& Therrien, 2018; Higgins, 2016). These two objectives are complementary and directly interrelated: Reliability provides objective credibility due to formal correctness and reproducibility and trust leads to subjective credibility due to individual confidence building (Fig. 2.1).

Consequently, two main characteristics of Open Science are transparency and openness that have to cover the whole research process from the design until the critical review after publication (Miguel et al., 2014; Nosek & Bar-Anan, 2012; Nosek et al., 2015). Transparency is a core value of science for credibility and is required to maximize insights, peer evaluation and evidences (Cook et al., 2018). Openness includes the sharing of research materials and data to facilitate their better understanding, verification, improvement and re-usage (Miguel et al., 2014; Molloy, 2011).

A third main characteristic of Open Science is reproducibility: Reproducibility indicates how robust and repeatable research findings are and includes the potential replicability (Goodman, Fanelli & Ioannidis, 2016; Nosek & Errington, 2017). Next to the research methods, reproducibility addresses the influence of decisions during the data analysis (e.g., on outliers and covariates) for consistent findings by different researchers, too (LeBel, McCarthy, Earp, Elson & Vanpaemel, 2018; Silberzahn et al., 2017). However, I agree with Goodman et al. (2016) that it is still unclear how reproducibility relates and leads to the development of cumulative evidence and commonly accepted truth in the research community. Overall, the research evidences from Open Science are considered more reliable and valid due to their increase of transparency, openness and reproducibility (Cook et al., 2018; Nosek et al., 2015).

Another core argument in favour of Open Science is that it enhances the trustworthiness of the research findings: Trustworthiness means to which extent research methods and data and the resulting findings can be called reliable and valid representations of the reality (Carnine, 1997; Odom et al., 2005). In this perspective, trustworthiness contributes directly to the first objective of Open Science (i.e., higher reliability and validity). And in the long-term view, it should support the second objective of Open Science (i.e., greater trust and confidence in research) by convincing both, the researchers, as well as the citizens and the whole society. This way, Open Science could play an important role to overcome fake news and to build a societal consensus and knowledge community.

2.3.3 Open Science in Scientific Research and Dimensions

Open Science is strongly growing currently and the term is used to describe many different concepts, means and practices across the whole science. Next to the commercialization of (higher) education, more problems were appearing in scientific practices and publications during the last decades (Chambers, Feredoes, Muthukumaraswamy & Etchells, 2014; Cook et al., 2018). There are also general concerns about whether science is self-correcting and that the progress of research is uneven (Shavelson & Towne, 2002).

Contrary interests of researchers against Open Science are secrecy, particularism, self-interestedness and organized dogmatism (Anderson, Ronning, DeVries & Martinson, 2007). They were first discovered by Mitroff (1974) through interviews with elite scientists from the Apollo lunar missions who conducted research in direct contradiction to the Merton's norms. The connected problems of pressures for publications and funding acquisition are demanding for researchers and under broad discussion (Casadevall & Fang, 2012; Giner-Sorolla, 2012; Gunsalus & Robinson, 2018; Nosek, Spies & Motyl, 2012).

In addition, it is proven that researchers have great freedom to manipulate research analysis and findings to achieve the most attractive and interesting results for easy publication and best recognition (Simmons, Nelson & Simohnson, 2011; Wicherts et al., 2016). Normally, researchers do not falsify data as it would be accused as scientific misconduct but several manipulations can easily be conducted and are reported as research practices such as data fishing and p-hacking (see https://projects.fivethirtyeight.com/phacking for an interactive demonstration), hypothesizing after results are known (called HARKing), and selectively reporting analyses and publishing studies with positive results labelled as reporting and publication bias (John, Loewenstein & Prelec, 2012; Simmons et al., 2011; Cook et al., 2018).

Replication studies are not often practiced and resulting in failures for the validation of the original findings (Camerer et al., 2016; Ebersole et al., 2016; Klein et al., 2014; Open Science Collaboration, 2015). One first major replication study tried to repeat 100 studies in psychology with 97 significant findings and could validate only 36 of them (Open Science Collaboration, 2015). That does not mean that the conclusions of the other studies were false-positive but that the reproducibility is more difficult than normally estimated and may lead to more cautious statements on research results (Randall & Welser, 2018).

The general idea behind Open Science including its concept of replication is the common sharing, analysis, peer-reviewing and evaluation of research and its results. Therefore, the Open Access to the research, its design, its data, its results and its publications is very important for Open Science. There are many types of Open Access (OA) that can be differentiated according to their availabilities and costs (Piwowar et al., 2018): They range from Libre OA (reading and re-usage of articles), Gratis OA (only reading of articles), Gold OA (journals with direct OA), Green OA (journals with permission of self-archiving), Hybrid OA (OA after paying an article processing charge), Delayed OA (OA after embargo time), Academic Social Networks (online communities) to Black OA (illegal pirate sites). To give researchers (as well as any other interested parties such as educators and learning providers) a better overview of what they can do with the OA publications, licenses such as Creative Commons (see above) were developed for different purposes.

Furthermore, Open badges can support the introduction of Open Science and Open Access as reported by Kidwell et al. (2016): *Psychological Science* was the first journal using open badges for marking articles following principles of Open Science and the number of articles with open data has increased from 3% (the two years before adopting open badges) up to 39% (1.5 years after adopting open badges). However, it remains questionable whether this increase is caused by the badges or maybe by the general increase of open access publications.

More directly and evidently, Open Science and Open Access can benefit from public authorities and policy developers. Taxpayers, respectively, the politicians on behalf of them and funding donors are increasingly demanding for Open Access of supported and funded research results such as the European Commission and national Ministries of Education like the Dutch one. In that way, research councils can play an important role in the establishment of future policies and practices of Open Science (Lasthiotakis, Kretz & Sá, 2015).

In addition, Open Science is focusing collaborative research in different approaches: First examples of collaborative research in Open Sciences are: the Human Genome Project that was open for expert organizations, the Polymath Project that asked for contributions from experts and senior researchers and the Galaxy Zoo that all citizens could join (Fecher & Friesike, 2014). In addition, the technological progress in distributed computing led to Open Science examples such as the Open Science Grid (Fecher & Friesike, 2014).

Open Science is already discussed and introduced in many different disciplines as identified and highlighted by van der Zee and Reich (2018): There are first examples of disciplines in social sciences such as criminology (Pridemore, Makel & Plucker, 2017) and sex research (Sakaluk & Graham, 2018), whereas the discussion is just starting in humanities, see, e.g., open science education (van der Zee & Reich, 2018; Stracke, 2019), while Open Science is practiced in many disciplines of (natural and formal) sciences such as animal welfare (Wicherts, 2017), biomedicine (Page et al., 2018), climate research (Muster, 2018), energy efficiency (Huebner et al., 2017), hardware development (Dosemagen, Liboiron & Molloy, 2017), high-energy

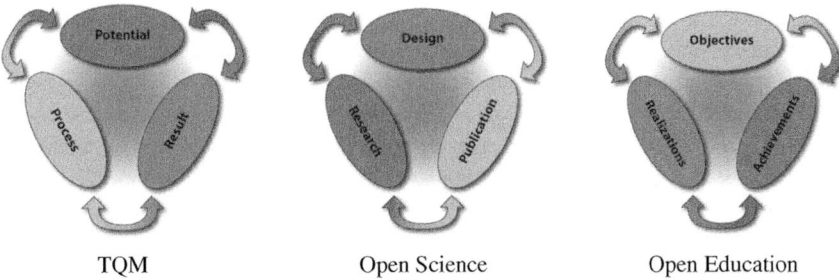

Fig. 2.2 Three dimensions of TQM and their adaptations to Open Science and Open Education

physics (Hecker, 2017), information science (Sandy et al., 2017), mass spectrometry (Schymanski & Williams, 2017), neuroscience (Poupon, Seyller & Rouleau, 2017) and robotics (Mondada, 2017).

Finally, Open Science is covering all dimensions and processes of scientific research from first idea development until the final revision and improvement of published results. To ensure such a broad focus and to constantly increase the scientific knowledge, Open Science can and should adapt and follow the philosophy of Total Quality Management (TQM) and its continuous improvement cycle (Juran, 1951, 1992, Deming, 1982, 1986; Stracke, 2011). The TQM philosophy distinguishes between the potential, the processes and the results as the three dimensions to be continuously evaluated and improved in iterative cycles (Stracke, 2006, 2014).

These three dimensions of TQM were transferred first to the health care sector by Donabedian (1980) and afterward to the education sector by Stracke (2006, 2015). They can also be adapted to science by differentiating the three dimensions of the research design, the research processes and the research publications as shown in Fig. 2.2. In the following, a short overview of the current practices of Open Science will be provided to present its variety and main focus today.

2.3.4 Openness in Scientific Design, Research and Publications

Open Science is combining and promoting different concepts, means and practices for all three science dimensions, sometimes introducing radical solutions. In the following, only a few examples can be highlighted that are consequently changing the way how science design, research and publications are realized.

First, Open Science is promoting Open Data to share data for their potential re-usage: The practices of data sharing are different across research communities and sometimes even within research communities (Borgman, 2012). Data should be open instead of free (as in "free beer" - or open, as well as free) as open data allow independent re-usage (Murray-Rust, 2008). It has to be noted that the importance and need for open data depends on the discipline (Fecher & Friesike, 2014). Thus, the question arises whether open data should be stored and accessible in general or in domain-specific repositories (Cook et al., 2018). That leads to discussions on data sharing that can be tipped only on the surface (like an iceberg):

The journal *Advances in Methods and Practices in Psychological Science* presents in its inaugural issue guiding principles in data sharing, primers, as well as discussion about sharing data that might contain sensitive information (Gilmore, Kennedy & Adolph, 2018; Levenstein & Lyle, 2018; Meyer, 2018). Guidelines (e.g., Inter-University Consortium for Political and Social Research, 2012) are available to assist researchers in formatting a variety of data types, including qualitative and quantitative, for their sharing. And an open and lively debate is also whether researchers or publishers are responsible (or guilty) for (not) sharing their data Murray-Rust (2008), Molloy (2011), Vision (2010), Boulton, Rawlins, Vallance and Walport (2011), Fecher and Friesike (2014). Wilkinson et al. (2016) recommend for sharing of data that researchers should follow their proposed "FAIR" principles to make data: findable, accessible, interoperable and reusable.

Second, Open Science is also requesting the public announcement and discussion of future research and its results that includes diverse options such as preregistration of research plans and questions, preprints of interim or final drafts of research results and publications and registered reports as a combination of both, the research design and the discussion of the results. Registered reports are splitting the traditional peer review of articles that are undertaken for the publication into two stages: the peer review of the research design before conducting the research and the peer review after the data analysis (Chambers et al., 2014). *The Lancet* was the first journal that introduced a prototype of registered reports, called "protocol review", in the year 1997 (Horton, 1997) that was ceased after revision in the year 2015 (Chambers, 2019): The editors noted the greater importance of open access to research protocols and encouraged the authors to publish on own institutional websites for general openness (The Lancet, 2015). Registered reports were introduced first in 2013 by the journal *Cortex* and in parallel with a related format at *Perspectives on Psychological Science* (Nosek & Lakens, 2014; Chambers, 2019). The number of journals offering registered reports increased quickly up to 108 in June 2018 and 207 in October 2019 (see the current list of journals on: https://cos.io/rr). Open questions and concerns about registered reports are answered by Chambers et al. (2014).

2.4 The Future for Open Science

Open Science can be traced back to the Middle Ages and is currently growing and entering the stage in many disciplines as introduced above. That is happening, in particular, due to the opportunities that worldwide internet and new technologies, tools and communication channels are offering. In the current second decade of the twenty-first century, science is facing the beginning of a post-truth age (Higgins,

2016): This development causes a lot of issues and concerns such as fake news and general denial of sciences and scientific facts. In the following, an overview will be presented how Open Science can evolve in the future and can contribute to overcome the post-truth age.

2.4.1 Benefits of Open Science

The future of Open Science depends on the facilitated benefits and on the problems and needs of researchers that Open Science can solve. Therefore, the following overview of the benefits of Open Science focuses on its support for the individual researchers and the whole science, too.

McKiernan et al. (2016) postulate that Open Science supports researchers to succeed by offering several benefits such as higher citations and recognition what is seconded by several authors (Dorch, 2012; Henneken & Accomazzi, 2011; Piwowar, Day & Fridsma, 2007; Piwowar & Vision, 2013). Three general benefits of Open Science are reported by Allen and Mehler (2019): First, greater faith in research, second, new helpful science systems and third, investment in the own future for researchers. Nosek et al. (2015) propose eight standards with three levels for promoting Open Science and its openness in research and science: two standards for rewarding authors, four standards for the scientific process and its reproducibility and two standards for values from preregistration.

In particular, Open Science and registered reports (RRs) are offering specific benefits (Cook et al., 2018). Registered reports enable more publications of null findings: Allen and Mehler (2019) have compared registered reports against traditional studies and found that they publish more null findings. Research studies with null findings are important for the scientific progress and avoid duplications of studies but are not often reported and published or not even submitted due to reporting and publication bias, in particular, in social sciences (Fanelli, 2010; Sterling, 1959, Cook & Therrien, 2017; Therrien & Cook, 2018; Franco, Malhotra & Simonovits, 2014; Greenwald, 1975). Furthermore, journals are often not accepting null findings leading to research evidences and literature basis that are exaggerating false-positive findings or positive effects (Ferguson & Heene, 2012; Ioannidis, 2012; Munafo et al., 2017).

In addition, Open Access is a necessity and an instrument to overcome the inequities among researchers and institutions in financial positions, among countries with different levels of developments and in general among all citizens from our global society. Several authors have analysed these inequities from different perspectives (Fecher & Friesike, 2014): Phelps, Fox and Marincola (2012) highlight the role of Open Access for the development of individual researchers, as well as of the society, through the broadest possible dissemination. Rufai, Gul and Shah (2012) in their study on library and information science recommend low-income countries to adopt Open Access. Cribb and Sari (2010) have stated the difference between the creation and sharing of research results: They conclude that while every five years the scientific knowledge doubles, the access to it remains limited in most cases. I agree with them that Open Access to scientific knowledge is a human right: It has to be tackled by the researcher, research institutions, funding bodies, public authorities and the whole society.

2.4.2 Challenges for Open Science

Three general challenges of Open Science are identified by Allen and Mehler (2019) when practicing Open Science: First, the restrictions on flexibility, second, the costs of (additional) time required for Open Science and third, the lack of an incentive structure. Furthermore, there are many more challenges for Open Science at different levels from which only two examples are selected to highlight the questions to be addressed and answered by Open Science.

First and at the general level, the opportunity for replication as encouraged and requested by Open Science can also cause a *constraint on generality* (Simons, Shoda & Lindsay, 2017). That is a substantial and generic question that is not easy to answer. The situation in (social) science has slowly enhanced since the rhetoric questioning of replications by Schmidt (2009). On the other hand, Simmons, Nelson and Simonsohn could prove the huge flexibility of the researcher when analysing data, often leading to unpredictable and non-replicable results (Simmons et al., 2011). Furthermore, meta-research has shown that most studies are still not fulfilling the requirements and standards of Open Science including the opportunity for replication even if they are claiming to do it (Nuijten, Hartgerink, van Assen, Epskamp & Wicherts, 2016).

Second and at the analysis level, Open Science has to deal with the same challenges as traditional research that became evident with the discussion in the year 2017 about the right level for statistical significance: Benjamin et al. (2017) proposed $p < 0.005$ (instead of $p < 0.05$) as a new level for better reproducibility and more accurate communication. In direct replicas, Lakens et al. (2017) recommend to avoid the term statistical significance and the use of standardized thresholds for p-values whereas McShane, Gal, Gelman, Robert and Tackett (2017) demands to abandon the importance of null hypothesis significance testing (NHST) and of statistical significance and its levels in general. This discussion demonstrates, on the other hand, a big advantage of Open Science. Researchers can quickly read preprints and answer them in the same way leading to a strong and lively community. Thus, Open Science offers new communication channels that avoid the waiting for review processes and facilitate more and direct responses.

2.5 Open Science and Openness in Education

Our society is entering a post-truth age causing a lot of issues and concerns as introduced above. That is happening in science, as well as in education and quantifies the size of the problems. Open Science education is considered to enable a change (van der Zee & Reich, 2018; Stracke, 2019). Open Science education can mean both: First, the education for introducing Open Science as subject (i.e., theories and practices of Open Science as an educational topic) and second, Open Education adapting and following Open Science principles (i.e., learning processes as innovative (pedagogical) methodologies). For the adaptation of Open Science, nine different dimensions of openness were defined and clustered in three dimensions (visionary, operational and legal) and applied to Open Education by Stracke (2017a, b, c). In special education, Cook et al. (2018) have requested to apply Open Science and related practices to advance the quality of research, as well as the future policies and practices and McBee, Makel, Peters and Matthews (2018) called for the same action in gifted education.

In his meta-analysis of meta-analysis studies, Hattie (2008), however, has proven that most studies claiming scientific and evidence-based results could not be verified and validated. The debate on the relevance and importance of these findings has just started in educational research and community. During the last four years, many educators and community organizations have collaborated to opening up education and its research. Under the leadership of the Slovenian government, the first draft for a UNESCO Recommendation on Open Education and Open Educational Resources (2019a) was developed and discussed in open consultations. Only three weeks ago (on 25th of November 2019), the 40th General Conference of UNESCO has adopted in global consensus the UNESCO Recommendation on Open Education and Open Educational Resources (2019b). It is a milestone as it is UNESCO's very first binding recommendation in the fields of Open Education and it requires annual progress reporting by all 193 UNESCO member states. I hope that it will be a glorious landmark and guide for the future of Open Education leading to a fundamental change in global learning and education for all.

2.6 Conclusions and Outlook

Open Science is a current phenomenon that can be traced back to the Middle Ages. Its growth is happening in many disciplines and in diverse facets in particular due to the worldwide internet and related new technologies, tools and communication channels. In the future, it is desirable that all researchers collaborate in Open Science to realize its benefits. The three main characteristics of Open Science (transparency, openness and reproducibility) strengthen science leading to the two core objectives of Open Science: more objective credibility due to increased (formal) reliability and more subjective credibility due to increased (personal) trust. In this way, Open Science can contribute and facilitate to overcome the post-truth age.

Therefore, all researchers should ensure that Open Science is introduced and established in all three science dimensions of research design, processes and publications. In consequence, Open Science can improve further development, recognition, reputation and progress of the different science disciplines, research practices and science in general. And in the long-term perspective, Open Science can and hopefully will improve the whole research, education, as well as our society.

References

Allen, C., & Mehler, D. M. A. (2019). Open science challenges, benefits and tips in early career and beyond. *PLoS Biology, 17*(5), e3000246. https://doi.org/10.1371/journal.pbio.3000246.

Anderson, M. S., Ronning, E. A., De Vries, R., & Martinson, B. C. (2007). The perverse effects of competition on scientists' work and relationships. *Science and Engineering Ethics, 13,* 437–461. https://doi.org/10.1007/s11948-007-9042-5.

Arabito, S., & Pitrelli, N. (2015). Open science training and education: Challenges and difficulties on the researchers' side and in public engagement. *Journal of Science Communication, 14*(4), C01_en, 1–4. https://doi.org/10.22323/2.14040301.

Benjamin, D. J., Berger, J., Johannesson, M., Nosek, B. A., Wagenmakers, E., Berk, R., ... Johnson, V. (2017, July 22). Redefine statistical significance. *PsyArXiv* [pre-print]. https://doi.org/10.31234/osf.io/mky9j.

Berlin Declaration on Open Access to Knowledge in the Sciences and Humanities. (2003). Retrieved March 1, 2019, from http://oa.mpg.de/lang/en-uk/berlin-prozess/berliner-erklarung/.

Bethesda Statement on Open Access Publishing. (2003). Retrieved March 1, 2019, from http://dash.harvard.edu/handle/1/4725199.

Bok, D. (2003). *Universities in the marketplace: The commercialization of higher education.* Princeton, N.J.: Princeton University Press.

Borgman, C. L. (2007). *Scholarship in the digital age: Information, infrastructure, and the internet.* Cambridge, MA: The MIT Press.

Borgman, C. L. (2012). The conundrum of sharing research data. *Journal of the American Society for Information Science and Technology, 63*(6), 1059–1078.

Boulton, G., Rawlins, M., Vallance, P., & Walport, M. (2011). Science as a public enterprise: The case for open data. *The Lancet, 377*(9778), 1633–1635. https://doi.org/10.1016/S0140-6736(11)60647-8.

Budapest Open Access Initiative. (2002). Retrieved March 1, 2019, from http://www.opensocietyfoundations.org/openaccess/read.

Camerer, C. F., Dreber, A., Forsell, E., Ho, T.-H., Huber, J., Johannesson, M., et al. (2016). Evaluating replicability of laboratory experiments in economics. *Science, 351,* 1433–1436. https://doi.org/10.1126/science.aaf0918.

Carnine, D. (1997). Bridging the research-to-practice gap. *Exceptional Children, 63,* 513–521. https://doi.org/10.1177/001440299706300406.

Casadevall, A., & Fang, F. C. (2012). Reforming science: Methodological and cultural reforms. *Infection and Immunity, 80,* 891–896. https://doi.org/10.1128/IAI.06183-11.

Chambers, C. (2019). What's next for registered reports? *Nature, 573,* 187–189. https://doi.org/10.1038/d41586-019-02674-6.

Chambers, C., Feredoes, E., D. Muthukumaraswamy, S. J., & Etchells, P. (2014). Instead of "playing the game" it is time to change the rules: Registered Reports at *AIMS Neuroscience* and beyond. *AIMS Neuroscience, 1,* 4–17. https://doi.org/10.3934/neuroscience.2014.1.4.

Cook, B. G., & Therrien, W. J. (2017). Null effects and publication bias in special education research. *Behavioral Disorders, 42,* 149–158. https://doi.org/10.1177/0198742917709473.

Cook, B. G., Lloyd, J. W., Mellor, D., Nosek, B. A., & Therrien, W. J. (2018). Promoting open science to increase the trustworthiness of evidence in special education. *Exceptional Children, 85*(1), 104–118. https://doi.org/10.1177/0014402918793138.

Cribb, J., & Sari, T. (2010). *Open science: Sharing knowledge in the global century.* Collingwood: CSIRO Publishing.

Czarnitzki, D., Grimpe, C., & Pellens, M. (2015). Access to research inputs: Open science versus the entrepreneurial university. *Journal of Technology Transfer, 40*(6), 1050–1063.

David, P. A. (1998). Common agency contracting and the emergence of 'open science' institutions. *American Economic Review, 88*(2), 15–21.

David, P. A. (2004a). Understanding the emergence of 'open science' institutions: Functionalist economics in historical context. *Industrial and Corporate Change, 13*(4), 571–589. https://doi.org/10.1093/icc/dth023.

David, P. A. (2004b). Can "Open Science" be protected from the evolving regime of IPR protections? *Journal of Institutional and Theoretical Economics, 160*(1), 9–34.

David, P. A. (2007). *The Historical Origins of 'Open Science'. An essay on patronage, reputation, and common agency contracting in the scientific revolution.* Stanford, CA: Stanford University.

Deming, W. E. (1982). *Quality, productivity and competitive position.* Cambridge, MA: MIT.

Deming, W. E. (1986). *Out of the Crisis.* Cambridge, MA: MIT.

Donabedian, A. (1980). *The definition of quality and approaches to its assessment* [Explorations in Quality Assessment and Monitoring, vol. 1]. Ann Arbor: Health Administration Press.

Dorch, B. (2012). *On the citation advantage of linking to data.* Retrieved from https://hal-hprints.archives-ouvertes.fr/hprints-00714715/document.

Dosemagen, S., Liboiron, M., & Molloy, J. (2017). Gathering for open science hardware 2016. *Journal of Open Hardware, 1*(1), 4. https://doi.org/10.5334/joh.5.

Ebersole, C. R., Atherton, O. E., Belanger, A. L., Skulborstad, H. M., Allen, J. M., Banks, J. B., et al. (2016). Many labs 3: Evaluating participant pool quality across the academic semester via replication. *Journal of Experimental Social Psychology, 67,* 68–82. https://doi.org/10.1016/j.jesp.2015.10.012.

European Commission. (2015). *Study on open science. Impact, implications and policy options.* Brussels: European Commission. Retrieved from https://ec.europa.eu/research/innovation-union/pdf/expert-groups/rise/study_on_open_science-impact_implications_and_policy_options-salmi_072015.pdf.

Fanelli, D. (2010). "Positive" results increase down the hierarchy of the sciences. *PLoS ONE, 5*(4), e10068. https://doi.org/10.1371/journal.pone.0010068.

Fecher, B., & Friesike, S. (2014). Open science: One term, five schools of thought. In S. Bartling, & S. Friesike (Eds.), *Opening science* (pp. 17–47). Cham: Springer. https://doi.org/10.1007/978-3-319-00026-8_2.

Ferguson, C. J., & Heene, M. (2012). A vast graveyard of undead theories: Publication bias and psychological science's aversion to the null. *Perspectives on Psychological Science, 7,* 555–561. https://doi.org/10.1177/1745691612459059.

Feyerabend, P. (1978). *Science in a free society.* London: New Left Books.

Franco, A., Malhotra, N., & Simonovits, G. (2014). Publication bias in the social sciences: Unlocking the file drawer. *Science, 345,* 1502–1505. https://doi.org/10.1126/science.1255484.

Gilmore, R. O., Kennedy, J. L., & Adolph, K. E. (2018). Practical solutions for sharing data and materials from psychological research. *Advances in Methods and Practices in Psychological Science, 1,* 121–130. https://doi.org/10.1177/2515245917746500.

Giner-Sorolla, R. (2012). Science or art? How aesthetic standards grease the way through the publication bottleneck but undermine science. *Perspectives on Psychological Science, 7,* 562–571. https://doi.org/10.1177/1745691612457576.

Goodman, S. N., Fanelli, D., & Ioannidis, J. P. A. (2016). What does research reproducibility mean? *Science Translational Medicine, 8*(341), 341ps12. https://doi.org/10.1126/scitranslmed.aaf5027.

Greenwald, A. G. (1975). Consequences of prejudice against the null hypothesis. *Psychological Bulletin, 82,* 1–20. https://doi.org/10.1037/h0076157.

Gunsalus, C. K., & Robinson, A. D. (2018). Nine pitfalls of research misconduct. *Nature, 557,* 297–299. https://doi.org/10.1038/d41586-018-05145-6.

Hattie, J. A. C. (2008). *Visible learning. A synthesis of over 800 meta-analyses relating to achievement.* London & New York: Routledge.

Hecker, B. L. (2017). Four decades of open science. *Nature Physics, 13*(6), 523–525. https://doi.org/10.1038/nphys4160.

Henneken, E. A., & Accomazzi, A. (2011). *Linking to data: Effect on citation rates in astronomy.* Retrieved from http://arxiv.org/abs/1111.3618.

Higgins, K. (2016). Post-truth: A guide for the perplexed. *Nature News, 540*(7631). https://doi.org/10.1038/540009a.

Horton, R. (1997). Pardonable revisions and protocol reviews. *The Lancet, 349,* 6.

Inter-University Consortium for Political and Social Research. (2012). *Guide to social science data preparation and archiving: Best practice throughout the data life cycle* (5th ed). Ann Arbor, MI: Author. Retrieved from https://www.icpsr.umich.edu/files/deposit/dataprep.pdf.

Ioannidis, J. P. (2012). Why science is not necessarily self-correcting. *Perspectives on Psychological Science, 7,* 645–654. https://doi.org/10.1177/1745691612464056.

John, L. K., Loewenstein, G., & Prelec, D. (2012). Measuring the prevalence of questionable research practices with incentives for truth telling. *Psychological Science, 23,* 524–532. https://doi.org/10.1177/0956797611430953.

Juran, J. M. (Ed.). (1951). *Quality control handbook.* New York: McGraw-Hill.

Juran, J. M. (1992). *Juran on quality by design. The new steps for planning quality into goods and services.* New York: Free Press.

Kagan, J. (2009). *The three cultures: Natural sciences, social sciences, and the humanities in the 21st century.* New York: Cambridge University Press.

Kidwell, M. C., Lazarević, L. B., Baranski, E., Hardwicke, T. E., Piechowski, S., Falkenberg, L. S., et al. (2016). Badges to acknowledge open practices: A simple, lowcost, effective method for increasing transparency. *PLoS Biology, 14*(5), e1002456. https://doi.org/10.1371/journal.pbio.1002456.

Klein, R. A., Ratliff, K. A., Vianello, M., Adams, R. B., Bahnik, Š., Bernstein, M. J., et al. (2014). Investigating variation in replicability. *Social Psychology, 45,* 142–152. https://doi.org/10.1027/1864-9335/a000178.

Kraker, P., Leony, D., Reinhardt, W., & Beham, G. (2011). The case for an open science in technology enhanced learning. *International Journal of Technology Enhanced Learning, 3*(6), 643–654. https://doi.org/10.1504/IJTEL.2011.045454.

Kronick, D. A. (1976). *A history of scientific & technical periodicals: The origins and development of the scientific and technical press, 1665–1790.* Metuchen, NJ: Scarecrow Press.

Kuhn, T. S. (1962). *The structure of scientific revolutions.* Chicago: University of Chicago Press.

Lakens, D., Adolfi, F. G., Albers, C. J., Anvari, F., Apps, M. A. J., Argamon, S. E., … Zwaan, R. A. (2017, September 18). Justify your alpha. *PsyArXiv* [pre-print]. https://doi.org/10.31234/osf.io/9s3y6.

The Lancet. (2015). Protocol review at *The Lancet:* 1997–2015. *The Lancet, 386,* 2456–2457.

Lasthiotakis, H., Kretz, A., & Sá, C. (2015). Open science strategies in research policies: A comparative exploration of Canada, the US and the UK. *Policy Futures in Education, 13*(8), 968–989. https://doi.org/10.1177/1478210315579983.

LeBel, E. P., McCarthy, R., Earp, B. D., Elson, M., & Vanpaemel, W. (2018). A unified framework to quantify the credibility of scientific findings. *Advances in Methods and Practices in Psychological Science, 1*(3), 389–402. https://doi.org/10.1177/2515245918787489.

Levenstein, M. C., & Lyle, J. A. (2018). Data: Sharing is caring. *Advances in Methods and Practices in Psychological Science, 1,* 95–103. https://doi.org/10.1177/2515245918758319.

Lin, T. (2012). Cracking open the scientific process. *The New York Times*, 16 January. Retrieved November 8, 2019, from https://www.nytimes.com/2012/01/17/science/open-science-challenges-journal-tradition-with-web-collaboration.html.

Macfarlane, B., & Cheng, M. (2008). Communism, universalism and disinterestedness: Re-examining contemporary support among academics for Merton's scientific norms. *Journal of Academic Ethics, 6*(1), 67–78. https://doi.org/10.1007/s10805-008-9055-y.

Makel, M. C., & Plucker, J. A. (Eds.). (2017). *Toward a more perfect psychology: Improving trust, accuracy, and transparency in research*. Washington, DC: American Psychological Association.

Markoff, J. (2005). *What the dormouse said: How the sixties counterculture shaped the personal computer industry*. New York: Viking.

McBee, M. T., Makel, M. C., Peters, S. J., & Matthews, M. S. (2018). A call for open science in giftedness research. *Gifted Child Quarterly, 62,* 374–388. https://doi.org/10.1177/0016986218784178.

McKiernan, E. C., Bourne, P. E., Brown, C. T., Buck, S., Kenall, A., Lin, J., ... Yarkoni, T. (2016). Point of view: How open science helps researchers succeed. *Elife, 5,* e16800. https://doi.org/10.7554/elife.16800.

McShane, B. B., Gal, D., Gelman, A., Robert, C., & Tackett, J. L. (2017). Abandon statistical significance. *The American Statistician, 73*(sup1), 235–245. https://doi.org/10.1080/00031305.2018.1527253.

Merton, R. K. (1973). *The sociology of science: Theoretical and empirical investigations*. Chicago: University of Chicago Press.

Merton, R. K. (1996). *On social structure and science*. Chicago: University of Chicago Press.

Meyer, M. N. (2018). Practical tips for ethical data sharing. *Advances in Methods and Practices in Psychological Science, 1,* 131–144. https://doi.org/10.1177/2515245917747656.

Miguel, E., Camerer, C., Casey, K., Cohen, J., Esterling, K. M., Gerber, A., et al. (2014). Promoting transparency in social science research. *Science, 343,* 30–31. https://doi.org/10.1126/science.1245317.

Mirowski, P. (2018). The future(s) of open science. *Social Studies of Science, 48*(2), 171–203. https://doi.org/10.1177/0306312718772086.

Mitroff, I. I. (1974). Norms and counter-norms in a select group of the *Apollo* moon scientists: A case study of the ambivalence of scientists. *American Sociological Review, 39,* 579–595. https://doi.org/10.2307/2094423.

Molloy, J. C. (2011). The open knowledge foundation: Open data means better science. *PLoS Biology, 9*(12), e1001195. https://doi.org/10.1371/journal.pbio.1001195.

Mondada, F. (2017). Can robotics help move researchers toward open science? [From the Field]. *IEEE Robotics and Automation Magazine, 24*(1), 111–112. https://doi.org/10.1109/MRA.2016.2646118.

Munafo, M. R., Nosek, B. A., Bishop, D. V. M., Button, K. S., Chambers, C. D., Percie, du Sert, N., ... & Ioannidis, J. P. A. (2017). A manifesto for reproducible science. *Nature Human Behaviour, 1*(1), 0021. https://doi.org/10.1038/s41562-016-0021.

Murray-Rust, P. (2008). Open data in science. *Serials Review, 34*(1), 52–64. https://doi.org/10.1016/j.serrev.2008.01.001.

Muster, S. (2018). Arctic freshwater—A commons requires open science. In *Arctic summer college yearbook* (pp. 107–120). New York, NY: Springer.

Nosek, B. A., & Bar-Anan, Y. (2012). Scientific utopia: I. Opening scientific communication. *Psychological Inquiry: An International Journal for the Advancement of Psychological Theory, 23,* 217–243. https://doi.org/10.1080/1047840X.2012.692215.

Nosek, B. A., & Errington, T. M. (2017). Making sense of replications. *ELife, 6,* e23383. https://doi.org/10.7554/eLife.23383.

Nosek, B. A., & Lakens, D. (2014). Registered reports: A method to increase the credibility of published results. *Social Psychology, 45*(3), 137–141. https://doi.org/10.1027/1864-9335/a000192.

Nosek, B. A., Spies, J. R., & Motyl, M. (2012). Scientific utopia: II. Restructuring incentives and practices to promote truth over publishability. *Perspectives on Psychological Science, 7,* 615–631. https://doi.org/10.1177/1745691612459058.

Nosek, B. A., Alter, G., Banks, G. C., Borsboom, D., Bowman, S. D., Breckler, S. J., et al. (2015). Promoting an open research culture. *Science, 348*(6242), 1422–1425. https://doi.org/10.1126/science.aab2374.

Nuijten, M. B., Hartgerink, C. H., van Assen, M. A., Epskamp, S., & Wicherts, J. M. (2016). The prevalence of statistical reporting errors in psychology (1985–2013). *Behavior Research Methods, 48,* 1205–1226. https://doi.org/10.3758/s13428-015-0664-2.

Odom, S. L., Brantlinger, E., Gersten, R., Horner, R. H., Thompson, B., & Harris, K. R. (2005). Research in special education: Scientific methods and evidence-based practices. *Exceptional Children, 71,* 137–148. https://doi.org/10.1177/001440290507100201.

OECD. (2015). *Making open science a reality, OECD science, technology and industry policy papers*. Paris: OECD Publishing (No. 25). https://doi.org/10.1787/5jrs2f963zs1-en.

Open Science Collaboration. (2015). Estimating the reproducibility of psychological science. *Science, 349*(6251), aac4716. https://doi.org/10.1126/science.aac4716.

Page, M. J., Altman, D. G., Shamseer, L., McKenzie, J. E., Ahmadzai, N., Wolfe, D., et al. (2018). Reproducible research practices are underused in systematic reviews of biomedical interventions. *Journal of Clinical Epidemiology, 94,* 8–18. https://doi.org/10.1016/j.jclinepi.2017.10.017.

Peters, M. A., & Roberts, P. (2012). *The virtues of openness: Education, science, and scholarship in the digital age*. Boulder, CO: Paradigm Publishers.

Phelps, L., Fox, B. A., & Marincola, F. M. (2012). Supporting the advancement of science: Open Access publishing and the role of mandates. *Journal of Translational Medicine, 10,* 13. https://doi.org/10.1186/1479-5876-10-13.

Piwowar, H. A., & Vision, T. J. (2013). Data reuse and the open data citation advantage. *PeerJ, 1,* e175. https://doi.org/10.7717/peerj.175.

Piwowar, H. A., Day, R. S., & Fridsma, D. B. (2007). Sharing detailed research data is associated with increased citation rate. *PLoS ONE, 2*(3), e308. https://doi.org/10.1371/journal.pone.0000308.

Piwowar, H., Priem, J., Larivière, V., Alperin, J. P., Matthias, L., Norlander, B., et al. (2018). The state of OA: A large-scale analysis of the prevalence and impact of Open Access articles. *PeerJ, 6,* e4375. https://doi.org/10.7717/peerj.4375.

Popper, K. (1959). *The logic of scientific discovery*. Abingdon-on-Thames: Routledge.

Poupon, V., Seyller, A., & Rouleau, G. A. (2017). The Tanenbaum Open Science Institute: Leading a paradigm shift at the Montreal Neurological Institute. *Neuron, 95*(5), 1002–1006. https://doi.org/10.1016/j.neuron.2017.07.026.

Pridemore, W. A., Makel, M. C., & Plucker, J. A. (2017). Replication in criminology and the social sciences. *Annual Review of Criminology, 1,* 19–38. https://doi.org/10.1146/annurev-criminol-032317-091849.

Randall, D., & Welser, C. (2018). *The irreproducibility crisis of modern science: Causes, consequences, and the road to reform*. New York, NY: National Association of Scholars. Retrieved from www.nas.org/images/documents/irreproducibility_report/NAS_irreproducibilityReport.pdf.

Royal Society. (2012). *Science as an open enterprise*. London: Royal Society. Retrieved November 8, 2019, from https://royalsociety.org/~/media/Royal_Society_Content/policy/projects/sape/2012-06-20-SAOE.pdf.

Rufai, R., Gul, S., & Shah, T. A. (2012). Open access journals in library and information science: The story so far. *Trends in Information Management, 7*(2), 218–228.

Sakaluk, J. K., & Graham, C. A. (2018). Promoting transparent reporting of conflicts of interests and statistical analyses at the Journal of Sex Research. *Journal of Sex Research, 55,* 1–6. https://doi.org/10.1080/00224499.2017.1395387.

Sandy, H. M., Mitchell, E., Corrado, E. M., Budd, J., West, J. D., Bossaller, J., et al. (2017). Making a case for open research: Implications for reproducibility and transparency. *Proceedings of the Association for Information Science and Technology, 54*(1), 583–586. https://doi.org/10.1002/pra2.2017.14505401079.

Schmidt, S. (2009). Shall we really do it again? The powerful concept of replication is neglected in the social sciences. *Review of General Psychology, 13*, 90–100. https://doi.org/10.1037/a0015108.

Schymanski, E. L., & Williams, A. J. (2017). Open Science for identifying "known unknown" chemicals. *Environmental Science and Technology, 51*(10), 5357–5359. https://doi.org/10.1021/acs.est.7b01908.

Shavelson, R. J., & Towne, L. (Eds.). (2002). *Scientific research in education*. Washington, DC: National Academy Press.

Shibayama, S. (2015). Academic commercialization and changing nature of academic cooperation. *Journal of Evolutionary Economics, 25*(2), 513–532.

Sidler, M. (2014). Open science and the three cultures: Expanding open science to all domains of knowledge creation. In S. Bartling, & S. Friesike (Eds.), *Opening science* (pp. 81–85). Cham: Springer. https://doi.org/10.1007/978-3-319-00026-8_5.

Silberzahn, R., Uhlmann, E. L., Martin, D. P., Anselmi, P., Aust, F., Awtrey, E. C., … Nosek, B. A. (2017). *Many analysts, one dataset: Making transparent how variations in analytical choices affect results, 1*(3), 337–356. https://doi.org/10.1177/2515245917747646.

Simmons, J. P., Nelson, L. D., & Simonsohn, U. (2011). False-positive psychology: Undisclosed flexibility in data collection and analysis allows presenting anything as significant. *Psychological Science, 22*, 1359–1366. https://doi.org/10.1177/0956797611417632.

Simons, S. J., Shoda, Y., & Lindsay, D. S. (2017). Constraints on generality (COG): A proposed addition to all empirical papers. *Perspectives on Psychological Science, 12*, 1123–1128. https://doi.org/10.1177/1745691617708630.

Stallman, R. (2005). Copyright and globalization in the age of computer networks. In R. A. Ghosh (Ed.), *CODE: Collaborative ownership and digital economy* (pp. 317–335). Cambridge, Mass.: MIT Press.

Sterling, T. D. (1959). Publication decisions and their possible effects on inferences drawn from tests of significance – or vice versa. *Journal of the American Statistical Association, 54*(285), 30. https://doi.org/10.2307/2282137.

Stracke, C. M. (2006). Process-oriented quality management. In U.-D. Ehlers & J. M. Pawlowski (Eds.), *Handbook on quality and standardisation in e-learning* (pp. 79–96). Berlin: Springer. https://doi.org/10.1007/3-540-32788-6_6. Retrieved from http://opening-up.education/publications/stracke-c-m-2006-process-oriented-quality-management.

Stracke, C. M. (2011). Competences and skills in the digital age: Competence development, modelling, and standards for human resources development. In E. García-Barriocanal et al. (Eds.), *Communications in computer and information science* (Vol. 240, pp. 34–46). Berlin: Springer. https://doi.org/10.1007/978-3-642-24731-6_4.

Stracke, C. M. (2014). How innovations and competence development support quality in lifelong learning. *The International Journal for Innovation and Quality in Learning (INNOQUAL), 2*(3), 35–44. https://doi.org/10.5281/zenodo.3608669.

Stracke, C. M. (2017a). The quality of MOOCs: How to improve the design of open education and online courses for learners? In P. Zaphiris, & A. Ioannou (Eds.), *Learning and collaboration technologies. Novel learning ecosystems. Lecture Notes in Computer Science*, (Vol. 10295, pp. 285–293). https://doi.org/10.1007/978-3-319-58509-3_23.

Stracke, C. M. (2017b). The quality of open online education and learning: A quality reference framework for MOOCs. In C. M. Stracke, M. Shanks, & O. Tveiten (Eds.), *Smart universities: Education's digital future. Official Proceedings of the International WLS and LINQ Conference 2017* (pp. 97–105). https://doi.org/10.6084/m9.figshare.9272657.

Stracke, C. M. (2017c). Open education and learning quality: The need for changing strategies and learning experiences. In *Proceedings of 2017 IEEE Global Engineering Education Conference (EDUCON)* (pp. 1044–1048). https://doi.org/10.1109/educon.2017.7942977.

Stracke, C. M. (2018a). 开放教育的学习质量和设计: OpenEd 框架 [The Learning Quality and Design of Open Education. The OpenEd Framework (translated by Junhong Xiao)]. *Distance Education in China, 11*, 5–18 + 78. http://cnki.net/kcms/doi/10.13541/j.cnki.chinade.20181108.005.html.

Stracke, C. M. (2018b). Como a Educação Aberta pode melhorar a qualidade de aprendizagem e produzir impacto em alunos, organizações e na sociedade? [How can Open Education improve learning quality and achieve impact for learners, organizations and in society?] In M. Duran, T. Amiel, & C. Costa (Eds.), *Utopias and Distopias da Tecnologia na Educação a Distância e Aberta* (pp. 499–545). Campinas: & Niterói: UNICAMP & UFF. Retrieved from http://opening-up.education/wp-content/uploads/2018/06/Stracke_2018_Educacao_Aberta_Qualidade_Impacto.pdf.

Stracke, C. M. (2019). Quality frameworks and learning design for open education. *The International Review of Research in Open and Distributed Learning, 20*(2), 180–203. https://doi.org/10.19173/irrodl.v20i2.4213.

Therrien, W. J., & Cook, B. G. (2018). Null effects and publication bias in learning disabilities research. *Learning Disabilities Research & Practice, 33*, 5–10. https://doi.org/10.1111/ldrp.12163.

UNESCO. (2019a). *Draft recommendation on open educational resources*. Retrieved from https://unesdoc.unesco.org/ark:/48223/pf0000370936?posInSet=22&queryId=304ed6aa-5635-4d73-aefd-92ed93ae3c48.

UNESCO. (2019b). *UNESCO recommendation on open educational resources*. 40 C/32 Annex. Paris: UNESCO. Retrieved from http://opening-up.education/wp-content/uploads/2019/12/RECOMMENDATION-CONCERNING-OPEN-EDUCATIONAL-RESOURCES.pdf.

van der Zee, T., & Reich, J. (2018). Open education science. *AERA Open, 4*(3), 1–15. https://doi.org/10.1177/2332858418787466.

Vazire, S. (2018). Implications of the credibility revolution for productivity, creativity, and progress. *Perspectives on Psychological Science, 13*, 411–417. https://doi.org/10.1177/1745691617751884.

Vicente-Saez, R., & Martinez-Fuentes, C. (2018). Open science now: A systematic literature review for an integrated definition. *Journal of Business Research, 88*, 428–436. https://doi.org/10.1016/j.jbusres.2017.12.043.

Vision, T. J. (2010). Open data and the social contract of scientific publishing. *BioScience, 60*(5), 330–331. https://doi.org/10.1525/bio.2010.60.5.2.

von Hippel, E. (2005). Democratizing innovation. The evolving phenomenon of user innovation. *Journal für Betriebswirtschaft, 55*(1), 63–78.

Wicherts, J. M. (2017). The weak spots in contemporary science (and how to fix them). *Animals, 7*(12), 90. https://doi.org/10.3390/ani7120090.

Wicherts, J. M., Veldkamp, C. L., Augusteijn, H. E., Bakker, M., Van Aert, R., & Van Assen, M. A. (2016). Degrees of freedom in planning, running, analyzing, and reporting psychological studies: A checklist to avoid p-hacking. *Frontiers in Psychology, 7*, 1832. https://doi.org/10.3389/fpsyg.2016.01832.

Wilkinson, M. D., Dumontier, M., Aalbersberg, I. J., Appleton, G., Axton, M., Baak, A., et al. (2016). The FAIR guiding principles for scientific data management and stewardship. *Scientific Data, 3*, 160018. https://doi.org/10.1038/sdata.2016.18.

Willinsky, J. (2005, August 1). The unacknowledged convergence of open source, open access, and open science. *First Monday, 10*(8). Retrieved from https://journals.uic.edu/ojs/index.php/fm/article/view/1265/1185.

Huebner, G. M., Nicolson, M. L., Fell, M. J., Kennard, H., Elam, S., Hanmer, C., … Shipworth, D. (2017). *Are we heading towards a replicability crisis in energy efficiency research? A toolkit for improving the quality, transparency and replicability of energy efficiency impact evaluations*. Retrieved from https://pdfs.semanticscholar.org/71e4/fde85949cf5f2d803657d6becfb080be1a57.pdf.

Ziman, J. (1994). *Prometheus bound. Science in a dynamic steady state*. Cambridge: Cambridge University Press.

Ziman, J. (2000). *Real science: What it is, and what it means*. Cambridge: Cambridge University Press.

Dr. Christian M. Stracke is ICDE Chair in OER and Associate Professor for Open Education and Innovations at the Open University of the Netherlands (OUNL). In addition he is an Advisory Professor at the East China Normal University (ECNU) in Shanghai, and an Adjunct Professor at the Korea National Open University (KNOU) in Seoul. Christian holds a Ph.D. in Economics (Dr. rer. pol.) from the University of Duisburg-Essen (Germany) and a Magister Artium (M.A.) in Educational Sciences from the University of Bonn (Germany). He is a senior researcher and strategy consultant with international reputation and excellent references (>150 publications).

As an internationally recognized expert and innovator, his main research and working fields are: Open Education, technology-enhanced learning, educational policies and philosophy, learning innovations and quality, impact assessment and competence development.

Christian has got 20+ years of business and research experience in HR and E-Learning in leading research teams and large-scale projects (>100 projects, >50 Mio. EUR) and in consulting and supporting ministries, public authorities and institutions to develop long-term policies and to improve learning innovations and quality.

He founded ICORE, the International Community for Open Education and Research and LINQ, the international conference on Learning Innovations and Quality

Open Access This chapter is licensed under the terms of the Creative Commons Attribution 4.0 International License (http://creativecommons.org/licenses/by/4.0/), which permits use, sharing, adaptation, distribution and reproduction in any medium or format, as long as you give appropriate credit to the original author(s) and the source, provide a link to the Creative Commons license and indicate if changes were made.

The images or other third party material in this chapter are included in the chapter's Creative Commons license, unless indicated otherwise in a credit line to the material. If material is not included in the chapter's Creative Commons license and your intended use is not permitted by statutory regulation or exceeds the permitted use, you will need to obtain permission directly from the copyright holder.

Chapter 3
The Ethical Issues of Learning Analytics in Their Historical Context

Dai Griffiths

Abstract The ethical context of Learning Analytics is framed by two related processes. Firstly, the amount of personal data available to organisations has been transformed by the computerisation and the subsequent development of the Internet. Secondly, the methods and ethical assumptions of Operations Research have been extended into new areas. Learning Analytics can be conceptualised as the extension of Operations Research methods to educational institutions, in a process facilitated by technological and social changes in the early twenty-first century. It is argued that the ethical discourse has viewed Learning Analytics as a discrete field, and focused on its internal processes, at the expense of its connections with the wider social context. As a result, contradictions arise in the practice of research ethics, and a number of urgent issues are not given due consideration. These include the partial erosion of the consensus around the Nuremberg code; the use of ethical waivers for quality improvement; the coercive extraction of data; the use of analytics as an enabling technology for management; and the educational implications of the relationship between surveillance and trust.

3.1 Ethics and Learning Analytics

As a first step in considering the ethical context in which Learning Analytics (LA) is carried out, it is necessary to discuss the declared purpose and modus operandi of the field. Writing at an early stage in the development of LA, Long and Siemens, two of the principal actors in the field, explained the rationale for the development of LA, arguing that research indicates that "data-driven decision-making improves organizational output and productivity", and that education is falling behind other fields in this respect.

> Higher education, a field that gathers an astonishing array of data about its "customers," has traditionally been inefficient in its data use, ... Organizational processes—such as planning and resource allocation— often fail to utilize large amounts of data on effective learning

D. Griffiths (✉)
The University of Bolton, Deane Road, Bolton BL3 5AB, UK
e-mail: d.e.griffiths@bolton.ac.uk

© The Author(s) 2020
D. Burgos (ed.), *Radical Solutions and Open Science*, Lecture Notes in Educational Technology, https://doi.org/10.1007/978-981-15-4276-3_3

practices, student profiles, and needed interventions. Something must change. For decades, calls have been made for reform in the efficiency and quality of higher education. Now, with the Internet, mobile technologies, and open education, these calls are gaining a new level of urgency. (Long & Siemens, 2011)

Long and Siemens (2011) go on to distinguish between LA, which is "exclusively on the learning process" (p.34) and 'academic analytics', which is "the application of business intelligence in education" to achieve what Siemens elsewhere referred to as "organisational efficiency" (Long and Siemens, 2011). Since then a great deal of work has been done to implement LA systems, which has been best documented by the Society for Learning Analytics Research (SOLAR), in its annual Learning Analytics and Knowledge (LAK) conference series, and in the Journal of Learning Analytics which SOLAR publishes. It soon became clear that this work raised ethical issues, and Gasevic, Dawson and Jovanovic (2016) comment that "questions related to privacy and ethics in connection to learning analytics have been an ongoing concern since the early days of learning analytics"), with major questions including protection of personal data and data sharing.

Slade and Prinsloo have taken a leading role in identifying the ethical challenges faced by the implementers of LA, and their papers provide a good picture of the issues which were of concern to the field. In an early paper they discussed a number of ethical issues and dilemmas faced by LA (Slade & Prinsloo, 2013), identifying and exploring three broad overlapping categories of ethical issues:

1. The location and interpretation of data
2. Informed consent, privacy and the de-identification of data
3. The management, classification and storage of data.

An influential checklist of ethical concerns proposed by Draschler and Greller (2016) serves as an elaboration of some aspects of the three categories. A fourth important aspect, the obligation to act on knowledge, was identified in Prinsloo and Slade (2017). A recent report by Slade and Tait indicates the current concerns in the field:

…Core Issues that are important on a global basis for the use and development of Learning Analytics in ethics-informed ways:

- Transparency
- Data ownership and control
- Accessibility of data
- Validity and reliability of data
- Institutional responsibility and obligation to act
- Communications
- Cultural values
- Inclusion
- Consent
- Student agency and responsibility
  (Slade & Tait, 2019, p.1)

Readers are directed to a recent paper by Kitto and Knight (2019) which cogently analyzes these ethical initiatives and discusses the practical implications for building LA systems.

The extent of the discussion of ethics in the LA community is testament to the importance which it has been given, and the desire of the participants to act ethically, and to create systems which will not be rejected by stakeholders. Important issues have been identified, the possible courses of action analyzed in depth, and recommendations are made. The designers of LA systems are tasked with providing particular functionality, and they need guidance on how to go about this in an ethically defensible way, and without alienating stakeholders. These are important matters, which have been addressed in the literature which I cite above. In this chapter, however, I am concerned less with the internal workings of the field of LA, and more with the ethical implications of the connections between LA and the wider social context in which it is situated.

In response to the ethical considerations which I have described above, a number of institutions have established codes of practice for LA, to make explicit what will and will not be done with student data, and the roles of those involved. Such policies include, in the UK, Jisc (2015) and The Open University (2014c); in Canada, The University of British Columbia (undated); and in Australia, Charles Stuart University (2015). These codes of practice have the great merit of making explicit the basis for LA design, and they are the results of many person-years of reflection by experts in the field. Nevertheless, contradictions can arise between ethical practices in LA and those prevailing in academic research. The Open University (OU) of the UK provides a good example, because of the exemplary clarity of its policies on research ethics and on LA. The OU FAQs on LA inform students that in order to have "a complete dataset" available to the University "…it is not possible, at present, to have your data excluded" (The Open University, 2014b). At the same time, the OU's Ethics Principles for Research Involving Human Participants assert that "Except in exceptional circumstances, where the nature of the research design requires it, no research shall be conducted without the opt-in valid consent of participants." and that "Participants … have a right to withdraw their consent at any time up to a specified date" (The Open University, 2014a). LA at the OU is intended to "identify interventions which aim to support students in achieving their study goals" (The Open University, 2014c), an aim which has traditionally been addressed by means of academic educational research. From these documents, it inescapably appears that an OU PhD student who is researching into teaching and learning outside the OU would need to obtain ethical approval and consent from participants before gathering any data, while the student's parent organisation carries out the same research on its own students without any such constraint. All three OU documents that I have cited are dated 2014, and so this contradiction is not a case of outdated policies failing to keep track of recent developments.

The OU is by no means alone in viewing very similar research activities through quite different ethical lenses. To take another example, the Charles Sturt University Learning Analytics Code of Practice states that data is collected without consent:

> Data is collected from learning and teaching systems, retained and utilised for the purposes of enhancing learning and teaching by: (…)
>
> – Contributing to research and scholarship in learning and teaching (Charles Sturt University, 2015)

At the same time the University ascribes to the National Statement on Ethical Conduct in Human Research, which states that

> Consent to participate in research must be voluntary and based on sufficient information and adequate understanding of both the proposed research and the implications of participation in it. (NHMRC, 2018)

I have actively promoted LA for a number of years, and it is not my intention here to proclaim *mea culpa*, or to condemn my colleagues for failing to abide by codes of practice for research with human participants. Rather I seek to achieve some understanding of the shifting context which has caused well-intentioned and conscientious people to find themselves in this tangle, and to provide a way of conceiving of the forces which are shaping the future of education. To do this, we need to examine the historical context within which LA has developed.

3.2 Two Traditions of Research Ethics

The academic community working on LA has defined itself as a distinct field of study. This makes it possible to maintain a scholarly community and discourse, but tends to disguise the degree to which the ethical issues of LA are not specific to the field, but rather are symptomatic of wider changes in which networked data is used to mediate and mould human relationships. To understand these changes, and their ethical implications, it is necessary to look back in the past, well beyond the development of the Internet. Knowingly or otherwise, practitioners of LA, academics and ethical review bodies have all situated themselves within ethical traditions which date back to the Second World War when framing the use of data in understanding and predicting the activities and performance of organisations and individuals.

Following the Nuremberg trials of those involved in Nazi atrocities during the Second World War, the Nuremberg Code (U.S. Government, 1949) was established to ensure that research would never again establish an abusive or exploitative relationship with its subjects. According to Shuster (1997), the Code has not been officially adopted by any nation or major medical association, but "Nonetheless, its influence on global human-rights law and medical ethics has been profound." Of particular relevance for this chapter is article 1 of the Code:

> The voluntary consent of the human subject is absolutely essential …the person involved should … be able to exercise free power of choice, there should be made known to him the nature, duration, and purpose of the experiment; the method and means by which it is to be conducted …. (U.S. Government, 1949)

The Code was originally conceived in response to horrific Nazi-sponsored medical research and it was in medicine that it was first applied. However, the application of the Code was soon extended to all research involving human subjects. This is reflected in all major policies and codes on ethics in the social sciences, including the influential Common Rule in the U.S.A. (U.S. Government, 2017). For example, the International Sociological Association (2001) code of ethics states that "The consent of research subjects and informants should be obtained in advance", while the British Educational Research Association Ethical Guidelines for Educational Research affirm that "It is normally expected that participants' voluntary informed consent to be involved in the study will be obtained at the start of the study" and stipulate that "It should be made clear to participants that they can withdraw at any point without needing to provide an explanation" (British Educational Research Association, 2018, p.9).

Also with its origins in the Second World War, a quite different ethical tradition has developed. During the War, researchers were employed to optimise the operation of the military and other essential government services. This was particularly the case in the application of new technologies, such as radar, which required the development of new collaborative sociotechnical processes to achieve optimal performance. Rau (2005) describes how work was carried out

> ...to develop new filtering methods, study the effects of the location of stations on radar performance and discover why some aircraft slipped through the radar network undetected. Rowe referred to this work as 'operational research' to contrast it with the developmental research' going on in the laboratories and workshops: in OR the work took place 'on site'.

'Operational', or more frequently 'Operations' Research (OR) continued in peacetime, with investigations being carried out in businesses, industrial organisations and the state sector, with the aim of establishing effective processes and management strategies. As Rau continues, "the subsequent influence that these wartime foundations had on OR are hard to overestimate". In the 1960s computer models started to be used extensively to support OR, with the development of Decision Support Systems (see Ferguson and Jones (1969) for an early example). 'Business Intelligence' can also be seen as a manifestation of OR, while Stafford Beer (1967) viewed the whole of Management Science as "the business use of operations research". It is therefore clear that we are looking at a continuous and influential tradition of research in these fields leading back (at least) to the Second World War, whatever disagreements there may be about how to name the parts and the whole.

Many in academia will, I suspect, be unfamiliar with the OR tradition and its related fields, and perhaps even doubt that its activities should be classified as 'research'. However, an early definition by Pocock describes OR as follows:

> Operations Research is a scientific methodology analytical, experimental, quantitative which, by assessing the overall implications of various alternative courses of action in a management system provides an improved basis for management decisions. (Pocock, 1956)

Thus, OR applies scientific methodologies to understand the world, and as such it seems undeniably to constitute 'research'. If it is unfamiliar in academia, outside areas such as management science and information systems, this may be because its objects of study have not overlapped with those of academic researchers. Once academics accept OR as 'research' in the full sense of the word, often working with human respondents, they may assume without further reflection that ethical codes of practice drawn from the Nuremberg Code will be applicable to it, but this has not been the case at any point in the history of OR. The lack of ethical scrutiny in OR is not simply a matter of ignorance or evasion. An athlete can keep records of their own performance, and use this data in optimising their diet and exercise regime, without the requirement for any ethical approval. Similarly, the organisation can be seen as a metaphorical (and, in many cases, legal) person that owns its own data, and has the freedom to do as it wishes with it to optimise its own performance. As Picavet comments "in operational research, efficiency is not usually viewed as something which conflicts with ethics. Quite simply, it does not refer to the same category of problems." (Picavet, 2009, p. 1122). Moreover, the methods and processes which result from this research may bring significant competitive advantage to the organisation. It is therefore not surprising that opening up this research to ethical scrutiny is not only seen as unnecessary, but is also actively unwelcome, as it threatens the secrecy required to protect competitive advantage. There has been ongoing discussion of ethics within the OR community over a number of years, see, for example Le Menestrel and van Wassenhove (2009). However, where ethical codes for OR exist, they make no mention of the key dispensations of the Nuremberg Code, in particular those of informed consent and of a right to withdraw. This is the case, for example in the ethical principles of the Operational Research Society (2019).

I have argued for the continuity of thinking on research ethics since the Second World War, but this thinking has also evolved over time, principally as a result of the impact of technological change, as I now discuss.

3.3 The Impact of Technology on Research Ethics

The massive expansion of the availability of data on human interactions generated by the Internet has had a profound impact on assumptions about the ethics of gathering data. To illustrate the nature of these changes it is sufficient to look back at the concerns about computing in the years before the emergence of the Internet. Culman and Smith (1995) describe the furore that surrounded Lotus Marketplace. Launched in 1990, this was a CD-ROM for sale at $695 containing information about 120 million Americans, including name, address, age, gender, marital status, household income, and lifestyle and purchasing propensities. Software was included to facilitate creation of mailing lists that targeted prospective customers. 30,000 letter writers and callers contacted Lotus, complaining that the product was a violation of privacy. The CEO of Lotus concluded that the company "would be ill-served by a prolonged battle over consumer privacy", and the product was cancelled in January 1991. Despite the reticence of Lotus, that battle has since taken place, and has resulted in an unqualified victory for commercial interests over personal privacy. Today the scale of data held by Lotus Marketplace, and the threat of increased junk mail which it presented, both seem insignificant. The supermarkets where we shop (Rowley, 2007) and the websites which we visit (Evans, 2009) hold and exchange vastly more detailed data about us than Lotus could have dreamed of. The revelations of Snowdon (Greenwald, 2014) have shown that governments have secretly developed vast infrastructures to monitor and analyze the communications of individuals. Cambridge Analytica, the firm accused of harvesting millions of people's data from Facebook, "said publicly that it held up to 5000 data points on each of over 230 million American voters." (Mr. Justice Norris, 2019). While this case ended in litigation, no effective opposition has emerged to the gathering of data on a massive scale by private companies, and its use in marketing, advertising and politics. Similarly, within the field of LA the InBloom analytics initiative was closed following a public reaction to intrusive data gathering (Bulger, McCormick & Pitcan, 2017), but this has not slowed the growth of the field.

Zuboff (2019) argues that Google has taken a leading role in these developments and provides a detailed analysis of the strategy established by Google Chief Economist Hal Varian to leverage the data gathered by the company. By 2014 Varian was confident enough to assert that these new procedures with private and personal data had become accepted practice rather than a matter for discussion:

> 'There is no putting the genie back in the bottle … Everyone will expect to be tracked and monitored, since the advantages, in terms of convenience, safety, and services, will be so great … continuous monitoring will be the norm (Varian, H, quoted in PEW Research (2014)).

Zuboff herself has painted a less optimistic view of this outcome:

> …our lives are unilaterally rendered as data, expropriated, and repurposed in new forms of social control, all of it in the service of others' interests and in the absence of our awareness or means of combat. (Zuboff, 2019, p.54)

Zuboff (2019) identifies as 'surveillance capitalism' the methods which have driven the expansion of the analysis of personal data since the emergence of the Internet. Its principal actors are commercial organisations and security agencies, its workings are shrouded in secrecy, and its purpose is to obtain personal or organisational advantage. LA, in contrast, is a self-declared community of academics working towards an explicit goal of improving education, and sharing their methods and insights in public conferences. This contrast means that the emergence of LA cannot be explained as simply a manifestation of surveillance capitalism. Nevertheless, LA shares some of the methods and assumptions of surveillance capitalism, and these carry with them assumptions about data gathering and use which may shed light on the ethical tangle which LA finds itself in. These assumptions were well summarised by Bill Schmarzo, chief technical officer of EMC Global Services: "I'm a hoarder, I want it all. And even if I don't yet know how I'll use that data, I want it … My data science team might find a use for it" (Bertolucci, 2014). Informed consent for a specified purpose, is clearly not compatible with such a strategy.

The changes which have taken place in the practice of data collection in society have had a substantial impact on the methodology of the social sciences, to the extent that it has been seen as constituting a 'watershed moment' (McFarland, Lewis and Goldberg, 2015). The increasing influence of 'big data' data-gathering strategies is blurring the line between OR and academic social science in two ways.

Firstly, OR is being applied in fields which were once the preserve of academic research. Until the emergence of the Internet, the data available to OR researchers was largely limited to that produced in-house by commercial and governmental organisations, such as production process data and internal communications. This led to a well-demarcated area of research, which studied the internal processes of organisations, and seldom clashed with academic research investigating wider social phenomena. Today, however, huge quantities of data are available, generated by clients and stakeholders' engagement with computer systems, which enable organisations to address a much wider range of OR questions, many of which are situated beyond the confines of the organisation per se. For example, retailers would in the past have conducted operations research on their organisation and communications, but would usually have relied on social scientists to analyze the social context in which they were operating. Now, however, an advertisement for analytics roles at TESCO says that successful applicants will "help the business to really understand our customers and suppliers" (TESCO, 2019). Similarly, 'predictive policing' practices are encroaching on the domain of academic criminology, using data analytics "to identify liktargets for police intervention and prevent crime or solve past crimes by making statistical predictions" (Perry, 2013 p. xiii), combining, for example, GPS tracking, license plate readers, and geographic profiling tools (Perry, 2013; Table 5.3).

Secondly, academic social science has adopted OR methods. According to Gary King, Director of the Harvard Institute for Quantitative Social Science, "Businesses now possess more social-science data than academics do" (Shaw, 2014). In the face of this shift in power, many social scientists appear to have accepted that a change in research practices is inevitable, with concomitant ethical implications which have yet to be spelt out. For example, the Social Science Research Council has entered into the Social Science One collaboration with Facebook. This development has been welcomed by some social scientists, for example Puschmann (2019), while the complaints of the European Advisory Committee for Science One (2019) are that "Facebook has still not provided academics with anything approaching adequate data access". In contrast Leetaru (2019) argues that Social Science One will make the personal and intimate data of two billion Facebook users available for data mining by researchers, with little information available about the details of aggregation, privacy or how the results of the research might be used in intervening in society. In the context of developments such as this, it is unsurprising that LA practitioners are unwilling to commit to the constraints which would be placed on their relatively small scale studies by compliance with policies on research ethics with human participants.

The argument made here is that within the wider context of the influence of data analytics on the social sciences, the development of LA can be best understood as the extension of the OR research tradition to the education sector. Furthermore, the contradictions identified above between ethical policies for academic research with human subjects, and ethical guidelines for the practice of LA, correspond closely to the tension between the ethical traditions of OR and academic research. I propose that the resolution of these ethical contradictions can only be achieved through an understanding of the implications of these changes for educational systems, institutions and the people who work and study in them, and then taking decisions in the light of that understanding. In the remainder of this chapter, I will consider some of the issues which will need to be addressed in order to achieve such an understanding.

3.4 Ethical Issues Raised by the Extension of Operations Research to Education

3.4.1 The Erosion of the Nuremberg Tradition

The multiple issues and challenges of the ethics of LA may be summarised in this quandary: is LA academic research (as it appears to be from its objects of study) or is it OR (as it appears to be from its institutional purpose)?

This quandary is easy to name, but hard to resolve. A resolution in favour of either alternative implies consequences that are unacceptable to many actors. If LA is research, and is governed by the Nuremberg code, then education institutions will be required to seek consent from students and teachers for any analytical activity, in advance, and to specify the purpose of the data gathering. As we have seen above, this flies in the face of universal education practice in maintaining records of student attendance and achievement, and would rule out many of the activities of LA. It would also have significant consequences for commercial suppliers of services to education. On the other hand, if, as I have argued, LA is most usefully conceptualised as the extension of OR to the institution, then there is a prospect that the entire ethical framework for educational research could become irrelevant. There are two ways in which this may take place. Firstly, in the medium term the availability of data on the systems of institutions and their commercial partners, and the ease of access and ethical approval through LA, will inevitably be an attraction to educational researchers, and a cause for cynicism about research ethics procedures. It is hard to see how this could not undermine the authority of research ethics procedures.

Secondly, educational research could simply move out of the academic sector. To take an example, researchers from Pearson presented a paper at the American Educational Research Association Annual Meeting (Belenky, 2018) which described a randomised control trial in different messages that were embedded in the MyLab Programming application, in order to see which would lead students to attempt and complete more problems. Five thousand students were unknowingly involved in the experiment. According to Herold (2018) "the research prompted a fierce debate over issues of ethics, privacy and consent" leading to a fall in stock value. Pearson then described the experiment as a "relatively minor product update" (Herold, 2018) No related research has been published by Pearson, but institutions who use their products cannot know if the company is no longer carrying out such work, or if such analytics work is simply not being reported. The same is true, of course, for other companies. The question for educational institutions is whether it is ethical to make use of educational services which are not sufficiently transparent in their use of data, when doing so means that they cannot ensure that their institutional codes of practice for both research ethics and LA are being respected.

The issues raised by the Pearson research are a particular case of a wider process. As discussed by Zuboff (2019 p.299–305) the issue was brought to prominence by a paper in Nature by University of California and Facebook researchers leveraging company data, entitled "A 61-million-person experiment in social influence and political mobilization" (Bond et al., 2012). The editor of Nature said in an interview that

> I was concerned … until I queried the authors and they said their local institutional review board had approved it—and apparently on the grounds that Facebook apparently manipulates people's News Feeds all the time. (Lafrance, 2019)

The editor also explained that the review board had approved the study because it used a 'pre-existing dataset'. Professor Chris Chambers summarised the concerns of many that

> the Facebook study paints a dystopian future in which academic researchers escape ethical restriction by teaming up with private companies to test increasingly dangerous or harmful interventions. (Chambers, 2014)

If, as I have argued, LA wholly or partly represents the extension of OR to the Education sector, then a primary ethical concern for the sector should be the disruption which this extension is causing to research ethics within education, and the likely implications of its future impact on education and educational research. A failure to conduct this discussion would mean that, despite all the good intentions and reflection in the LA community, the ethics of LA would be those of a power grab: 'we grant ourselves an ethical exemption because we can, and let the social consequences fall as they will'.

3.4.2 Ethical Waivers and Exemptions

The medical field has been confronted with very similar ethical issues to those raised by LA, but for rather longer because until recently much more data was generated in the health sector than in education. In many jurisdictions, including the United States, the same problem that we have identified in LA arises, i.e. deciding whether an investigation qualifies as 'research' (which is governed by ethical review boards) or as 'quality improvement' OR (which has a waiver or exemption from ethical review), as discussed by Goldstein et al. (2018). Taylor et al. (2010) describe how in the 1990s "questions were raised as to whether quality improvement initiatives ought to be considered human subject research and reviewed and regulated as such", and they provide a number of examples.

These questions remain open, as McLennan writes:

> The ethical oversight system in Switzerland currently places a higher standard of ethical oversight on "research" in comparison with "quality control" activities using the same quality data. However, these activities cannot often be reliably differentiated from each other and the inconsistent ethical oversight of these activities needs to be reconsidered. (McLennan et al., 2018)

Here we have a more mature field which is wrestling with the same issues as LA, and it is surely worth examining the parallels to see what can be usefully learned, but very little connection has been made between LA and medical ethics. In particular, the concept of an ethical waiver or exemption for quality improvement maps well onto the contradiction between LA and academic research in education. From this perspective, it is not sufficient for LA to publish codes of practice. The ethical challenge for LA is to discuss in one framework both the codes governing research with human subjects and those governing LA, and to justify the exemptions which are granted to LA. This discussion may result in desirable changes to the governance of research with human subjects, as well as adjustments to LA. It will have to take into consideration wider changes in society regarding the use of data, and so will have social and political dimensions. It therefore cannot take place only in the LA academic community within which most of the ethical discussion of LA has so far taken place.

3.4.3 Coercive Extraction of Data

Citizens in many countries share data in many aspects of their lives. Every time they drive a car their license plate may be captured, when they walk in a public space their face may be automatically processed. Every time they send an email, actors such as GCHQ and Google monitor its content. Unless they take elaborate precautions, many websites that they visit will share their record of interactions with an advertising network such as Google's Adsense. The citizen has little choice but to acquiesce in this data collection, because their daily lives depend on carrying out these activities.

School-age education is compulsory around the world, and higher education is, increasingly, also a requirement for life in a developed economy. In an environment where all educational institutions monitor the data generated by all students, citizens and children are confronted by the coercive analysis of data which goes well beyond the traditional data generated in the course of educational administration. It is perhaps in recognition of this that Charles Sturt University (2015) explicitly excludes the use in LA of data from email and other private online communication. Nevertheless, while educational institutions refuse to exclude students from datasets (for example The Open University, 2014b), LA codes of practice cannot be seen only as the individual choice of an institution, but rather also as symptomatic of a society-wide coercive extraction of data from its citizens, for good or ill. An analysis of the ethics of LA that aspires to go beyond the comparison of implementation approaches should recognise that the field is part of this wider trend, and take a position on it.

3.4.4 Learning Analytics Entwined with Governance

While wanting to avoid suggesting that there was a golden age in which lecturers and students were aware of, and able to contribute to, institutional management processes, there is no doubt that Shattock is correct to assert that in the UK

> from 2000 to 2016, the policy turmoil that accompanied the increasing marketisation of the higher education system and the introduction of a league table culture has led to the growth of powerful vice-chancellor-led executive teams, which have transformed governance practice and decision-making in many universities. (Shattock, 2017)

This concentration of power is also to be seen in many institutions across Europe, as described by Paradeise and Thoenig (2013), and is in many respects a global phenomenon driven by the New Public Management movement (see Lapsley, 2009). LA represents a potential or actual source of data to feed into the Key Performance Indicators and other methods which are used by managers to control the institutions which they are running. Whether or not learners and teachers are keen to use an LA intervention, they may nevertheless find that they have to do so if they are to maintain their studies or jobs. A corollary of this argument, if it is accepted, is that 'learning' and 'academic' analytics (see Long & Siemans, 2011) cannot be kept separate for ethical purposes. Education institutions compete on the basis of their effectiveness in teaching, and an essential business target is for them to meet the key performance indicators in teaching and learning set out for them by government agencies. Similarly, management decisions about teaching contracts and pay are influenced by teaching achievement.

As I have argued elsewhere (Griffiths, 2017), LA generates models of the institution and its operation. These models are conceived from particular perspectives and for particular purposes, generally by or for people in a management role, in part because it is managers who control budgets and who have access to data. These models then become an active element in the management of the institution and of the activities of lecturers and students, and can change relationships in the institution. Brans and Gallo offer two ways of viewing the ethics of OR practice which can be applied to this situation. One perspective is that of "those whose view on ethics is mainly internal, i.e. those who focus on the relation between OR/MS professionals and clients and on the way the modelling work is carried on" (Brans & Gallo, 2007), emphasising technical correctness and honesty. Within LA, such correctness would include respecting the relevant codes of practice and regulations covering the management of data. Brans and Gallo identify others for whom ethical professional behaviour "means taking always into account the effects on society and nature of the decisions derived from their analyses and models" (ibid). From this perspective a person concerned with the ethics of an LA implementation needs to look at the systemic impact of LA on the institution as a whole, and on all of the people who will be directly or indirectly affected by it. Given the complex intertwining of LA with systemic change in education, it seems incumbent to pay attention to these wider consequences of model making in LA, both positive and negative, in assessing the ethics of LA implementations.

3.4.5 Surveillance, Trust and Learning

Long and Siemens describe how Learning analytics can assist all stakeholders to penetrate "the fog that has settled over much of higher education" (Long & Siemens, 2011, p. 40). Increasing visibility is generally understood as a good thing, but could it also be that the fog can sometimes be an essential enabler of education? Fried argued that

> There can be no trust where there is no possibility of error. More specifically, man cannot know that he is trusted unless he has a right to act without constant surveillance so that he knows he can betray the trust. Privacy confers that essential right. (Fried, 1970, p.56)

Trust is not the same as a lack of surveillance, but surveillance acts to reduce trust. It is trust shown towards students that enables them to demonstrate autonomy and initiative, and to learn from their own mistakes. It can therefore be argued that while dispelling the fog in education may have befits, and it also changes the behaviour of students. Writing about the educational application of online forums before the emergence of LA, Dawson (2006) noted that "behaviour is altered when students are aware of surveillance techniques" and that "attention must be given to the manner in which online discussion forums efficiently construct new subjects that are both 'productive' and 'docile'".

I describe as 'cognitive engineering' this use of technology to construct a productive and docile subject who learns what is prescribed. It is the fulfilment of Skinner's dream of a teaching machine (Skinner, 1958). To the extent that we can know and specify what is best for others to learn, and how they should learn it (and this can certainly be argued in some situations), then this approach may be justified, indeed perhaps ethically obligatory. However, the application of such an approach as a technocratic imperative, and the lack of trust which that would bring with it, would not only clash with political and ideological ideas of personal freedom, but also fly in the face of the requirements for education as they have been set out in the twenty-first century. For example, the key competences set out by the European Commission in the New Skills Agenda for Europe (Kraatz, 2017) include learning to learn, social and civic competences and a sense of initiative and entrepreneurship. It is hard to see how such reflective communication skills and intellectual autonomy can be developed if error is not allowed or, indeed, encouraged.

LA is not incompatible with trust, but trust raises ethical questions for the design and implementation of LA. To what degree should the fog of education be dispersed in order to monitored and optimise students' behaviour? To what extent is a particular LA implementation a constraint on students' personal development and autonomy? To what degree are privacy and trust (of students by lecturers, and of lecturers by managers), necessary in order for them to develop as autonomous learners and human beings? To what extent does a cognitive engineering approach imply an abandonment of teachers' responsibility for their learners? These are practical questions for LA, and they all have significant ethical implications. The answers will be as complex and as socially situated as the arguments around the pedagogy which LA seeks to support.

3.5 Concluding Remarks

Throughout this paper, I have argued that the discourse of the ethics of LA should not be only that of a community of educationalists and technologists reflecting on its own practice within a discrete field with its own ethical imperatives. It is also necessary to view LA as a manifestation in the education sector of wider trends which are transforming society, and to theorise where these trends have come from, where they are going to and what the place of LA is within them.

I have made reference to the extensive and valuable work has been done to articulate codes of practice and to define the ethical conduct of LA. My purpose has not been to critique that work, but rather to place it in context, to provide a diagnosis of the causes of the ethical tensions which it is wrestling with, and to identify wider ethical issues which, in my view, are raised by LA.

Technology has enabled an on-going transformation of educational relationships, and continues to do so. LA is situated at the point of contact between technological developments in society as a whole, and the particular practices of education, and so offers an opportunity to inquire into the ethical dimensions of that emerging relationship. With this in mind, I hope to have shown that the ethics of LA concerns not only the self-contained act of data collection, or the details of data governance, but also more complex and relative issues of who is doing what for whom, how and with what ends. This requires an engagement with pedagogy, politics and ideology which has so far been more conspicuous by its absence than its salience in the discourse around the ethics of LA.

Socrates said that when we speak of ethics "what we are talking about is how one should live." (Williams, 2011). As the second decade of the twenty-first century reaches its close, there is puzzlement on all sides about why we live as we do, and how we should respond. How did xenophobic nationalism re-emerge in democracies? How did we let the ocean become filled with plastic? Why are we unable to do anything about climate change? Why do we work more hours every year? Why were we so unprepared for the coronavirus? The answer to these questions is, I suspect, that our attention has been misdirected towards problems of marginal importance, while unnoticed processes have been radically transforming our way of life. If we want to understand the ethics of "how one should live" with data analytics in education, then we need to ask if our attention is well directed, or if, as I suspect, we are failing to examine links between our use of technology and wider processes that are transforming the way that students and teachers live their lives. Such a failure would risk the emergence of unintended consequences which would horrify many enthusiasts for the powerful and potentially beneficial technology of LA.

References

Beer, S. (1967). *Management science: The business use of operations research*. New York: Doubleday & Co. Inc.

Belenky, D. M. et al. (2018). Embedding research-inspired innovations in EdTech: A Randomized Controlled Trial of Social-Psychological Interventions, at Scale. In Abstacts of the AERA Annual Meeting, Apr 13–17, New York. http://www.aera.net/Publications/Online-Paper-Repository/AERA-Online-Paper-Repository. Accessed 30 Sept 2019.

Bertolucci, J. (2014). When data hoarding makes sense. In: InformationWeek. https://www.informationweek.com/big-data/big-data-analytics/when-data-hoarding-makes-sense/d/d-id/1297474. Accessed 30 Sept 2019.

Bond, R. M. et al. (2012). A 61-million-person experiment in social influence and political mobilization. *Nature, 489*(7415).

Brans, J. P., & Gallo, G. (2007). Ethics in OR/MS: Past, present and future. *Annals of Operations Research, 153*(1), 165–178.

British Educational Research Association. (2018). *Ethical guidelines for educational research*, 4th ed. https://www.bera.ac.uk/wp-content/uploads/2018/06/BERA-Ethical-Guidelines-for-Educational-Research_4thEdn_2018.pdf. Accessed 5 Apr 2020.

Bulger, M., McCormick, P., & Pitcan, M. (2017). The legacy of InBloom, data & society research institute working paper. https://datasociety.net/pubs/ecl/InBloom_feb_2017.pdf. Accessed 6 Oct 2019.

Chambers, C. (2014). Facebook fiasco: Was Cornell's study of "emotional contagion" an ethics breach? In: The guardian, 1st July. https://www.theguardian.com/science/head-quarters/2014/jul/01/facebook-cornell-study-emotional-contagion-ethics-breach. Accessed 30 Sept 2019.

Charles Sturt University. (2015). CSU learning analytics code of practice VERSION 3.2. http://www.csu.edu.au/__data/assets/pdf_file/0007/2160484/2016_CSU_LearningAnalyticsCodePractice.pdf. Accessed 29 Sept 2019.

Culman, M. J., Smith, H. J. (1995). Lotus marketplace: Households ... managing information privacy concerns. In *Computers, Ethics, and Social Values, Prentice Hall* (pp. 269–277).

Dawson, S. (2006). The impact of institutional surveillance technologies on student behaviour. *Surveillance & Society, 4*(1/2).

Drachsler, H., Greller, W. (2016). Privacy and learning analytics—a delicate issue: A checklist for trusted learning analytics. In *LAK'16 Proceedings of the 6th International Conference on Learning Analytics & Knowledge* (p. 89). ACM.

European Advisory Committee of Social Science One. (2019). Public statement from the Co-Chairs and European Advisory Committee of Social Science One. https://socialscience.one/blog/public-statement-european-advisory-committee-social-science-one. Accessed 5 Apr 2020.

Evans, D.-S. (2009). The online advertising industry: Economics, evolution, and privacy. *Journal of Economic Perspectives, 23*(3), 37–60.

Ferguson, R.-L., & Jones, C.-H. (1969). A computer aided decision system. *Management Science, 15*(10), B550–561.

Fried, C. (1970). Privacy: A rational context. Reprinted in Ermann, M. D., Williams, M. B., Gutierrez, C. (Eds) (1990). *Computers, Ethics, & Society* (pp. 51–63). Oxford University Press.

Gasevic, D., Dawson, S., & Jovanovic, J. (2016). Editorial: Ethics and privacy in learning analytics. *Journal of Learning Analytics, 3*(1), 1–4.

Goldstein, C.E., et al. (2018). Accommodating quality and service improvement research within existing ethical principles. *Trials, 19*(334), 334.

Greenwald, G. (2014). *No place to Hide*. New York: Metropolitan Books.

Griffiths, D. (2017). The use of models in learning design and learning analytics. *Interaction Design and Architecture(s)*, (33), 113–133.

Herold, B. (2018). Pearson tests growth-mindset messages in software. In: Education week. https://www.edweek.org/ew/articles/2018/05/02/pearson-tests-growth-mindset-messages-in-software.html?print=1. Accessed 30 Sept 2019.

International Sociological Association. (2001). Code of ethics. https://www.isa-sociology.org/en/about-isa/code-of-ethics/. Accessed 30 Sept 2019.

Jisc. (2015). *Code of practice for learning analytics*. https://www.jisc.ac.uk/sites/default/files/jd0040_code_of_practice_for_learning_analytics_190515_v1.pdf. Accessed 5 Apr 2020.

Kitto, K., Knight, S. (2019). Practical ethics for building learning analytics. *British Journal of Educational Technology, 50*(6).

Kraatz, S. (2017). New skills agenda for europe: State of implementation. European parliament. http://www.europarl.europa.eu/RegData/etudes/BRIE/2017/607334/IPOL_BRI(2017)607334_EN.pdf. Accessed 30 Sept 2019.

Lafrance, A. (2019). Even the editor of facebook's mood study thought it was creepy. Atlantic. https://www.theatlantic.com/technology/archive/2014/06/even-the-editor-of-facebooks-mood-study-thought-it-was-creepy/373649/. Accessed 8 Oct 2019.

Lapsley, I. (2009). New public management: The cruellest invention of the human spirit? *Abacus, 45*(1), 1–21.

Leetaru, K. (2019). Forget "Russian" FaceApp - Facebook and social science one are the real Russian data danger. In: Forbes. https://www.forbes.com/sites/kalevleetaru/2019/07/19/forget-russian-faceapp-facebook-and-social-science-one-are-the-real-russian-data-danger/. Accessed 5 Apr 2020.

Le Menestrel, M., & Van Wassenhove, L. N. (2009). Ethics in operations research and management sciences: A never-ending effort to combine rigor and passion. *Omega 12, Special Issue on Ethics and Operations Research, 37*(6), 1039–1043.

Long, P., & Siemens, G. (2011). Penetrating the fog: Analytics in learning and education. Educause review (Sepember/October) pp. 31–40.

McFarland, D. A., Lewis, K., & Goldberg, A. (2015). Sociology in the era of big data: The ascent of forensic social science. *The American Sociologist, 47*(1), 12–35.

McLennan, S., et al. (2018). The inconsistent ethical oversight of healthcare quality data in Switzerland. *Swiss Medical Weekly, 148,* w14637.

Mr Justice Norris. (2019). Approved judgment. Royal courts of justice. Case No: CO/7774/2010; CO/7850/2011.

NHMRC. (2018). Conduct in human research national statement on ethical conduct in human research, 2007 (Updated 2018). Australian Government: National health and medical research council. https://www.nhmrc.gov.au/about-us/publications/national-statement-ethical-conduct-human-research-2007-updated-2018. Accessed 29 Sept 2019.

Paradeise, C., & Thoenig, J.-C. (2013). Academic institutions in search of quality: local orders and global standards. *Organization Studies, 34*(2), 189–218.

Perry, W. L. et al. (2013). Predictive policing: the role of crime forecasting in law enforcement operations. RAND safety and justice program. RAND corporation research papers. https://www.rand.org/pubs/research_reports/RR233.html. Accessed 30 Sept 2019.

PEW Research Center. (2014). Digital life in 2025. http://www.pewinternet.org/2014/03/11/digital-life-in-2025/. Accessed 30 Sept 2019.

Picavet, E. (2009). Opportunities and pitfalls for ethical analysis in operations research and the management sciences. *Omega, 37*(6), 1121–1131.

Pocock, J. W. (1956). Operations research, special report no. 13. In *Operations Research: Challenges to Management.* American Management Association.

Prinsloo, P., & Slade, S. (2017). An elephant in the learning analytics room: The obligation to Act. In Proceedings of the Seventh International Learning Analytics and Knowledge (pp. 46–55). ACM.

Puschmann, C. (2019). An end to the wild west of social media research: A response to Axel Bruns. *Information, Communication & Society, 22*(11), 1582–1589.

Rau, E.-P. (2005). Combat science: The emergence of operational research in world war II. *Endeavour, 29*(4), 156–161.

Rowley, J. (2007). Reconceptualising the strategic role of loyalty schemes. *Journal of Computer Marketing, 24*(6), 366–374.

Shattock, M. (2017). The Four Ages of UK University Governance. Times Higher Education. https://www.timeshighereducation.com/blog/four-ages-uk-university-governance. Accessed 8 Oct 2019.

Shaw, J. (2014). Why "Big Data" is a big deal. Harvard Magazine (March-April).

Shuster, E. (1997). Fifty years later: The significance of the Nuremberg code. *New England Journal of Medicine, 337*, 1436–1440.
Skinner, B.-F. (1958). Teaching machines. *Science, 128*(3330), 969–977.
Slade, S., & Prinsloo, P. (2013). Learning analytics: Ethical issues and dilemmas. *American Behavioral Scientist, 57*(10), 1510–1529.
Slade, S., & Tait, A. (2019). Global guidelines: Ethics in learning analytics. International council for open and distance education. https://www.learntechlib.org/p/208251/report_208251.pdf. Accessed 9 October 2019.
Taylor, H. A., et al. (2010). The ethical review of health care quality improvement initiatives: Findings from the field. *Commonwealth Fund Issue Briefs, 95*(August), 1–12.
TESCO. (2019). TESCO careers. https://www.tesco-careers.com/office/data-science-and-analytics/analytics/. Accessed 30 Sept 2019.
The Open University. (2014a). Ethics principles for research involving human participants. http://www.open.ac.uk/research/ethics/sites/www.open.ac.uk.research.ethics/files/files/ecms/web-content/Ethics-Principles-for-Research-involving-Human-Participants.pdf. Accessed 29 Sept 2019.
The Open University. (2014b). Ethical use of student data for learning analytics policy FAQs. https://help.open.ac.uk/documents/policies/ethical-use-of-student-data/files/23/ethical-student-data-faq.pdf. Accessed 29 Sept 2019.
The Open University. (2014c). Policy on ethical use of student data for learning analytics. Available at. https://help.open.ac.uk/documents/policies/ethical-use-of-student-data/files/22/ethical-use-of-student-data-policy.pdf Accessed 29 Sept 2019.
The Operational Research Society. (2019). Statement of ethical principles. https://www.theorsociety.com/who-we-are/board/ethical-principles/. Accessed 9 Oct 2019.
The University of British Columbia. (undated). *Learning analytics: Ethics and policy*. https://learninganalytics.ubc.ca/ethics-policy/ Accessed 5 Apr 2020
U.S. Government. (1949). *Trials of war criminals before the nuremberg military tribunals under control council. Law No. 10* (Vol. 2).
U.S. Government. (2017). Federal policy for the protection of human subjects. Federal register. 19 Jan 2017.
Williams, B. (2011). *Ethics and the Limits of philosophy*. London and New York: Taylor and Francis.
Zuboff, S. (2019). *The age of surveillance capitalism: The fight for a human future at the new frontier of power*. London: Profile Books.

Open Access This chapter is licensed under the terms of the Creative Commons Attribution 4.0 International License (http://creativecommons.org/licenses/by/4.0/), which permits use, sharing, adaptation, distribution and reproduction in any medium or format, as long as you give appropriate credit to the original author(s) and the source, provide a link to the Creative Commons license and indicate if changes were made.

The images or other third party material in this chapter are included in the chapter's Creative Commons license, unless indicated otherwise in a credit line to the material. If material is not included in the chapter's Creative Commons license and your intended use is not permitted by statutory regulation or exceeds the permitted use, you will need to obtain permission directly from the copyright holder.

Chapter 4
A Hidden Dream: Open Educational Resources

Saida Affouneh and Zuheir N. Khlaif

Abstract Open-source materials are being used for education in a variety of contexts, and educators can reuse them to achieve different objectives in both higher education and public education. Educators in Palestine are using open education resources for professional development to improve their performance and learning. There are different advantages to open education resources; for example, they can reduce training costs, as well as the time and effort required by students and educators. Different open resources have emerged in Palestine, such as MOOCs and open learning objects for K-12.

Keywords Open education resources · MOOCs · Professional development

4.1 Introduction

Searching for new knowledge, good practices, recent articles and upcoming conferences is an interesting and rich experience nowadays. With one click, you can download hundreds of pages of eBooks and tens of articles in a few minutes. This was not the case in the early eighties, where you had to travel for miles to libraries and bookshops in order to be able to copy an article or the cover page of a recent book. It is only possible due to the current information and technology revolution, which has affected all aspects of human life, such as education, communication and work.

My own experience seems very exciting. From the time I was a child, I was eager to learn. I was born into a big family with many siblings and limited resources, and was always trying to save money in order to buy books to read (Saida's own experience). That led me to read very cheap books or any affordable magazines; many times, I read the newspapers or my mom's novels, which were usually not suitable for children. My passion for reading was enough to motivate me to continue

---

S. Affouneh (✉) · Z. N. Khlaif
An-Najah National University, Old Building, Nablus, Palestine
e-mail: s.affouneh@najah.edu

Z. N. Khlaif
e-mail: zkhlaif@najah.edu

© The Author(s) 2020
D. Burgos (ed.), *Radical Solutions and Open Science*, Lecture Notes
in Educational Technology, https://doi.org/10.1007/978-981-15-4276-3_4

searching for a way to learn. Suddenly I discovered the public library, where I could be a member by paying low fees. In those days, going to the library was not usual for people my age. Teenagers went there to meet their boyfriends or girlfriends, and not to read, so I faced questions all the time. But going home with books convinced my mom of my passion for reading.

Borrowing books or copying them was the other way to own a copy of a book. Sometimes I just enjoyed my own notes or summary of a book and to read it several times. Enrolling in university made my journey in learning easier due to the fact that each student needed to have a library card and had access to all existing resources. The limited resources in the library at that time forced me to spend hours and hours there every day, since there was only one copy of many of the resources, and that copy was either reserved or it could not be taken outside the library itself. Everyone knew that I would be in the library between classes, reading, studying textbooks and/or searching for new resources.

When I compare my experience while doing my thesis and those of my masters students today, I can feel the differences, and I really feel the blessing of the open resources that are available everywhere and at any time through open databases, libraries and D-space repositories.

4.2 The Evolution of Open Education

4.2.1 Definition of Open Education

Previous researchers have studied the concept of open education, and have done qualitative and quantitative research into the practices of different countries and universities in that area. Open education refers to practices including the sharing of information and ideas liberally, as well as the sharing of other platforms or methods used in the process of learning and teaching through technology (Blessinger & Bliss, 2016). Other researchers have defined open education as the process of making knowledge available to and easily accessible by the public by minimizing geographical, economic and other borders through the enhancement and development of technology. This is one of the reasons that, to some extent, people refer to open education as distance education, and within higher education, the nomenclature of 'open' is incorporated in the names of universities such as the Open University, Indonesia's Universitas Terbuka (meaning 'Open University'), the Open University of Hong Kong, University of the Philippines Open University and Allama Iqbal Open University. (Berti, 2018; Mossley, 2013).

Berti (2018) has defined open education as 'an emerging trend facilitated by the confluence of technology and imagination' (p. 25). The European Commission's Science and Knowledge Service has offered an explanation that expands on her definition, framing open education as that which guarantees different methods of formal and informal education, regardless of any barriers for learners, to maximize the possibility for students to succeed, and which makes higher education accessible by eliminating the cost of educational resources. In the 2012 Paris OER declaration, the definition was refined and strengthened to 'teaching, learning, and research materials in any medium, digital or otherwise, that reside in the public domain or have been released under an open license that permits no-cost access, use, adaptation and redistribution by others with no or limited restrictions. Open licensing is built within the existing framework of intellectual property rights as defined by relevant international conventions and respects the authorship of the work' (Mishra, 2017, pp. 275–276).

The adoption of OER has generally been a response to educational challenges, such as equity in education, sustainability and new trends. It has been supported by intergovernmental agencies, such as UNESCO and the Commonwealth of Learning, and philanthropic organizations, such as the Hewlett Foundation (Arinto et al., 2017). Open educational resources are teaching, learning or research materials that are in the public domain or released with an intellectual property license that allows for free use, adaptation and distribution (Vlasenko, n.d).

Open education and open educational resources grant the opportunity for instructors, students or self-learners to access the information available online for everyone, free of charge. For example, the resources include full programs, curricula, materials from teaching sessions in different formats, assessment resources, lab and classroom activities, pedagogical academic development materials and many more (Belawati, 2014).

Open access material aims to be globally and permanently reachable by groups of intellectuals, students and staff on both the physical campus of a university and in distance learning environments. However, there are also intellectual property rights and equity issues that are particularly relevant to the context of open and distance learning, where access to resources related to research articles and data is frequently problematic for students and staff (Krelja Kurelovic, 2016).

Distance education is defined as a method of teaching where the student and teacher are physically separated. It can employ a combination of technologies, including the Internet, multimedia, audio, text, animation, video and computer accessories. Today's version of distance education is online education, which uses computers and the Internet as the delivery mechanisms, with at least 80% of the course content delivered online (Allen & Seaman, 2011; Sengupta, Reshef, & Blessinger, 2019).

We, as Palestinians who are living in a unique environment where restrictions on mobility and checkpoints exist across the occupied land (Khlaif, Gok, & Kouraïchi, 2019; Traxler et al., 2019), define an open education resource as any learning object (digital or traditional) that can be reused in multiple contexts that educators can adapt to mitigate educational difficulties due to occupation and that can be used to achieve a specific learning goal or training aim. For that reason, the Palestinian Ministry of Education and Higher Education launched a website for public education teachers to upload their learning objects so that other teachers could use them in their classrooms. Furthermore, higher education institutions in Palestine (universities and community colleges) adapted open sources for learning management systems (LMS). These initiatives in Palestine reduced the running costs of developing learning objects for different stages in the education system. In addition, they fostered collaborative work among teachers at schools in different districts.

Palestinian students, public education teachers and staff at universities use OER to acquire new knowledge and skills related to their fields of practice and study, since it can reduce the costs of training and save them time and effort. Because of political issues in Palestine, the MoE is using open resources to train teachers in Gaza, providing training objects and using Zoom, Skype and other tools (Khlaif, 2018).

4.2.2 Challenges of OER

Adopting OER in daily life is not without problems, because it affects the traditional rules, cultures, feelings and modes of learning in both public and higher education (Hood & Littlejohn, 2017). Moreover, the reuse of OER is challenging for users because these objects are stored in various repositories without a general description of their content or without metadata (Wang & Towey, 2017). The quality of OER is an emerging issue in the Palestinian context, because teachers and educators upload their objects and the system accepts these objects without peer review, or any public scrutiny (Okada, Mikroyannidis, Meister, & Little, 2012). There are also concerns about sustainability and business models (Algers, 2015; Downes, 2007), and a lack of trust in academic institutions and among educators that use them to create OER (Clements & Pawlowski, 2012).

According to our experience and based on the Palestinian context, a number of competencies are needed for exploring the tools to enable learning by using OER, to adapt content to societal rules (e.g., clear vision, a clear policy and legislation regarding public education as well as higher education), to identify learning goals and to gather the related content in the institutions. All these should be considered to ensure the ethical use of OER.

In Palestine, the term 'open education' was usually used to refer to Al Quds Open University (QOU), which was established in 1990 in order to offer education to Palestinian students who have suffered from closures and sieges and who have been prevented from traveling abroad due to Israeli military instructions. Despite all the challenges that Palestinians face due to the political and economic situation, they continue to value their educations and consider them tools for a better life. QOU was one of the earliest experiments in open education, following the model of Open University in the UK and Australia. Education was offered through different campuses and using textbooks and other resources. My work at QOU for many years, trying to develop new open practices through introducing more technology into teaching and learning, shows that there are many different practices that could be collected under this umbrella. The university was first established to provide adult education and then moved to serve young students who have fewer opportunities to attend regular universities, either for economic reasons or because they obtained low scores on secondary school exams.

In the twenty-first century, as a result of the information and telecommunication revolution, education has evolved in order to meet the technological needs of the new generation. Long discussions have been held between higher education policymakers, and many questions have been raised by educators, practitioners and policymakers about open education, e-Learning, online learning and digitalisation of education. Different terminology has been used to describe using different forms of technology to improve the quality of teaching and learning. Can technology improve the quality of education? Are we ready for this reform? What type of capacity-building do we need to do for our teachers? How much will that cost? These and many other questions have been asked, and no agreement has been reached. Pioneers at my university have taken the lead in implementing different types of blended learning in order to pilot it in their courses.

Many other higher education institutions have started to use open resources such as MOOCs for education. For example, An-Najah National University, which is located in Nablus, Palestine has been developing MOOC courses since 2014. Different open courses in different languages are available on the university website. These courses are open to the public to give people more information about Palestine, and are funded by the Ministry of Culture. Other universities have launched MOOC courses about wild plants in Palestine. The adoption of OER in the Palestinian context has been in response to educational challenges and to meet international and regional standards in higher education. However, we have concerns about the assessment process for OER, as well as the quality of these resources.

Our roadmap for integrating OER in both practice and policy in education is linked to the institutional and strategic plan of the Ministry of Higher Education in Palestine and the required process for implementation, including the timeframe, priority level and the expected results and impact of using OER over the short and long term.

4.2.3 Advantages of Open Education

There are a lot of benefits to using open education and open resources in different aspects of the educational system in any country. For example, open education has extended the possibilities and provided new opportunities for educators and students to broaden their knowledge and skills in different fields, with fewer costs. Open education has introduced learners to nontraditional ways of learning by sharing and reusing knowledge and information between different institutions to achieve specific goals. Furthermore, OER have linked informal and formal education by using different resources. Many OER allow teachers and learners to access learning materials with permission to edit and modify the content to meet their needs and expectations. Students, educators, non-profit organizations and job seekers can benefit from open education by joining the right programs, which can facilitate the recruitment process. Open education helps faculty and students reach out to other institutions and universities, which can improve collaboration between learners and universities in different parts of the world. It should also be taken into consideration that open education is cost-effective, since it is not necessary to print textbooks, and that it promotes informal learning by not requiring credentials. Judith and Bull (2016) have stressed the importance of open education's enhancing the quality of learning by allowing more participants to be involved in it, which results in a more personalized and efficient learning process (Berti, 2018).

4.2.4 The Dilemma of Policy and Practice

Conole (2010) concentrated on using a suggested framework to bridge the gap between policy and practice in e-learning in higher education. He compared different contexts and factors that influence the width of this gap and found ten main points that have a real impact which are congruent with Conole's study (2007). I served as the head of the national committee to develop e-learning policy for the Ministry of Education and Higher education. With my team, I developed the policy for e-learning, which was discussed in the Prime Minister's Cabinet and was included and reflected in higher education as a new law. Furthermore, I was the founder of the e-Learning Center at An-Najah National University. My main objective for the e-Learning Center was to change the culture of open education to be part of the university. My team developed the university policy for e-Learning and open education through:

- Preparing two MOOCs
- Training faculty members on best practices in open education
- Participating in many conferences and workshops.

An-Najah National University now has thousands of recorded lectures and hundreds of open courses. In addition, its D-space repository includes all papers, eBooks and theses as open resources for learners. All the scholarly work it produces is shared online and free to access by students and colleagues.

4.3 Reflections on Life Experience

I was very lucky to go through such a rich learning experience despite the fact I did it the difficult way, where I learned all the time through doing and working very hard. Open education was just a dream, not only for me, but also for my country and the Arab region. People appreciated radical teaching and sat in rows in classrooms with blackboards and tough teachers with loud voices, tough hands and loving hearts.

Working at Open University and implementing open education practices in an environment where everyone is ready for that differs from working from scratch to build the culture of open education. In a convenient university, the experience needs to change attitudes, practices, policies and expectations. Trying to convince everyone, starting from the management level and moving to the teachers' levels, is very challenging due to the fact that everyone is questioning learning quality. The easiest answer to the quality issue was to ask the same question of how you ensure quality in traditional classrooms, and then reflect that in open education where all the material is accessible by everyone, anytime and anywhere, with no conditions. Unfortunately, however, you cannot convince everyone, and that question continues to be raised in relation to open education.

Other strategies including trying to shift the teachers' minds from considering developing open resources (OR) as a burden to considering it as a way to improve their professions (and as PR material for their CVs) is another way to address the quality question. Using ORs to introduce ourselves as experts and good practitioners to the scholar community is a strong argument to lead and is also easier since teachers can directly see its impact on their career development.

4.4 Limitation of Open Education and Open Educational Resources

Open education has indeed made the learning process more flexible for learners. However, it still faces some challenges as it still emerging, and its adoption process is still in the early stages. OP requires a clear system to help people adapt to its concept and to ensure the quality of the resources offered online. Another limitation is the traditional mindsets of organizations regarding sharing information within those organizations and between the students and teachers. There should be awareness campaigns explaining the necessity of global sharing. Limitations due to the cost of resources are also a challenge, as many organizations are financed by governments, which restrict content development by teachers. The latter often requires more funding, since it involves special software and hardware. The language barrier can further restrict the process of open education development. The Paris OER Declaration (2012) suggests that localization of the language in content development can ensure the flexibility and diversity of content. Some countries' scarce resources and their intention to use traditional teaching methods due to the lack of digital competencies can be an additional barrier. Finally, the biggest challenge is the mindset of the people, which needs to be shifted to be more open to adapting to new methods of learning (Krelja Kurelovic, 2016).

A case study found that there are several challenges that accompany adopting OER within a course in a higher education curriculum. The major ones include limited staff knowledge of OEP, copyright issues, discoverability issues driven by diffuse nature of OER repositories, finding context-suitable resources and adapting material across contexts (Judith & Bull, 2016).

According to Vlasenko (n.d.), there are limitations and disadvantages of open education and distance education:

1. The individuality of work and limitation of interactions with other students, since group work is limited and there is little or no oral communication with

other classmates and teachers, which results in the lack of the critical thinking and problem-solving skills that are developed by interacting in a classroom.
2. The limitations of technology and accessibility can be a barrier, especially for people who are still terrified of using technology. Moreover, a computer and high-speed internet are requirements for open education and distance learning, so it can cost a lot to set up facilities, especially those for live communication. Since, distance learning programs sometimes need high-tech tools which could be expensive. These tools can be used to develop new learning materials for courses, updating them, and marketing the courses.
3. Some students live outside the study area, which, in a traditional learning process, requires them to order some materials that need to be mailed to them. However, in distance learning, they do not need these materials to be mailed to them.
4. Distance learning is different than traditional learning in the sense of feedback. In distance learning, students do not get immediate feedback; they have to wait for review and comments from their teachers.
5. Distance learning is not recognized worldwide. Some employers might not accept online degrees, or it can be less suitable for some fields (Vlasenko, n.d.).

4.5 Usage of Open Education

Massive open online courses (MOOCs), open digital textbooks, and video lectures are the most popular open educational resources. The greatest number of MOOCs in Europe is provided in Great Britain (234 courses), followed by France (137 courses) and Germany (111 courses). At the global level, 27% of MOOCs originate from the USA, 17% from India, 13% in China, and 4% each from Great Britain, Australia and Canada, while the remaining 31% come from other countries (http://www.moocs.co/). Accordingly, mostly OERs in well-known repositories are in the English language: 96% on OER Commons, 94% on Curriki, 89% on Merlot, 70% on Coursera and 83% on edX. However, the MIT Open Courseware repository, the leader in the OER initiative, has translated some courses and other educational materials into at least 10 languages (Gutonber blog, 2018).

OER received support in a recent study by Inside Higher Ed (2018) survey on school leaders and teachers' opinions on technology. Presidents strongly agreed (61%) or agreed (30%) that 'textbooks and course materials are too expensive'. 85% of presidents also agreed (85%) or strongly agreed (52%) that colleges should adopt free and openly licensed online educational materials. Presidents of doctoral universities, whether public or private, were slightly less likely than their counterparts in other institutions to agree, at 49% and 40%, respectively.

Distance and open education are the best solutions for students who have trouble attending traditional classes; they allow those students to attend educational programs according to their schedules without affecting their personal or professional lives. A person only needs a computer and an internet connection to finish an online program anywhere and anytime. Moreover, the numerous option a person can find online can have a significant advantage of giving them their choice of education and providing them with different specializations in different fields. Like other researchers, Vlasenko (n.d) has mentioned that open education offers students cost savings by not requiring them to spend money and time on commuting. In addition, Open education offers free movement and availability for students. A student can also learn while working; they fit their learning programs to their schedules, which gives them more income and stability without the financial stress that comes with the traditional learning (Gregson & Hatzipanagos, 2015).

4.6 Conclusion

The purpose of the current chapter was to introduce the Palestinian experience in using open education resources in both higher and public education, as well as the challenges of developing this new paradigm. Educators in Palestine have defined open education resources as reusing learning objects in a different context in the learning process as well as in the professional development programs. Many national initiatives on the level of universities and the Ministry of Education have been adapted to develop open education resources such as MOOCs, recording lectures and using a digital repository to upload theses and academic papers that can be freely accessed by students, non-profit organizations and local communities.

Despite developments in OER, there are many challenges confronting open education, including trust, source quality and lack of developer competencies. More efforts are needed in order for Palestine to be a part of the open education world, and especially to increase and enrich the content of open resources in Arabic. Universities and other higher education institutions should have a clear vision and plan to develop and use OER. It is a culture issue that takes a long time to be resolved, since attitudes and practices are not easy to change unless the change is part of national policy and institutional plans.

REFERENCES

Allen, I. E., & Seaman, J. (2011). *Going the distance: Online education in the United States, 2011.* Newburyport, MA: Sloan Consortium.

Algers, A. (2015). *Open learning in life sciences—Studies of open educational resources in animal welfare and work-based learning in food science* (Doctoral dissertation). University of Gothenburg, Gothenburg, Sweden. http://hdl.handle.net/2077/40580.

Arinto, P., Hodgkinson-Williams, C., King, T., Cartmill, T., & Willmers, M. (2017). *Research on open educational resources for development in the Global South: Project landscape.*

Belawati, T. I. A. N. (2014). Open education, open education resources, and massive open online courses. *International Journal of Continuing Education and Lifelong Learning, 7*(1), 2–15. Retrieved from https://oerknowledgecloud.org/sites/oerknowledgecloud.org/files/tian02eng.pdf.

Berti, M. (2018). Open educational resources in higher education. *Issues and Trends in Educational Technology, 6*(1), 1–9.

Blessinger, P., & Bliss, T. J. (2016). *Introduction to open education: Towards a human rights theory.* Retrieved from https://books.openedition.org/obp/3539?lang=en.

Clements, K. I., & Pawlowski, J. M. (2012). User-oriented quality for OER: Understanding teachers' views on re-use, quality, and trust. *Journal of Computer Assisted Learning, 28*(1), 4–14.

Conole, G. (2007). Describing learning activities: Tools and resources to guide practice. In *Rethinking pedagogy for a digital age* (pp. 101–111). London: Routledge.

Conole, G. (2010). Facilitating new forms of discourse for learning and teaching: Harnessing the power of Web 2.0 practices. *Open Learning: The Journal of Open, Distance and e-Learning, 25*(2), 141–151.

Downes, S. (2007). Models of sustainable open educational resources. *Interdisciplinary Journal of Knowledge and Learning Objects, 3,* 29–44.

Gregson, J., & Hatzipanagos, S. (2015). The role of open access and open educational resources: A distance learning perspective. *Electronic Journal of e-Learning, 13*(2), 97–105.

Gutonber blog. (2018, March 29). *Pros and cons of using open educational resources.* [Blog]. Retrieved from https://blog.gutenberg-technology.com/en/pros-cons-open-educational-oer.

Hood, N., & Littlejohn, A. (2017). Knowledge typologies for professional learning: educators' (re)generation of knowledge when learning open educational practice. *Educational Technology Research and Development, 65*(6), 1583–1604.

Judith, K., & Bull, D. (2016). Assessing the potential for openness: A framework for examining course-level OER implementation in higher education. *Education policy analysis archives, 24,* 42.

Khlaif, Z. (2018). Teachers' perceptions of factors affecting their adoption and acceptance of mobile technology in K-12 settings. *Computers in the Schools, 35*(1), 49–67.

Khlaif, Z., Gok, F., & Kouraïchi, B. (2019). How teachers in middle schools design technology integration activities. *Teaching and Teacher Education, 78,* 141–150.

Krelja Kurelovic, E. (2016). Advantages and limitations of usage of open educational resources in small countries. *International Journal of Research in Education and Science (IJRES), 2*(1), 136–142.

Mishra, S. (2017). Open educational resources: removing barriers from within. *Distance Education, 38*(3), 369–380.

Mossley, D. (2013). *Open educational resources and open education* (pp. 6–7). Retrieved from https://www.heacademy.ac.uk/system/files/resources/oer_toolkit_0.pdf.

Okada, A., Mikroyannidis, A., Meister, I., & Little, S. (2012). "Co-learning"—Collaborative networks for creating, sharing and reusing OER through social media. In *Proceedings from OCWC Global 2012: Innovation and Impact—Openly Collaborating to Enhance Education.* Cambridge, UK. Retrieved May, 2018, from http://oro.open.ac.uk/33750/2/59B2E252.pdf.

Sengupta, E., Reshef, S., & Blessinger, P. (2019). Creating a borderless world of education for refugees. In *Language, teaching, and pedagogy for refugee education* (pp. 181–191).

Traxler, J., Khlaif, Z., Nevill, A., Affouneh, S., Salha, S., Zuhd, A., et al. (2019). Living under occupation: Palestinian teachers' experiences and their digital responses. *Research in Learning Technology, 27,* 1–18.

Vlasenko, L. (n.d.). *Advantages and disadvantages of distance learning.* National University of Food Technologies, Ukraine.

Wang, T., & Towey, D. (2017, December). Open educational resource (OER) adoption in higher education: Challenges and strategies. In *2017 IEEE 6th International Conference on Teaching, Assessment, and Learning for Engineering (TALE)* (pp. 317–319). IEEE.

Saida Affouneh is an associate professor and Dean of Faculty of Education and Teacher Training and is the founder and director of the E-Learning Center (ELC) at An-Najah National University. Dr. Affouneh also worked as a consultant to develop a national policy paper for open education, a Project sponsored by AQAQ (Accreditation and Quality Assurance Commission) and AMIDEAST. She was the chairperson of the 2014 International Conference for Learning and Teaching in the Digital World, which was organized by the e-Learning Center at An-Najah National University and had 1200 attendees. She was also the chairperson of the 2017 International Conference for Learning and Teaching in the Digital World (Smart World). She received a grant from the Sloan Consortium to participate in an online leadership program in 2013, as the first scholar from the Middle East to do so.

Zuheir N. Khlaif research interests are in the areas of technology integration and microlearning in both K-12 and higher education. Zuheir has extensive experience in training teachers to use and design technology activities for classrooms, and has conducted many workshops for training teachers to use open resources in their practice. He has published many articles in international journals. He is now designing activities and conducting research related to STEM projects.

Open Access This chapter is licensed under the terms of the Creative Commons Attribution 4.0 International License (http://creativecommons.org/licenses/by/4.0/), which permits use, sharing, adaptation, distribution and reproduction in any medium or format, as long as you give appropriate credit to the original author(s) and the source, provide a link to the Creative Commons license and indicate if changes were made.

The images or other third party material in this chapter are included in the chapter's Creative Commons license, unless indicated otherwise in a credit line to the material. If material is not included in the chapter's Creative Commons license and your intended use is not permitted by statutory regulation or exceeds the permitted use, you will need to obtain permission directly from the copyright holder.

Chapter 5
Who Benefits from the Public Good? How OER Is Contributing to the Private Appropriation of the Educational Commons

Tel Amiel, Ewout ter Haar, Miguel Said Vieira, and Tiago Chagas Soares

Abstract The idea of Open Educational Resources (OER) has a history and is embedded in social contexts that influence its practice. To get a handle on tensions between different conceptualizations of "open" we discuss some of the battles surrounding the usage of the term. We note the origin of the concept of OER and how the emergence of the OER movement fits into the discourse of educational improvements through technologies and techniques. We argue that there is a relation between an uncritical stance toward technology and the appropriation of education activities by private oligopolies, a phenomenon that could be mitigated by a larger awareness of recent history and current sociotechnical analysis. We point out how these dilemmas play out in the Brazilian context of the implementation of OER in public policies and conclude by mentioning some programs and projects that point to the way forward.

Keywords Open educational resources · Open education · Private sector

---

T. Amiel (✉)
University of Brasília (UnB), Campus Universitário Darcy Ribeiro, Faculdade de Educação, Cep: 70.910-900 Brasilia, Brazil
e-mail: amiel@unb.br

E. ter Haar
Universidade de São Paulo, Instituto de Física – USP, Rua do Matão 1371, CEP 05508-090 Cidade Universitária, São Paulo, Brazil
e-mail: ewout@usp.br

M. S. Vieira
Universidade Federal do ABC, Av. dos Estados 5001, 09210-580 Santo André, São Paulo, Brazil
e-mail: miguel.vieira@ufabc.edu.br

T. C. Soares
Universidade de São Paulo, Rua Antônio João Tonella 179, Bosque de Barão Geraldo, CEP 13082-756 Campinas – SP, Brazil
e-mail: tiago@oplanob.com

© The Author(s) 2020
D. Burgos (ed.), *Radical Solutions and Open Science*, Lecture Notes in Educational Technology, https://doi.org/10.1007/978-981-15-4276-3_5

5.1 Introduction

In 1945, the magazine The Atlantic published an essay named "As We May Think" (Bush, 1945). Its author was Vannevar Bush, the then Director of the Office of Scientific Research and Development of the US Government. Bush had been responsible for the bulk of the technoscientific effort led by the US throughout World War II, an effort that led to a deep restructuring of how the country's research would be developed and networked from then on (Turner, 2010).

After World War II, with the Allied victory over the nazi–fascist threat, Bush was faced with a new and immediate challenge: to reconfigure, in peacetime, the sociotechnical apparatus mobilized at wartime. In a world struggling to be rebuilt from scratch, how should one set in motion a new architecture where information and science would foster individual freedom and the emancipation of knowledge? The answer sketched by Bush in his essay addresses this challenge through a new, radical rationale for cataloging, storing, and accessing of information. A system, that in its ideal form, would envision terminals to large repositories granting open access, at different levels of retrieval, to the whole of human knowledge—in print, audio, and film alike. To this networked, universal library, Bush gave the name *Memex*. The notion articulated by Bush in his *Memex*—of high technique as something in service of knowledge made universal—underlies, to some extent, what the internet came to be perceived as in the public imagination.

In the second half of the twentieth century, access to information and knowledge has taken the forefront of civic discourse and in the development and emancipation of individuals and communities alike. The emergence and fast development of computers, from the large mainframes of the 1960s to individual networked terminals, has opened a universe of possibilities intertwining the social and the technical. Through ideals such as free software, open source, copyleft, and remix culture, access to knowledge more often than not comes to mean also the mastery of new digital tools.

With the widespread expansion of the commercial Internet and the emergence of the World Wide Web from the 1990s onward, the centrality of the internet for the circulation of knowledge and in the transformation of educational practices fueled high expectations. This was theorized by authors who would become canonical of an optimistic outlook, including Castells (2011), Levy (2010), and Negroponte (1995). This ethos would become institutionalized in initiatives such as the W3C, articulating the civil society as a guardian of the internet in its technical and policy aspects.

In 2001, amidst this movement to institutionalize new standards, best practices, and joint objectives, the Massachusetts Institute of Technology (MIT) made the decision to open up teaching content through an online platform (Taylor, 2007). The initiative was copied by multiple other institutions, in what is sometimes referred to as the beginning of the Open Educational Resources (OER) movement. The terminology was consolidated during a 2002 UNESCO forum on educational resources (UNESCO, 2002), which evolved during the next decade into OER being defined as:

Learning, teaching and research materials in any format and medium that reside in the public domain or are under copyright that have been released under an open license, that permit no-cost access, re-use, re-purpose, adaptation and redistribution by others (UNESCO, 2019).

The OER movement has joined other efforts on the opening up of information, culture, and knowledge. Platforms such as Wikipedia and YouTube have become synonymous with shared knowledge creation and the democratization of access to educational content. Creative Commons (CC), a set of free licenses that has quickly become the global standard for free culture, and almost synonymous with "openness", is the license suit that is most used by these and other services in a converging movement between platform expansion and growth of open licensing initiatives.

According to official CC data, the number of resources made available with its licenses has grown from 140 million in 2006 to over 1 billion in 2016. Such expansion at first glance points to a huge increase in size, capillarization, and practices informed by the idea of OER. Notwithstanding some criticism of the methodology used to calculate the number of works with CC licenses (Downes, 2015), the movement has indeed grown, which is evident not only from its sheer number of cultural artifacts, but also from the number of licensed open access journals using CC licenses, and the political movement fostered by OER initiatives around the world.[1] In Brazil, the public sector (at the federal, state, municipal, and institutional levels alike) has been mobilized to enable public policies in OER, with significant successes (Amiel, Gonsales, & Sebriam, 2018). In fact, in a recent survey (Amiel & Soares, 2016), the state seems to be, at least in Latin America, the main catalyst in the construction of projects, policies, and initiatives to make educational resources available.

In light of these principles and goals, it can be hard to find someone who is against the idea of "open". But to what extent such an idea, as well as the movement it has set into motion, is free of tensions and unimpeded by roadblocks? What are the possible gaps and breaches that could be found in these movements' multiple possibilities of implementation, debate, and elaboration? And to what extent could these methods and tools serve as tools of liberation while they promote practices which are undesirable to specific educational communities?

In this paper, we focus on these issues by examining the practices of OER. In doing so, we find ourselves obliged to bring out the way different areas associated with openness relate to each other, and to address issues usually ignored by those who (like us) advocate for OER. We begin our discussion by discussing the concept of "open" in different spheres and the general context of the battle surrounding the usage of the term. We follow with brief notes on the origin of the concept of OER and how the OER movement fits—from a historical perspective—into the discourse of educational improvements through technologies and techniques, and—in the current scenario—into the phenomena of the appropriation of education activities by private oligopolies. We point out some Brazilian dilemmas in the implementation of OER in public policies and end up by mentioning some programs and projects that point us to fruitful paths.

---

[1] A source of multiple policy initiatives is the OER World Map (http://www.oerworldmap.org).

5.2 The Battle for Open

The construction of the public sphere in the second half of the twentieth century was based on technology, in particular on the new promises of Information and Communication Technology (ICT), that would enable the free expression of ideas. This project was seen in the light of liberal ideals, being a sort of vaccine against the emergence of the erosion of democracy and authoritarian power. Thinkers like Popper (2002) and Kuhn (2012) constructed models of the advancement of science that pointed to equality of access to knowledge and the tools for acquiring it as essential tools for liberty. But this kind of discourse, structured around ideals of equality and openness can be misleading when the political and economic assumptions of "open" projects must be given concrete meaning, when actors have to make sense of conflicting goals, means and results (Hansen & Reich, 2015).

Weller (2015) suggests that there's a (metaphorical) battle being waged on the meaning of the word "open", when it comes to the internet and cyberculture in general. As certain interpretations gain hold, actors with countervailing interests try to modify and bend these meanings toward their own ends. One example is "openwashing"[2]: the use of the expression "open" by actors, generally corporate market participants working with a profit motive, that wish to associate themselves with the positive connotations of the concept but without adopting the collaborative and transparent practices that are also typically associated with it. One example would be organizations that advertise open courses without permitting the reuse of course materials, or only as samples of commercial materials.

At stake in the battle for the meaning of "open" is the conception of what is a common good and who the commons serves. One answer to the phenomenon of openwashing is creating bright-line, rigid definitions that separate open from non-open.[3] A legalistic approach certainly gives clarity to the actors involved and aids policymaking. But these definitions are inevitably made in certain situated, local and political contexts, for certain ends. Being rigid, these rules may not attend to the needs of other communities at different times and contexts. And, as we shall see, even rigid rules can't always impede the subversion of the commons by outside interests.

Although there is a battle for its meaning, the adjective "open" in technical contexts still refers mostly to the collaborative or collective aspects of the production of digital goods. One of the most influential analyses of the sociotechnical possibilities of digital and internet technologies is the book *The Wealth of Networks* by Benkler (2006), in which he coined the expression *commons-based peer production*. Among

---

[2] An expression that derives from *greenwashing* is used to describe practices that look like they are ecological and sustainable but in reality are not.

[3] See, for example, the definition of open at http://opendefinition.org, or, for OER, the "5R" criteria that was created by one of the pioneers of the OER movement to precisely open content (http://www.opencontent.org/definition/). Some even identify open with the use of particular Creative Commons license such as CC-BY: https://open.bccampus.ca/2016/11/04/open-textbook-community-advocates-cc-by-license-for-open-textbooks/.

the set of practices to which this concept refers are those adopted by communities responsible for the production of commons and public goods like Wikipedia, or open and/or free software like the code for the Apache Web server. Similarly, most early participants in the OER movement were motivated by the idea that OER could contribute to social justice and that the practices associated with the "open" ethos would fit in naturally with educational theories and values like collaboration, transparency, horizontality, and other values of the commons.

But there is another side to the concept of open, not less powerful in its capacity to mobilize attention. Where Benkler emphasizes collaboration, and the empowerment of local communities through the commons, other proponents of open practices defend its role in efficiency gains and interoperability, concepts that are associated with traditional market mechanisms (cf. Evangelista, 2010). For example, in the area of transparency and open government, calls for more openness are targeted differently for audiences with different political outlooks. For a conservative audience focused on so-called free markets and traditional liberal and individual rights, open advocacy can emphasize the economic efficiency gains of initiatives like opening government data to market actors. For this audience, open government fits in perfectly with an ideology of the minimal state and free markets. But at the same time, open government advocacy can also be targeted to people with other political convictions, for example as being about the empowerment of civil society, favoring participatory democracy and the collective construction of common services.[4] If the same concept is capable to serve to rhetorical necessities of both sides of the political spectrum, the question arises: for whom and to what end the expression "open" is being put into play?

It's commonplace—at least in the social sciences—to affirm that technologies are not neutral, that their use and meaning is at least in part political (Winner, 1993). Analogously, we can say that the concept of "open" and the sociotechnical discourses around it are loaded with political values, even though these are not expressed explicitly. Technologies, especially complex ones like those that mediate the creation and dissemination of cultural products, cannot be considered to be mere tools that can be used for good or for bad purposes. These technologies have structure, they facilitate certain uses and discourage others. Therefore, if open government can be used to advance distinct political and economic models, then the idea of "open" in education should also be analyzed critically with respect to the underlying assumptions that influence its goals and results. Open licenses, in particular, can be seen as a kind of legal technology that needs to be interrogated in this manner.

To show that these considerations are not merely theoretical, we now exemplify the risks of not doing the necessary critical analysis by pointing to some cases in areas that directly inspired the OER movement: open access, open source, and open culture in general.

Wikipedia is the canonical example of how the internet made possible large scale collaborative processes. Its success is undeniable in terms of volume of the material produced, and to a lesser extent in terms of its quality. However, research has shown that the project suffers from a lack of diversity of its contributors which in turn is

---

[4]See, for example, the Open Government Partnership (https://www.opengovpartnership.org/).

reflected in the kinds of content produced. Large biases exist toward content that is of interest to a certain kind of audience: young, white men (Simonite, 2013).

The same lack of diversity exists among the contributors of open source software, to an even larger extent than in the IT industry as a whole.[5] The GNU/Linux operating system is a project that, at the beginning of the century, was seen as a model of production independent of traditional systems of property rights and markets. Today, however, most contributions to the project are made by IT professionals employed by and working in the interest of large companies (Yegulalp, 2014). Open source and internet technologies certainly brought new distributed and collaborative models to the corporate world. But companies took from the original vision of commons-based peer production only the parts that made their processes of accumulation more efficient. In many of these projects the formal equality of opportunity does not translate to real equality of participation. Not only do inequalities remain, in the absence of active interventions they are even amplified in some important dimensions.

A last case, especially relevant to the OER movement, is the subversion of the ideas and proposals of the open access movement by commercial publishers of scientific journals. Many publishers have used their monopoly on editorial validation to maintain control of the scholarly communication infrastructure, re-configuring their business models to slowly adapt to the latter, not the spirit, of open-access public policies. They have been able to articulate a model in which authors and funding agencies pay to publish while keeping prices high through artificial scarcity, marketing in prestige quantified through citation metrics. The resulting competition and the natural concentrating effect of market dynamics keep control over scholarly communication in the hands of just a few private actors. In the emerging "author pays" model, the price paid for the benefit of open access licensed scholarly articles is the exclusion of those academics without the capability to get funding to publish. The model also leads to conflicts of interests in the peer-review process and creates opportunities for bad actors to promote so-called predatory journals that publish without due regard for peer-review and academic merit. The open-access case is a prime example of how a narrow emphasis on the legal technology of licenses distracts from the real issue at hand, in this case the essential tension between public and private control over scholarly communication.

It's important to note that the collateral effects noted in the cases above are not caused by the projects and movements being "open" (in the sense of being participatory, collaborative, and culturally progressive). What the examples show is that without expressing clearly the meaning and goals of their "open" values, the movements are at the mercy of the status quo.

---

[5]For a general analysis of this matter see (Nafus, 2012). Three studies (David, Waterman, & Arora, 2003; Ghosh, Glott, Krieger, & Robles, 2002; Kuechler, Gilbertson, & Jensen, 2012) found a 1–2 % participation rate of women in free software projects; a fourth study found a rate of 11 %, but presented selection bias, as admitted in the study (Arjona-Reina, Robles, & Dueñas, 2014). These numbers are low, even compared to the small fraction of women in the IT industry as a whole, estimated to be 26 % in the US (Ashcraft, McLain, & Eger, 2016).

Open licenses alone are insufficient to promote social justice, to create a commons or even just to achieve economic efficiency. Claiming openness does not automatically call into being a neutral or progressive space free of political tensions. Without explicitly addressing their political values, open movements are at risk to have these values subverted. If a project seeks to promote social justice, for example, it will need to take into account existing power relations between relevant actors. Without recognizing existing social inequalities, providing access, providing equal opportunities, or "democratizing" technology will not be effective and can even amplify these inequalities.

5.3 The Battle for OER

Open education and OER are ideas with great protagonism in discussions surrounding the future of education. Issues related to the personalization of teaching in online platforms, the digitization of teaching material, access to online practice exams, and online tutoring videos, among others, are promoted with a common message of equity and access to education for all. On the one hand, these resources can help promote the "hacker ethic" in education (Pretto, 2012) with an emphasis on questioning, criticality, remixing, recombination, and collaboration. On the other hand, the democratization of access to educational resources has been used to promote an education centered on the logic of efficiency and training of students for specific tasks, so that they may, only instrumentally, overcome more efficiently the continuous certification from basic to higher education. OER as we know it, a child of the web, is permeated by the historical tensions we have presented. It is important to sketch a brief history of the concept in order to understand why, despite arguments for their educational benefits that appeal to common sense, we chose to say that we are in a "battle for OER".

Online learning, and in particular "Learning Objects" (LO) gained much attention during the 90s with the web and the rise of resource-based-learning (Hannafin & Hill, 2008). LOs are small educational resources, usually focused on a single learning objective, designed so as to be combined with other resources to create a larger entity, focusing on a particular context of use. According to this logic, a small set of educational resources would be able to be used and reused in many different contexts (Downes, 2001). Some authors have emphasized the use of LOs in constructivist environments (Wiley, 2001); others have emphasized that in their actual implementations LOs were more naturally used in instructionist teaching with a training perspective (Friesen, 2004).

As Benkler (2005) points out, the use of repositories of small adaptable LOs to form a larger and contextualized collection would be appropriate for the type of education in which educators have autonomy to curate and select their own teaching materials. This scenario is more typical in higher education, with a professional creating a singular experience for students. How educators in other contexts—with more rigid institutional constraints, less technical support, limited digital competencies, among other factors—could make use of repositories was an important question for LOs (Sicilia & Garcia, 2003). This remains the case today for OER.

On the other side of the modularity spectrum, that of textbooks and completes courses, Benkler also points to possible difficulties of applying his model of commons-based peer production, explaining that this model works best for resources with some natural modularity (like the encyclopedia entries of Wikipedia). The collaborative nature of peer production concept may be difficult to apply to resources that must conform to externally imposed quality standards, that are large volumes expected to maintain coherence or that need a distinct authorial voice (Benkler, 2005). We think that many of these concerns surrounding the use of LOs and debates around adequate policies for their adoption in educational environments should continue to be discussed as relevant agendas in the OER movement.

The introduction of new forms of educational technology, such as LOs and OER, is often seen as an obvious or inevitable development—or a sign of social progress. Examples of this mentality include the contested concept of the "digital natives"; the now largely debunked idea that Massive Open Online Courses (MOOCs), often associated with OER, would absolutely transform higher education[6]; and the idea that education through personalized algorithms would make teachers more efficient or even obsolete. For each of these narratives, convincing counter-arguments exist. Specialists have demonstrated the inadequacy and the lack of evidence for the idea of a "generational difference" associated to growing in an environment saturated by the internet (An & Carr, 2017; Reeves & Oh, 2008). The availability of many educational resources and courses from renowned universities online soon gave way to the recognition that education is more than transmitting and optimizing the delivery of lectures, no matter how charismatic the teacher may be. Finally, critics have indicated that behind the automation of the classroom there often is a deskilling (Chakraborty, 2013) of the job of the teacher, and a promotion of an instrumental perspective on education directed at the job market, in line with theories of learning focused on training instead (and sometimes with disregard) of the development of full citizenship. In each of these examples, one is able to identify commercial interests by vendors of educational technologies who might be less transparent than necessary about their motivations.

And so, what we have here is another view of OER, one that leads to caution. We cannot assume that the undeniable pedagogical potential of OER will naturally lead to changes that are aligned with pedagogical and political objectives, whichever these might be. Of course, association is not causation and the realization that educational technologies might have been poorly used in the past should not lead us to have preconceived notions in regard to OER. Nevertheless, the overly optimistic expectations of LOs, MOOCs, and educational technology, in general, should lead to caution with regard to how OER will be used in educational settings. We once again emphasize need to deploy educational technologies with a clear vision as to

---

[6]In a Wired article, Sebastian Thrun prophesied that in a near future there would only be 10 institutions providing higher education: https://www.wired.com/2012/03/ff_aiclass/.

their risks and potentialities and the importance of having a well developed political and pedagogical vision. Without this, there is a risk that projects may naturally align themselves in directions that may diverge from what was originally intended. We continue below, with further examples that exemplify the tensions within the discourse around OER.

5.3.1 OER and Oligopolies

The fact that OER may appeal to different perspectives and economic interests helps us explain how the movement has diverged globally. The motivation for educational change is often associated with the conservatism of educational institutions, portrayed as traditional and lethargic—and always a target for radical change. Critics often point to old practices, inefficiency, and the resistance in updating practices as evidence of the lack of alignment of formal education to contemporary demands. Weller (2015) contextualizes this old and recurring critique, as part of the "Silicon Valley narrative", points out that the argument that "education is broken" has become such an acceptable point of view, that it has the semblance of hard truth (Weller, 2015, p. 2). Accepting this perspective opens up a path to "disruptive" change in contrast to incremental change in education.

Still, the educational literature demonstrates that, in fact, incremental change seems to the most consistent path to educational change (Tyack & Cuban, 1997), and that the conservative nature of these institutions is only one side of the coin. Inbar (1996) argues that since public education has high level of permanence, guaranteed by a constant influx of students, funding and legislation, it might lead indeed to conservatism and inaction. On the other hand, these same guarantees create institutional safety, which can and (in many cases does) lead to an interest in innovation, change, and experimentation—but perhaps not as "disruptive" as some might wish.

Radical action is best exemplified by a Silicon Valley motto: "move fast and break things" which Dana Boyd recently characterized as "…an abomination if your goal is to create a healthy society" (Boyd, 2019). This mentality is often associated with the startup culture and the ecosystem surround what Smyrnaios (2016) considers and oligopoly perpetuated through large sums of capital and intellectual property: Google, Amazon, Facebook, Apple e Microsoft (GAFAM). Their aggressive focus on this market can be seen in all levels of formal education around the world.[7]

Singer (2017) indicates that, according to Google, more than half of all elementary school students in the United States (more than 30 million children) use Google applications, criticizing what she calls "Googlification" of the classroom. Brazil has moved in a similar direction. There is data that indicates a similar scenario in Brazil

---

[7] Within the #GoOpen program in the USA, the implementation guide discusses the use of Google applications, see: https://tech.ed.gov/open/.

(da Cruz, Saraiva, & Amiel, 2019).[8] Agreements and by-in from local governments have expanded and promoted access to GAFAM by schools. As an example, The São Paulo State Secretariat of Education regularly[9] promotes its partnership with Microsoft, offering Office 365 free of charge to students, teachers, and managers, simply by creating an email through an official channel (Digital School Office, in free translation; SED), accessible only by using an account registered with Microsoft. The State Secretariat also established a partnership with Google to offer, through SED, access to the Google Education service. The scope of these partnerships is not restricted to the online space: to use the school's computer labs (named *Acessa Escola*), it is necessary to create an institutional email (a Microsoft account). This imposition effectively restricts the use of a public space and public equipment in a public institution; or at the very least, the imposition that one shares personal data to a foreign company to enjoy a public good.

In higher education, similar partnerships have taken effect, offering "free access" to services from companies such as Google and Microsoft. Access to these platforms is promoted as an added option to existing services, with an emphasis on being "free" and promoted as a clear benefit to higher education institutions. They do, however, ignore the costs of "free", its impact on the current software ecosystem in institutions, and the consequences of inducing the use of foreign corporate platforms, often in conflict with internal institutional policies (Parra, Cruz, Amiel, & Marchado, 2018). The services offered go beyond email, and incorporate well-known productivity applications in the cloud (spreadsheets, text editors, etc.) as well as specific tools for education, such as grading sheets, shared calendars, activities, and tasks.

We have at least two potential scenarios. For some institutions, the partnership with companies might make "one more resource" available, that is, an alternative set of tools that in essence competes with existing solutions (such as a Moodle instance). In other cases, we begin to see evidence that the communication infrastructure of institutions is being taken over by companies such as Google and Microsoft, access to institutional communication tools (such as email) and file hosting (with institutional data) is no longer managed by higher education institutions. This stands in stark contrast to existing public or paid models that remain under the control of public administration (Parra et al., 2018). In both cases, given the economic power and the "free" provision of services offered by GAFAM, there is no room for effective competition with public entities, squashing the possibility of the coexistence of different platforms and services.

An almost inevitable consequence of this outsourcing of educational services is an atrophy in institutions and local educational businesses (unless aligned with larger corporate platforms), and the capacity to develop and support educational technology solutions that are adapted to local needs. As pointed out by Taplin (2017), antitrust

---

[8] Up to date information on the Brazilian landscape is available in the Education Under Surveillance project website (educacaovigiada.org.br)

[9] See, for example: https://www.educacao.sp.gov.br/noticias/alunos-e-professores-podem-baixar-o-pacote-office-365-da-microsoft-gratuitamente-2/ (2017); and https://www.educacao.sp.gov.br/noticias/ferramentas-da-microsoft-facilitam-a-rotina-do-professor/ (2016).

ideas from the 1960s and 1970s do not transfer well to the reality of twenty-first century informational markets. When products are "free" to the consumer, the real cost of monopolies is harder to ascertain.

As these services become institutionalized, and the de facto storage and communication systems, there is room for all sort of institutional information to be moved to these "partner" institutions: email exchanges between researchers, research data, personal student and teacher data, students grades and academic work, as well as (open) educational resources of all types. Google, for example, has said it does not use data from educational accounts for advertising purposes,[10] educational accounts, though there is strong evidence that data is collected and processed in multiple forms.[11] Privacy and copyright policies are notoriously difficult to navigate and understand. When these policies combine institutional regulation and private business policies, this becomes even more complicated (see Parra et al., 2018 for the description of two cases). When this partnership becomes institutionalized the acceptance of these policies is mandatory if one wants to use public services.

It is important to remember that beyond mining and collecting data, there are other ways in which businesses monetize "free". The continuous use of tools and platforms creates a cycle of familiarity and a content portfolio that created fidelity to the same platforms and tools in other areas of their life. In the words of the Head of Google Education for Brazil, "one of the advantages of offering services to schools is that we can create user fidelity early on" (Romani, 2019; our translation).

The voracity with which businesses such as Google and Microsoft (and Amazon, evidenced by their interest in OER through Amazon Inspire) promote their platforms to the educational sector leads us wonder how these "free" services benefit from user-generated content and interaction, particularly educational resources? First, one must consider what constitutes an educational resource. Certainly, the lesson plans, books, presentations, quizzes and all sorts of resources that constitute the content of classes in proprietary platforms can be considered educational content. So it is worth asking: in what way does the production and dissemination of educational resources—in many cases OER—in closed or "free" platforms offered by large corporations contribute to the consolidation of these oligopolies? Keeping in mind the values of openness and transparency valued by OER, one should question how much its proponent contributes to the status quo when they suggest, induce or do not question the use of these platforms in their teaching or within their organizations. One could cite as examples the ability to easily connect content to Google Classroom from well-known sites like Currwiki and OER Commons.[12]

---

[10] See https://support.google.com/edu/classroom/answer/6025224?hl=en.

[11] See the "Spying on Student" report from the Electronic Frontier Foundation (EFF) at https://www.eff.org/wp/school-issued-devices-and-student-privacy.

[12] See http://www.curriki.org/curriki-oer-library-is-now-lti-compliant-and-has-integrated-the-google-classroom-share-button/ and https://www.oercommons.org/authoring/13855-share-your-oer-with-google-classroom/view.

The intersection of OER and privacy is an emerging and still under-investigated field. The strategy supports the availability and capillarity of OER as they establish connections with platforms that control the distribution and storage of content. Another example of ambiguity is the partnership between Lumen Learning (headed by one of the pioneers of the OER movement in the United States of America) and Follett, "world's largest single source of books, entertainment products, digital content and multimedia for libraries, schools and retailers".[13] This partnership could lead to increasing the visibility and use of open content through established channels while also reducing the plurality and diversity of players. One must also question the rhetoric that openness, when restricted to legal and licensing concerns, might actually lead to changes in education, beyond the possible reduction of cost.

It is still not possible to foresee the consequences of these partnerships and their role in the consolidation of existing oligopolies in these industries and their impact on privacy, control, and transparency. The same scenario can be seen in Brazil, as we will present next.

5.4 Investigating Benefits and Risks

It is important then, to reflect on the specific effects that an OER strategy can have on education. One of the most commonly used arguments I favor of OER is the reduction of costs to educational resources (for example, Fischer, Hilton, Robinson, & Wiley, 2015). Educational resources are unquestionably important in any educational content, and have significant cost (in 2016, it was R$1,8 billion—half of the National Fund for the Development of Education (FNDE) budget—and almost 2 % of the Ministry of Educations' budget). With the upsurge of copyright legislation in recent decades, where rights reside mostly in the hands of publishers and conglomerates, the use of these resources is increasingly subject to restrictions—conditioned to authorization of payment—and frequently both.

Paradoxically, the influence of these restrictions is not limited to use and circulation of good, but also affect the production of these resources. For a small publisher that develops resources on literature, for example, it is increasingly difficult (and expensive) to include sections of literary works in their textbooks.[14] OER allow for the creation of a collection of resources with fewer restrictions and have the potential to reduce the cost in both the starting and endpoints of this process: for the "final users" of educational resources and its initial producers.

This OER advantage is full of complexities and possible negative consequences that must not be dismissed lightly. We will examine two of these risks: the displacement of production, and the imbalance in the distribution of gains with the reduction of costs.

---

[13] See https://www.follett.com/lumen/.

[14] Benkler (2006, p. 37) attributed this situation to a characteristics of informational goods: fact that they are both outputs and inputs of creative work.

5.4.1 Production Offshoring

The freedom to reuse OER can create two distinct situations in the development of textbooks. To exemplify those situations, let us imagine, a book on geography that contains some maps reproduced from other works (whose rights-holders demand authorization and royalties), and other maps that were produced specially for that book. In the first situation, which corresponds to reproduced maps, the use of OER would save costs on royalties, while also avoiding the need for authorization. In the second situation, the use of OER would save the costs of producing original maps.

It is in this second situation that relevant risks related to offshoring production arise. Although the cost savings that it allows could have positive effects, it also tends to encourage actors in peripheral countries to reduce their production of original material, replacing it by translating or merely reusing OER produced by actors in central countries, which will more frequently have the resources to produce original material. This trend can be particularly sharp in the commercial sector, since the actors making such use of OER will have a competitive advantage due to the cost savings. This can also imply the reduction of quality, in certain respects, of the materials produced. After all, even if the translated or adapted OER is of a very high pedagogical quality, it will rarely be able to reach the same level of context awareness (and meaningfulness to its public) than that of an original material produced by local experts, knowledgeable about the nuances of the sociocultural environment for which it is intended.

Although this trend is still relatively hypothetical, there are current examples that suggest it is important not to dismiss it. In Brazil, one of these examples can be seen in the parallel between the partnership negotiations between the Ministry of Education and the founder of Khan Academy for the translation of a vast amount of content in English,[15] on the one hand, and the reduced amount and quality of digital materials purchased through the PNLD program[16] on the other hand.

It is possible that this trend of concentration in content production—and in its related technical capabilities—may offer medium-term advantages to actors in large urban centers, and even to large local companies that follow this strategy; for instance, granting them dominance in those markets where existing OER are not a solution, or where there is a demand for complete educational systems (and not only for standalone educational material). It is nevertheless reasonable to consider if the availability of good quality, free to reuse educational resources would not compensate this asymmetry for under-resourced or peripheral actors. Without delving deeper in this debate, what seems beyond doubt is that there is no reason for the public sector to subsidize OER production by actors from large centers (or large local companies),

---

[15]This is only one of many translation projects supported by the Lemann Foundation. See http://www.fundacaolemann.org.br/khan-academy/ and http://www.fundacaolemann.org.br/para-aprender/.

[16]PNLD (National Program for Textbooks and Didactic Materials) is a federal program (one of the largest in the world) that buys textbooks from publishers and distributes them free of charge to schools.

even more so if they can already obtain commercial advantages by doing so. What would make sense is subsidizing—or directing—OER production by peripheral or under-resourced actors. As Divardin and Amiel (2018) show, the pioneering purchase of digital multimedia resources under the PNLD in 2014 led to a restructuring and strengthening of existing players to cope with this novel demand. The structure of the call, associating the purchasing of multimedia to the usual print textbooks meant that the usual players acquired, outsourced or incorporated into their structures mechanisms for production of digital resources—the program tended to favor already dominant companies.

Before concluding this discussion about the risk of offshoring, a caveat should be added. The reasoning made here about this risk is somewhat simplified: we know there is an imprecise continuum—and not a binary distinction—between the production of original material, on the one hand, and reuse of an OER, on the other hand. It is thus perfectly possible to reuse OER in an authorly manner, adapting and remixing it creatively and with high context awareness. Similarly, the decontextualized use of translated and poorly adapted material is not a phenomenon brought about by OER, but rather a practice that already happened in the past.[17] The production of original material is also not a panacea: it may well happen that an original material ends up being inferior to an existing OER, particularly with regard to its content or pedagogical approach. That, however, does not negate the fact that OER also open possibilities for more mechanical reuse practices, encouraging them by the cost reduction, and consequently introducing the risks of technical and pedagogical impoverishment (of the producers and resources, respectively) in subaltern regions and countries. Therefore, although the reasoning about the risk of offshoring should not be unduly generalized, and the particular circumstances of each case should be evaluated when discussing specific uses of OER, this argument also reveals a trend that can be problematic, particularly when considering its wide scale impacts.

5.4.2 *Concentration of Gains from Cost Reduction*

As mentioned above, the benefits that OER can offer to society must be weighed against the risks it implies, such as those from production offshoring. The second type of risk we will discuss involves the possibility that producers of educational resources might withhold those benefits, without sharing them with consumers or the public sector.

Indeed, in markets that are already concentrated (such as the textbook market in Brazil), competition might not be enough to force those who reduce costs (through

---

[17] Evidently the risk of lack of contextualization are not a issue only with OER. Contextualization has been a concern within the PNLD, through textbooks on History and Geography, for example. Still, looking at the recent 2016 purchase of these books, only 10 states were contemplated by specific texts (and some, like Mato Grosso do Sul and Espírito Santo were not even covered by more general textbooks, such as those who discussed the Amazon region or all of the Northeast (Brasil, 2015).

the use of third party OER) to pass on such reductions to consumer prices. Thus, in the Brazilian example, it is possible that a growth in OER adoption among publishing houses participating in the PNLD might not represent a reduction in public spending with educational resources, or that such reduction is not a fair share of the savings those companies achieved in their costs; in that scenario, the social benefits brought by OER would be captured by publishing houses, and transformed into an increase in their profit margins.

One cannot deny that, on the one hand, OER generate an equalizing effect that allows to reduce an important barrier for the participation of small publishing houses in a government program as PNLD: the capital needed to invest in original material production (capital which smaller firms frequently do not have). It so happens, though, that this is only one of the many barriers that small publishing houses face in such programs. In PNLD, for instance, publishing houses are responsible for printing and distributing the works, tasks that demand a robust structure and sophisticated relationships with other companies, and that larger publishing houses are much more prepared to undertake. That causes a paradox: in case the equalizing effect of OER is not enough to allow smaller firms to compete effectively in PNLD, the possible concentrating effect of OER (which happens, as discussed in the previous paragraph, when the company captures the cost savings generated by the use of OER and turns into an increase of its profit margin) reinforces the asymmetry of this market, feeding back into the risk discussed here.

The example of the PNLD is not the only one in which this risk of private capture of OER benefits manifests itself; it can also be seen when the educational resource is not the final product to be commercialized, but an input in a larger "package". As such, it is also possible that, in for-profit education, a company may start adopting OER in order to save costs (making the production of textbooks that are already included in the tuition fees cheaper), but end up not passing on this cost reduction to consumer prices, but rather incorporating it in its profit margin.

In Brazil, that scenario is very feasible in higher education, which is another extremely concentrated sector in the country—the largest educational company in the world (Cogna, formerly known as *Kroton Educacional*)[18] is Brazilian—as well as in the case of so-called "teaching systems", in which a company sells schools an ensemble of educational services (including not only textbooks, but also training, technological solutions, consulting, etc.), blurring the exact pricing of educational resources.

---

[18]The company became the largest in the world in 2014, after it merged with *Anhanguera*, another Brazilian educational company.

5.5 Finding Equilibrium

The majority of the risks we identified here are related to the capture of the potential benefits of OER by private actors involved in the production of educational resources (or those who make use of them to offer educational services). Even though there is room for state activity in this sector, we do not wish to defend the idea that educational resources should be produced solely by public actors. Without entering the discussions on the comparative efficiency of the public and private sectors, it is difficult to imagine that the centralization of this production within the state's apparatus could produce the kaleidoscope of necessities of the Brazilian educational system. As it stands, the state already has substantial sway in large content distribution programs, such as the PNLD; even though the PNLD is an example of a program that favors diversity, we suspect that exacerbating this power in the hands of the state could be detrimental in the case of totalitarian regimes, or when progressive and democratic values might be trumped in favor of specific ideologies.

Exclusivity would also neutralize one of the great potentials of OER: finding new models for the production of educational resources, so that they may be treated as a common good. In other words, a model that would allow anyone that demands so, to have access to them, and that encourages and permits anyone to contribute to its improvement. The creation of this type of legislation, infrastructure, and benefits is within the reach of the public sector—mechanisms that might promote and protect this "commons" and to create policies that induce those actors who today are in a privileged status to adopt strategies that will nourish this commons and make capturing it more difficult.

Initiatives in this direction have already taken place. The call for PNLD 2019 and 2020 demand that a portion of the digital resources submitted by publishers be licensed openly. To take the latter as an example, all "extra" resources which are used by teachers (quizzes, lesson plans, etc.) and 75 % of all audiovisual resources must have an open license (CC-BY-NC). A specific clause also allows for publishers to negotiate the complete (patrimonial) rights of submitted works, so that these rights are transferred to the Ministry of Education.[19]

While still recent and relatively small in scope, this proposal instigates a discussion on open licensing and distribution within the publishing industry, and promotes the availability of quality open content to the public without an expiration date on availability. It also opens up discussions on new models for the acquisition of educational resources with public monies, which might lead to a greater variety of participants in these calls and new models for purchasing content.

Within the Board for Distance Education (*Diretoria de Ensino a Distância*; DED/CAPES, which is responsible for the management of Open University of Brazil (*Universidade Aberta do Brasil*; UAB) there has been a strong and concerted effort in the direction of open resources. Since late 2016, all resources created by those receiving funds through the UAB (teachers, tutors, staff) must be openly licensed.

---

[19]Learn more at: http://aberta.org.br/materiais-educacionais-comprados-pelo-mec-terao-licenca-creative-commons/.

The UAB is a consortium of over 130 public institutions serving over 900 municipal centers throughout the country.[20] This policy, coupled with training, workshops, and the creation of network of OER Ambassadors in over a dozen higher education institutions[21] have created substantial momentum.

Another positive example is Ministry's new educational resources site for basic education.[22] As a repository, it only accepts resources which are openly licensed. It also includes detailed terms of service, which has been created to be an instructional material that can help users and contributors understand the difference between free, closed, and open content.

Also within the federal level, the Science Cloud Computing platform is under development by the National Network for Teaching and Research (*Rede Nacional de Ensino e Pesquisa*; RNP). Among other services, RNP is piloting a solution for file sharing for public higher education institutions and government educational agencies in a public cloud. Even though it is not strictly an initiative for the sharing of educational resources, it demonstrates that creating public infrastructures for collaborative work is possible. The case is also interesting because it demonstrates how this infrastructure can integrate itself to a larger ecosystem not only for servers but also for clients. It is based on free and open-source software (OpenStack, Owncloud) for which the institution also made contributions to the code (Ribeiro Filho et al., 2015). These are just some of the recent initiatives that already do, or might soon impact how educational resources are purchased, shared and created, due in great part to the activism of public servants, civil society organizations, educators and researchers fighting for the common good.

5.6 Conclusion

One of our main goals with this chapter is to demonstrate that open educational resources, like all digital or online technologies, are not neutral or apolitical. If they don't make explicit their premises, projects or movements run the risk of finding themselves adrift, at the mercy of the winds existing powers. If technology is to provide educational and social benefits, and not mere efficiency gains or monetary gains, they should be configured explicitly for these ends. There are risks in applying the "open" concept in a naive way, especially when it's configured by incumbent market actors. The delocalization of the production of teaching materials, the concentration of profit, and the strengthening of the position of big corporations are examples of these risks. In a paradox characteristic of globalization, OER from "the center" become ubiquitous, leading to atrophy of the capacity of the periphery to produce and to disseminate its voice.

---

[20] Visualize a map of the institutions and the municipal centers here: http://uab.educacaoaberta.org/.

[21] See the official CAPES page on OER and the Ambassadors at: http://www.capes.gov.br/uab/rea/.

[22] See https://plataformaintegrada.mec.gov.br/. It functions both as a referatory to both open and closed content, and as a repository, hosting exclusively open content.

When OER are financed by private interests and hosted on platforms owned by oligopolies that feed of their metadata and the personal data of their users, the mere possibility *de jure* of adaptation and remix won't save the local production of educational resources. A global commons that is structured on the terms of transnational corporations won't attend to the necessities of local communities of schools, educators, and students around the world.

OER and the ideas sustained by the various open movements like those of Open Access, Open Science, Transparency and Open Government or Open Data can and should be used to promote the autonomy of educators, a diversity of ideas and the creation of collaborative spaces. As pointed out by Peters and Britez (2008), OER mean freedom, citizenship, knowledge for all, social progress, and the transformation of individuals. Can a critical analysis of the project and an honest assessment of its limitations help realize the potential of this valuable movement for education? We sincerely believe so.

Acknowledgments If you wish to acknowledge persons who contributed or sponsoring agencies, do so here in this optional section.

References

Amiel, T., & Soares, T. C. (2016). Identifying tensions in the use of open licenses in OER repositories. *The International Review of Research in Open and Distributed Learning, 17*(3). https://doi.org/10.19173/irrodl.v17i3.2426.

Amiel, T., Gonsales, P., & Sebriam, D. (2018). Recursos Educacionais Abertos no Brasil: 10 anos de ativismo. *EmRede, 5*(2), 246–258.

An, D., & Carr, M. (2017). Learning styles theory fails to explain learning and achievement: Recommendations for alternative approaches. *Personality and Individual Differences, 116,* 410–416. https://doi.org/10.1016/j.paid.2017.04.050.

Arjona-Reina, L., Robles, G., & Dueñas, S. (2014, January). The FLOSS2013 Free/Libre/Open Source Survey. Retrieved March 26, 2017, from http://web.archive.org/web/20140212132153/, http://floss2013.libresoft.es/results.en.html.

Ashcraft, C., McLain, B., & Eger, E. (2016). *Women in tech: The facts.* Retrieved from https://www.ncwit.org/sites/default/files/resources/ncwit_women-in-it_2016-full-report_final-web06012016.pdf.

Benkler, Y. (2005). *Common wisdom: Peer production of educational materials.* Retrieved from http://www.lemill.org/trac/raw-attachment/wiki/BookList/162436.pdf.

Benkler, Y. (2006). *The wealth of networks: How social production transforms markets and freedom.* New Haven [Conn.]: Yale University Press.

Boyd, D. (2019, September 17). *Facing the great reckoning head-on.* Retrieved September 20, 2019, from https://onezero.medium.com/facing-the-great-reckoning-head-on-8fe434e10630.

Brasil. (2015). *Guia de livros didáticos: PNLD 2016: Apresentação: Ensino fundamental anos iniciais.* Retrieved from http://www.fnde.gov.br/centrais-de-conteudos/publicacoes/category/125-guias?download=9598:pnld-2016-guia-apresentacao.

Bush, V. (1945, July). As we may think. *The Atlantic.* Retrieved from https://www.theatlantic.com/magazine/archive/1945/07/as-we-may-think/303881/.

Castells, M. (2011). *The rise of the network society: The information age: Economy, society, and culture.* New York: Wiley.

Chakraborty, S. (2013). Deskilling of the teaching profession. In J. Ainsworth (Ed.), *Sociology of education: An A-to-Z guide*. https://doi.org/10.4135/9781452276151.n106.

da Cruz, R., Saraiva, F., & Amiel, T. (2019). Coletando dados sobre o Capitalismo de Vigilância nas instituições públicas do ensino superior do Brasil. In *VI Simpósio Internacional LAVITS*. Presented at the LAVITS, Salvador. Retrieved from https://www.integra.unb.br/s/5zWiygrHPcXFitD.

David, P. A., Waterman, A., & Arora, S. (2003). FLOSS-US the free/libre/open source software survey for 2003. Stanford Institute for Economic Policy Research, Stanford University, Stanford, CA (http://www.stanford.edu/group/floss-us/report/floss-us-report.pdf). Retrieved from https://pdfs.semanticscholar.org/f040/542f2d2ab3c188fac82b5d039ad7aa31a97d.pdf.

Divardin, D., & Amiel, T. (2018). A produção de contéudos digitais para o PNLD. In *Proceedings of the XIII Latin-American Conference on Learning Technologies*. Presented at the LACLO, São Paulo. Retrieved from http://cleilaclo2018.mackenzie.br.

Downes, S. (2001). Learning objects: resources for distance education worldwide. *The International Review of Research in Open and Distributed Learning, 2*(1). Retrieved from http://www.irrodl.org/index.php/irrodl/article/view/32.

Downes, S. (2015). *State of the commons report*. Retrieved January 26, 2017, from http://www.downes.ca/post/64762.

Evangelista, R. de A. (2010). *Traidores do movimento: Política, cultura, ideologia e trabalho no Software Livre* (Unicamp [dissertação de doutorado]). Retrieved from http://www.bibliotecadigital.unicamp.br/document/?code=000477515.

Fischer, L., Hilton, J., Robinson, T. J., & Wiley, D. A. (2015). A multi-institutional study of the impact of open textbook adoption on the learning outcomes of post-secondary students. *Journal of Computing in Higher Education, 27*(3), 159–172.

Friesen, N. (2004). Three objections to learning objects and e-learning standards. In *Online education using learning objects* (pp. 59–70). London: Routledge.

Ghosh, R. A., Glott, R., Krieger, B., & Robles, G. (2002). *Free/libre and open source software: Survey and study*. International Institute of Infonomics, University of Maastricht. Retrieved from http://www.math.unipd.it/~bellio/FLOSS%20Final%20Report%20-%20Part%204%20-%20Survey%20of%20Developers.pdf.

Hannafin, M., & Hill, J. (2008). Resource-based learning. In M. Spector, D. Merrill, J. van Merrienboer, & M. Driscoll (Eds.), *Handbook of research in educational technology* (3rd ed.). New York: Lawrence Erlbaum.

Hansen, J. D., & Reich, J. (2015). Democratizing education? Examining access and usage patterns in massive open online courses. *Science, 350*(6265), 1245–1248. https://doi.org/10.1126/science.aab3782.

Inbar, D. E. (1996). *Planning for educational innovation* (Vol. 37). Retrieved from http://unesdoc.unesco.org/images/0011/001119/111952eb.pdf.

Kuechler, V., Gilbertson, C., & Jensen, C. (2012). Gender differences in early free and open source software joining process. In *Open source systems: Long-term sustainability* (pp. 78–93). https://doi.org/10.1007/978-3-642-33442-9_6.

Kuhn, T. S. (2012). *The structure of scientific revolutions: 50th anniversary edition*. Chicago: University of Chicago Press.

Levy, P. (2010). *Cibercultura*. Editora 34.

Nafus, D. (2012). "Patches don't have gender": What is not open in open source software. *New Media & Society, 14*(4), 669–683. https://doi.org/10.1177/1461444811422887.

Negroponte, N. (1995). *Being digital*. Vintage Books.

Parra, H., Cruz, L., Amiel, T., & Marchado, J. (2018). Infraestruturas, economia e política informacional: O caso do Google Suite for education. *Mediações, 23*(1), 63–99. https://doi.org/10.5433/2176-6665.2018v23n1p63.

Peters, M. A., & Britez, R. G. (2008). Introduction: Open education and education for openness. In R. G. Britez & M. A. Peters (Eds.), *Open education and education for openness* (pp. xvii–xxii). Taipei: Sense Publishers.

Popper, K. R. (2002). *Conjectures and refutations: The growth of scientific knowledge*. London: Routledge.
Pretto, N. (2012). Professores-autores em rede. In B. Santana, C. Rossini, & N. D. L. Pretto (Eds.), *Recursos Educacionais Abertos: Práticas colaborativas e políticas públicas* (pp. 91–108). São Paulo: Casa da Cultura Digital/Edufba.
Reeves, T. C., & Oh, E. (2008). Generational differences. *Handbook of Research on Educational Communications and Technology, 3,* 295–303.
Ribeiro Filho, J. L., Nunes, A. C. F., Makino, R. N. dos S., Araújo, G. B., Martins, G. M. L., & Guimarães, L. M. de O. (2015). Structuring and implementing the Brazilian Academic Cloud: Strategy, modelling, challenges and services. In *Proceedings and Report of the 8th UbuntuNet Alliance Annual Conference*. Presented at the 8th UbuntuNet Alliance annual conference, Maputo. Retrieved from http://www.ubuntunet.net/sites/default/files/Ribeiro%20Filho.pdf.
Romani, B. (2019, February 17). Gigantes da tecnologia entram na briga por novo espaço: A sala de aula. *Estado de São Paulo*. Retrieved from https://link.estadao.com.br/noticias/cultura-digital,gigantes-da-tecnologia-entram-na-briga-por-novo-espaco-a-sala-de-aula,70002724698.
Sicilia, M.-A., & Garcia, E. (2003). On the concepts of usability and reusability of learning objects. *The International Review of Research in Open and Distributed Learning, 4*(2). Retrieved from http://www.irrodl.org/index.php/irrodl/article/view/155.
Simonite, T. (2013). *The fight to save wikipedia from itself*. Retrieved August 29, 2017, from https://www.technologyreview.com/s/520446/the-decline-of-wikipedia/.
Singer, N. (2017). How Google took over the classroom. *New York Times, 13*. Retrieved from https://www.nytimes.com/2017/05/13/technology/google-education-chromebooks-schools.html.
Smyrnaios, N. (2016). L'effet GAFAM: stratégies et logiques de l'oligopole de l'internet (pre-print). *Communication & Langages, 2016*(188), 61–83.
Taplin, J. (2017, April 22). *Is it time to break up Google?* Retrieved from https://www.nytimes.com/2017/04/22/opinion/sunday/is-it-time-to-break-up-google.html.
Taylor, J. C. (2007). Open courseware futures: Creating a parallel universe. *Journal of Instructional Science and Technology, 10*(1), 9.
Turner, F. (2010). *From counterculture to cyberculture: Stewart brand, the whole earth network, and the rise of digital utopianism*. Chicago: University of Chicago Press.
Tyack, D., & Cuban, L. (1997). *Tinkering toward utopia: A century of public school reform*. Boston, MA: Harvard University Press.
UNESCO. (2002). *UNESCO promotes new initiative for free educational resources on the internet*. Retrieved from http://www.unesco.org/education/news_en/080702_free_edu_ress.shtml.
UNESCO. (2019). *Draft recommendation on Open Educational Resources*. Retrieved from https://unesdoc.unesco.org/ark:/48223/pf0000370936.
Weller, M. (2015). MOOCs and the silicon valley narrative. *Journal of Interactive Media in Education, 2015*(1). Retrieved from http://jime.open.ac.uk/articles/10.5334/jime.am/.
Wiley, D. A. (2001). *The instructional use of learning objects—Online version*. Retrieved from http://www.reusability.org/read/.
Winner, L. (1993). Social constructivism: Upon opening the black box and finding it empty. In R. C. Sharff & V. Dusek (Eds.), *Philosophy of technology: The technological condition* (pp. 233–243). Malden, MA: Blackwell.
Yegulalp, S. (2014, February 3). *Who writes Linux? Corporations, more than ever*. Retrieved August 29, 2017, from https://www.infoworld.com/article/2610207/open-source-software/who-writes-linux--corporations--more-than-ever.html.

Tel Amiel completed his Ph.D. in Instructional Technology at the University of Georgia. He is currently professor at the School of Education at the University of Brasília where he coordinates the UNESCO Chair in Distance Education (educacaoaberta.org). He was previously coordinated the UNESCO Chair in Open Education (Unicamp). More information at amiel.info.

Ewout ter Haar obtained his Ph.D. in condensed matter physics from the University of Leiden. He works since 2006 with Educational Technology at the University of São Paulo.

Miguel Said Vieira is a professor at the Federal University of ABC (UFABC, Brasil), where he works at the Center for Educational Technologies and teaches in the Public Policies and Sciences and Humanities programs. His research deals with the relations between knowledge, technology, collaboration and commodification, with a special interest in the theme of commons (including theoretical approaches and specific practices such as OER, free software and open access), and the areas of STS and philosophy of science. His publications can be found at http://impropriedades.wordpress.com.

Tiago C. Soares holds a Ph.D. in History of Economics from the University of São Paulo. A long-time activist, he's been involved with the Open Education and Free/Libre and Open Source Software movements for nearly two decades. He is an associate with the UNESCO Chair in Distance Education (Universidade da Brasília).

Open Access This chapter is licensed under the terms of the Creative Commons Attribution 4.0 International License (http://creativecommons.org/licenses/by/4.0/), which permits use, sharing, adaptation, distribution and reproduction in any medium or format, as long as you give appropriate credit to the original author(s) and the source, provide a link to the Creative Commons license and indicate if changes were made.

The images or other third party material in this chapter are included in the chapter's Creative Commons license, unless indicated otherwise in a credit line to the material. If material is not included in the chapter's Creative Commons license and your intended use is not permitted by statutory regulation or exceeds the permitted use, you will need to obtain permission directly from the copyright holder.

Chapter 6
Online Technology in Knowledge Transfer

Daniel Burgos

Abstract The transfer of knowledge entails a challenge for any research activity. It drives the promise and results towards implemented and replicable facts. The transfer is frequently crystallised in contracts and patents, but not solely: scientific communication, general publication, property rights, or public R&D + innovation projects generated in the heat of research are also transference products and tools. This article lays out the benefits and weaknesses of these devices, underlining the participation of technology, especially online tech, when appropriate. We found that there are a variety of resources for transference, and that technology is only valid in some of them.

Keywords Transfer · Commodification · Impact · Sustainability · Online technology

6.1 Transference Versus Commodification of Results

Spain is a powerhouse of quality researchers and cutting-edge research; the rest of Europe, too. We have strong teams, individuals, and institutions in health sciences, educational innovation, social policies, IT security, and other fields who interpret and shape daily reality and a promising future. However, tangible contributions, including the contact with civil society, complicity with companies and other agencies, and the actual use of products, services, and results by standing users or entities, are somewhat more elusive. Transference is sometimes not effective.

As researchers, we bear some of the blame. We follow the rules established by each call or accreditation step in order to fulfil the requirements, obtain a favourable review, and connect with a new project or activity that will enable continuing the line of investigation or group within a department. But we fail at the actual commodification of the results in the marketplace through serious dialogue with other stakeholders. Funding and accrediting agencies must facilitate the administrative

D. Burgos (✉)
Research Institute for Innovation & Technology in Education (UNIR iTED),
Universidad Internacional de La Rioja (UNIR), Logroño, La Rioja, Spain
e-mail: daniel.burgos@unir.net

steps that, paradoxically, often consume practically all the energy and most of the budget and time instead of facilitating the object of the call, whether it is research, development, or innovation. But at the same time, researchers must integrate our work in an obligatory and coordinated manner, into agencies, the market, and society, in order to ensure the usable and applicable transfer of results and knowledge.

6.2 Meaning of Knowledge Transfer

It is challenging to speak of transference. It is like speaking about innovation; everyone considers it crucial but there is no uniform definition or a minimally common consensus about it (Cooper, 1998; Goswami & Mathew, 2005; Baregheh, Rowley, & Sambrook, 2009). For some, transfer in academia means contracts between the university and companies. Thus, we find researchers focused on the industrial sector, measuring it by weight, quantity of projects, or the sum of associated contracts. By-products include the creation of industrially applied results-though not necessarily products—such as regulations, guidelines, specifications, or standards, and of course, industrial or intellectual registrations, by way of patents or utility models, and copyright clearance. For others, transfer means an impact on society, measured by, among other possibilities, target audience, end users, or Internet downloads. There are also scientific publishers, who insist on including specialised scientific production under the transfer umbrella, i.e. articles in scientific publications, chapters in books focused on a specific trade, and doctoral theses, or even conference communications. Conversely, we can find communicators who measure transference by hits obtained in unspecialised media and the budget conversion implied by crossover ads. We also have entrepreneurs, who defend the creation of companies in the wake of other initiatives, either as spin-offs, or as start-up incubators (Mowery, Oxley, & Silverman, 1996; Argote & Ingram, 2000; Agrawal & Henderson, 2002; Easterby-Smith, Lyles, & Tsang, 2008; Paulin & Suneson, 2015).

Although it is true that everyone is correct, because there is no singular definition, or a solid framework within which to include or exclude the concept of transfer, the fact is that most of the time the scientist is happy to link a new publicly-funded project in the wake of a prior finished project. And this, too, is considered transfer.

We can therefore group transfers into eight blocks or modalities (Fig. 6.1): (1) industrial, (2) property registration, (3) regulatory, (4) social impact, (5) scientific communication, (6) general publishing, (7) entrepreneurship, and (8) secondary public funding.

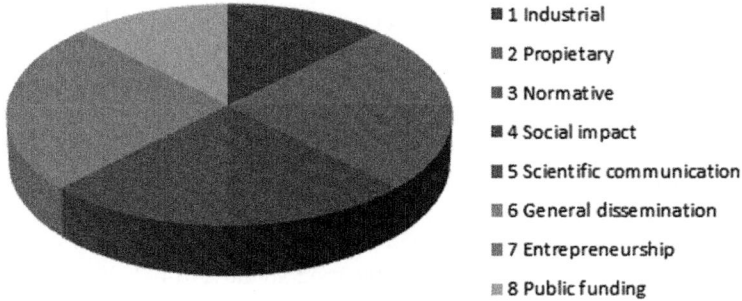

Fig. 6.1 Eight blocks of knowledge transfer

6.3 Advantages and Disadvantages of the Modalities

6.3.1 Industrial

Each of the blocks exhibits benefits and weaknesses that become more or less evident according to the block's success in matching the type of knowledge to be transferred with the chosen device. For example, the industrial block, focused on business contracts, has the advantage of returning the results of research, development, or innovation to the market and society through productive use (Ivascu, Cirjaliu, & Draghici, 2016). When this development has been funded or financed with regional, national, or international public funds, a tangible and measurable process of commodification that resonates in other subsequent productive processes is usually demanded. A contract with a company is a clear indication of this demand. Conversely, if the result is privately funded, the backers will certainly seek a way to recover that investment through industrial commodification. This block presents weaknesses, however, such as industrial ownership and the beneficiary of the commodification. If a public agency subsidises research that produces applicable results in a university using public funds, let's say state funds, and that commodification is attained by way of a contract between the university and a company, the economic benefit of the commodification will be ceded to the school. Public funds originate a benefit that reverts to the public university, but which does not necessarily return, either in full or partly, to the funding agent. In this context, the funding agency (the State, for example) functions as a driver or breeding ground at a sunk cost.

The case is sharper if the public body subsidises research in a private university, meaning that the contract between the private university and an outside company may generate a benefit reverting to that university. That is, public funds subsidise at sunk cost a result that generates a benefit to the private sector; in this case, the State invests, but private individuals benefit. Although it is true that the pillars of both public and private universities are portrayed as research and integration to society, leveraging contracts between the school and companies, as in Art. 83 of the Organic Law for Universities 6/2001 (dated 21 December) or any other type, fosters this integration but generates doubts regarding commodification; this is also true of rights, as described in the following section.

For example, the European Commission requires that all results from a subsidised project (e.g. Horizon 2020 or Erasmus+) should be open access (European Parliament, 2017), and curiously, this requirement is not only for citizens of Europe but for any individual in any country. That means Europe invests €77 billion (theoretically) in the Horizon 2020 program, split between subsidies for research, scholarships, support for SMEs, synergy between universities, etc. (CDTI, 2014). The results of this investment during the seven years of the programme (2014–2020) are accessible from any country, on any continent. Therefore, Europe provides free access to all its subsidised knowledge, born of its residents' taxes. This knowledge, those results, and those products are European, but they can be accessed by anyone in an instant. Intellectual property remains in Europe, but free access does not. Quite the opposite occurs in other continents or countries; Canada, Japan, the United Arab Emirates, the United States, or Colombia do not systematically yield their research for free, and therefore there is no reciprocity of access to information or to its possibilities for transfer.

Conversely, the right of commodification in Europe is regulated within agreements made by a consortium of European partners. If any spin-off commodification is decided or a contract is obtained with an administration, the beneficiary of that profit will be stipulated in the contract but will not reach the European Commission. That is to say, once again, Europe finances or subsidises a product, a result that generates a contract or a commodification of any kind but does not receive any payment in the case of positive production.

These two examples present a system that favours research in exchange for an expected return (productivity, publication, impact on society, etc.) but not at an economic level. The positive aspect is that a contract with a company generates wealth and, with luck, boosts that research and a productive layer. The not-so-positive aspect shows an unbalanced design where private business can happen at the expense of public funding, with no return to that source of funding.

6.3.2 Property Registration

Intellectual property proves to be a useful and effective mechanism to register certain aspects related to technology, such as content. Software proves to be somewhat more elusive, as it is also registered as text and is subject to the same norms of similarity ratios when faced with a copy (Joyce, Ochoa, Carroll, Leaffer, & Jaszi, 2016; Bettig, 2018; Stokes, 2019); this is undoubtedly a pending issue in support of developers. Industrial property follows a long procedure with multiple stages that means registration of technology or processes that lead to software development is obtained too late, with too-large budgets, and generally in an ineffective manner. Both Moore's Law (Waldrop, 2016) and the biannual logic of updating and modifying software and hardware mean that the 2-to-3-year process of patent registration exhausts any possibility of real commodification before the stamp is obtained (Mancini, 2019). A more agile, affordable, and equally robust mechanism is required in the face of possible plagiarism or misappropriation.

But not everything must be registered by copyright or patent. The open movement, mentioned earlier, has been extending its influence since 1975: software, content, education, access, etc. (Nyberg, 1975; D'Antoni, 2009; Downes, 2007; McAndrew, 2010). Code registered as Open Source, as in GitHub, GitLab, or SourceForge warehouses (Coelho & Valente, 2017), or in the Software Heritage project (Di Cosmo & Zacchiroli, 2017), provides immediate recognition of authorship, under the premises of fair and balanced use. The same is true of content and Creative Commons, preprints of scientific publications, or open education (Wong, 2017). The latter also cements its activity in technology together with other pillars (9 in all) such as access, research results, research data, content, educational policies, use licenses, accreditation, and inter-operability (Burgos, 2017). Society, in the shape of some users, has decided that there are alternative means of registration, warehousing, product use and recognition, and development and services which differ from the officially stipulated ones; this is an agreement between parties, with full operational effectiveness, which enables and more, stimulates, according to context, goal, and target audience, the exchange of information, knowledge, and resources among end users, whether they individual or institutional.

It is true that the open movement, on all levels, presents great grey areas. The definitions of open, unrestricted, free-of-charge, and universal tend to be commonly confused. Oftentimes, through a mere out-of-context translation of the English word "*free*" which can mean either "at no cost" or "unrestricted", or both, the multiple meanings are sometimes harmful to the appropriate use of the listed resource. The main objection lies in the approach of an over-inclined sector advocating for the unrestricted, free-of-charge, and unregistered use and enjoyment of external resources, without any type of compensation or financing from the user (Schimmer, Geschuhn, & Vogler, 2015). Content generation is the clearest example but this objection can be applied to any of the other nine pillars mentioned in the preceding paragraph. If a university official generates a course during their workday, the resource must be cost-free (Jahn & Tullney, 2016). The official is already paid for this effort from public funds and should not overburden the budget for private interest or use. If the university, as an institution, wishes to manage additional services (accreditation, tutoring, extra activities, etc.) or wishes to commercialise the course under certain parameters, there is certainly a viable and sustainable framework of commodification, but an institutional one, not for the official personally. If an individual generates a course in their free time, they have the right to offer it at no cost or for a fee, and they own their content and the means of distribution. Lastly, if an employee of a private institution (e.g. a university, research facility, or foundation) generates a course during their work time the institution will decide the commodification of the product, and whatever compensation it considers for the employee. In other words, if a product derives from public funding it cannot be doubly appraised. If it derives from private funds, the owner of those funds decides on access and costs. However, a wide sector of the open movement holds that everything must be open in education and academia, regardless of whether it is the result of personal, public, or private funds. Everything must be available for the free and unbound enjoyment of any user, regardless of which other user or institution has put up the funds.

Something similar occurs with registration. If an institution offers a free course, they cannot request registration information, depending on the sector, not even for academic tracking, licenses (any user can use, reuse, modify, and interpret what is published freely and without restrictions), or technology, including software; and so on, for many more resources (Fecher, Friesike, & Hebing, 2015; Ardi & Heidemann, 2019).

6.3.3 Regulatory

The creation of regulations, norms, standards, or technological specifications, among other productions, implies a form of transfer applied to the medium and long terms (Lerner & Tirole, 2015; Verhoeven, Bakker, & Veugelers, 2016). The possibility of regulating by defining the patterns of definition, use of, behaviour toward, and relation to a determined technology or technological process, enables *replicability* according to calibrated metrics, which should guarantee minimal levels of quality and control. The problem lies in the timing. Setting up any of these instruments requires years of preparation, and above all, approval, making streamlined transfer impossible and suggesting an almost impossible return within a prudent timeframe. The designer or group of designers must be willing to keep to the average years-long processing time before expecting to see any type of return.

6.3.4 Social Impact, Scientific Communication, and General Publication

Regarding user communication and interaction, transfer is centred on moving results and knowledge to different sections and groups of target audiences (Beck, S., Mahdad, Beukel, & Poetz, 2019; Cosgrove, Cristea, Shaughnessy, Mintzes, & Naudet, 2019). From a schoolteacher to a corporate lawyer, to a newspaper vendor; from a researcher in the same field to a critic of our theories, to a legislator; they are all valid, if rather limited, audiences, and all become possible interlocutors. This term, interlocutor, is wilfully chosen because those potential users do not act merely as receivers, but are emitters and replicators of communication in turn, at least potentially. Thus, a user becomes the focus, objective, initiator, medium, and even message, disrupting the usual chain in the communication process (Evans, 2010). They shift from merely passively observing to being a defining force (Hummel et al., 2005).

In this context, technology, especially online technology, represents a major trump card. Ever since a more popular Internet was launched through web service in 1996, and learning management systems like Moodle, Sakai, LAMS, and Claroline, and content managers like Drupal or PHPNuke, user communities such as the ubiquitous Facebook, instant messaging services like Messenger, file exchange services like eMule, and many other services flourished after 2000—since everything that has happened in these last fifteen years, the beast's evolution has been relentless. Any online service becomes a de facto social network: Ali Express, Telegram, WhatsApp, TripAdvisor, Booking, etc. (Karapanos, Teixeira, & Gouveia, 2016). From travel agencies to supermarkets to forums about automobiles or in journals, all services, or most of them, require user traffic and visits, and transform their original objective in order to embrace volume which will enable higher invoicing, obtain more publicity, or increase their value in a sale or a place on the stock exchange. In all of them it is common to use forums, downloads, ratings (the poorly named gamification which trivializes a useful yet complicated process for improvement and advancement, merely by attributing little stars born of a fleeting feeling and a simplified system) (de Sousa Borges, Durelli, Reis, & Isotani, 2014), assessment, file exchange, access to privileged information according to different metrics, and other tools. The entire ecosystem of interaction becomes crucial to knowledge transfer when designed with the appropriate approach. In the case of publication, the argument seems obvious: generating a community of users (or sharing the results of research, development, or innovation by way of an already-established community of users) implies an immediate and broad scope of possible impact. The trend is confirmed by universities' increasingly common use of networks or services with communities, such as LinkedIn, YouTube, Twitter, or Yammer.

These communities may be general or categorised by a thousand filters, ranging from language or gender to geography or experience, to personal interest or income range; those obtained through means both legitimate and subtly or directly illegal, as in the case of Cambridge Analytica (Cadwalladr & Graham-Harrison, 2018); through Alessia or Siri, or through thousands of unnecessary cookies. They may also be thematic communities focused on research, such as Research Gate or Academia; on dataset repositories, like Mendeley; or on publication indexing, like Scopus ID or Orcid. In any case, they all group and connect users according to the system's or user's own criteria, often with recommendations based on behaviour and profile, in the same spirit as Newton Learning, Netflix, or Amazon. Thus, they become powerful tools not only for knowledge transfer, but also for cultivating ideas, maintaining relationships, screening profiles, and enabling the creation of partnerships for new projects. On the other hand, exposing personal data or individual or collective behaviours allows the recovery or cataloguing of information for multiple uses. Characterisation of the user or the group favours a more direct and precise identification according to search criteria, which can be used towards noble ends (educational supervision, psychological support, sports training, etc.) or for other-not necessarily or expressly authorised- services, such as consumer profiling, political campaigning, triage of current or future patients, identity theft, and many other purposes (Tene & Polonetsky, 2012).

6.3.5 Entrepreneurship

The creation of spin-off companies from universities, as well as the use of incubators and accelerators to support start-ups and other entrepreneur initiatives, imply a determined step towards linking that fantastic university-business duo which is so idolised (Aceytuno & Báñez, 2008; Shapero & Sokol, 1982). Part of any university's function is to create knowledge and professionals that may be satisfactorily integrated into the business world, or better yet, help to form it. Without dramatising it, because not all universities should be dedicated to this singular goal (for example, certain Humanitarian or Arts careers) (Pilegaard & Neergaard, 2010), and because not all graduates should seek the same thing (for example, adult studies due to intellectual concerns or double degrees as a complement), the enterprising and integrating function in the market constitutes an important pillar of the modern university spirit. And in that context, technology and health play a key role. Fifty percent of the 949 companies created from universities in Spain between 2008 and 2016 are technology-based (REDOTRI, 2017; IUNE, 2019); 18% of them are engaged in ICT. The remaining 50% pursue diverse non-technical activities (Gómez-Miranda & Román-Martínez, 2016). Given these percentages, it is imperative to support technology as the driver, object, and result of transfer. If we focus on online technology, we find Internet products or services: communications (voice, text, and images), storage, anti-theft, security, secure transference (e.g. Blockchain), mobile networks, etc. With this spectrum of possibilities so completely enmeshed in daily life, a university's achievement in these fields is powerfully represented by the influence and success of its technological transfer in the form of the businesses which are established.

6.3.6 Secondary Public Funding

Considering publicly funded research projects as the only way to support lines of work is quite a common problem. The possibility of applying to so many open programs at the European Commission, Mineco, CDTI, regional invitations, and other institutions makes it possible, somewhat accidentally, somewhat purposefully, to maintain tasks and perspectives without the pressing need to diversify the origin of said funds.

Let's use the 7th Framework Programme, from 2007 to 2013, and the Horizon 2020 programme, from 2014 to 2020, as examples. Both have generated projects financed with €130 billion. Europe has invested over €191 billion in framework programmes (Fig. 6.2) (Feldman & Lichtenberg, 2000; Hoekman, Scherngell, Frenken, & Tijssen, 2013) altogether, beginning with the 1st Framework Programme which only lasted four years (1984–1987) and which contributed €3.75 billion.

A detailed analysis of Framework Programme VII (FP7), which allows us to focus on a closed and extensively studied cycle, presents spectacular numbers: 29,000 partners in 170 different countries financed by Europe, 136,000 applications reviewed,

Years	Framework Programme	Euros	M Euros
1984-1987	I	3.750.000.000	3.750
1987-1991	II	5.400.000.000	5.400
1991-1994	III	6.600.000.000	6.600
1994-1998	IV	13.100.000.000	13.100
1998-2002	V	14.960.000.000	14.960
2002-2006	VI	17.500.000.000	17.500
2007-2013	VII	50.000.000.000	50.000
2014-2020	VIII	80.000.000.000	80.000
TOTAL		191.310.000.000	191.310

Fig. 6.2 Budget per European framework programme, I–VII (Horizon 2020). *Source* http://www.jeupiste.eu/horizon-2020-and-around/historical-timeline-framework-programme, 2016

25,000 projects financed, with 70% support to universities and 30% to businesses, with the ICT sector as the greatest beneficiary, in addition to how ICT also appears in ancillary form in other spheres such as Health, Energy, or Transportation. Analysing more deeply, the numbers express a finer reading about knowledge transfer (European Commission, 2015, 2016). This programme produced 197,951 publications, including the mandatory scientific reports per project (deliverables), and evidencing a significant variation: anywhere between 1 and 1,412 reports from one project to another. There were also 1,700 requests made for patents, with companies owning 50% of them. Sadly, there is no tracking of filing registration or resolution to determine their progress. Similarly, 7,400 commodification designs were made, which are never monitored by the financing agent. From a scientific point of view, 50,000 researchers were registered in a system that identifies research (RTD type) as everything that is not management (MGT). Included in the non-MGT categories are software development, product maintenance, publication, etc., without it all necessarily being scientific. Lastly, 10,000 doctoral students were registered and 1,480 theses (14.8%) were presented for review.

These data show a wide capacity for generating interest in universities, generous funding of projects and partners, and concordant scientific production. However, the conversion does not support this. Neither the number of theses, nor the number of patents registered, nor the number of commodification plans, etc., permits accurate follow-up or analytical tracking, leading to a blurry conclusion regarding its relevance. With the data in hand, the conclusion centres on the imbalance between the resources invested and the benefits reported, allowing us to infer that real knowledge transfer has a relative effect.

What is certain is the linking of research projects. For instance, in research on Technology-Enhanced Learning (TEL, online learning or eLearning), Derntl & Klamma (2012), and later de la Fuente Valentín, Carrasco, Konya, & Solans, (2013) showed the concentration of public funding recipients in this sphere of research: an analysis of 77 and 93 projects in these two studies, respectively, from the FP6, FP7, and eContentplus (ECP) programmes, led to the conclusion that a half-dozen partners pooled most of the projects and financing, forming 27 common work pairs among them: Open Universiteit Nederland (Netherlands), The Open University (United Kingdom), the Catholic University of Leuven (Belgium), IMC AG (Germany), the University of Hannover (Germany), and the University of Jyväskylä (Finland). Curiously, the data sources of these analyses are no longer accessible except for a few analytical reports, so it is impossible to compare the information. Another case in the area of innovation (Competitiveness and Innovation Framework Programme—CIP-) is Intrasoft, a Luxembourg-based company that linked projects about the same subject during FP7 (education in science, technology, engineering, and mathematics, or STEM), for more than €25 million (CORDIS, 2019). There are similar cases organised by category, country, programmes, and professional areas (Health, Aeronautics, Security, etc.). This effective linking implies an inbred pseudo-transference of knowledge, like a cycle where one project's results feed the next, but have no effective impact outside the circuit. It is undoubtedly a case of circular economy, currently much in fashion, but with a creative interpretation.

We find a clear cause in the lack of post-project follow-up. At best, a project is approved and final funding is collected (after partial disbursements) after review by external experts with no need of subsequent reports. On the other hand, the absence of an effective mechanism for collecting subsidies for provable results obtained during the project and after its completion implies that the project's limit should be its own timeframe for implementation, without considering the commodification of the results. At most, a theoretical plan for transferring the knowledge is required, but will never be proven, as stated earlier. The solution lies in a series of measures, which are not necessarily popular ones: (1) implement these mechanisms and reserve a part of the subsidy, as per accomplishment metrics, for effective commodification once the implementation period has ended; (2) pay by objectives reached and verified, together with—for at least part of the total- an *ex-post* follow-up and impact verification; (3) reward successful commodification with future R&D+i funding; (4) establish a ranking of partners that weighs the participants according to metrics, including results and applied products and services, as well as effectively verified transfer; (5) separate the assessment and review of projects from the financing agency; (6) ensure no connection between reviewers and evaluators with funded partners exists, with sufficient margins for the absence of a relationship (revolving doors); and (7) demand a calibrated scientific and commodification review beyond the minimal viable product, not only an administrative one.

6.4 Conclusions

There are many possibilities for knowledge transfer in academia. Technology can be the object of this transfer but it can also become an instrument, especially in the case of online technology; one example of the former is patents and contracts, and one example of the latter is scientific communication and general publication. Special mention should be given to public financing. In this article we break down the circle of linked funding in a specific regional context, as a sample, and with a concrete object focused on online technology for education. We conclude that a proper selection of the instrument according to the final objective, product, and available medium is a determining component of transfer success.

Acknowledgments The original chapter in Spanish was firstly published in Nueva Revista, issue #171, November, 2019, available at www.nuevarevista.net. I thank this journal, along with the editor in chief, the guest editor (Prof. Dr. Guillermo Calleja), and their product manager (Mrs. Pilar Soldevilla) for their friendly and efficient support along the process.

References

Aceytuno Pérez, M. T., & Báñez, P. (2008). La creación de spin-off universitarias: el caso de la Universidad de Huelva.
Agrawal, A., & Henderson, R. (2002). Putting patents in context: Exploring knowledge transfer from MIT. *Management Science, 48*(1), 44–60.
Ardi, C., & Heidemann, J. (2019). Precise detection of content reuse in the web. *ACM SIGCOMM Computer Communication Review, 49*(2), 9–24.
Argote, L., & Ingram, P. (2000). Knowledge transfer: A basis for competitive advantage in firms. *Organizational Behavior and Human Decision Processes, 82*(1), 150–169.
Baregheh, A., Rowley, J., & Sambrook, S. (2009). Towards a multidisciplinary definition of innovation. *Management Decision, 47*(8), 1323–1339.
Beck, S., Mahdad, M., Beukel, K., & Poetz, M. (2019). The value of scientific knowledge dissemination for scientists—A value capture perspective. *Publications, 7*(3), 54.
Bettig, R. V. (2018). *Copyrighting culture: The political economy of intellectual property*. London: Routledge.
Burgos, D. (Ed.) (2017) Open education policy. UNIR: Logroño, La Rioja (Spain). Open Access from http://bit.ly/unir-openpolicy (English) and http://bit.ly/unir-educacionabierta (español).
Cadwalladr, C., & Graham-Harrison, E. (2018). The Cambridge analytica files. *The Guardian, 21,* 6–7.
CDTI. (2014). Retrieved September 5, 2019, from http://eshorizonte2020.cdti.es/recursos/doc/Programas/Cooperacion_internacional/HORIZONTE%202020/29236_2872872014135311.pdf.
Coelho, J., & Valente, M. T. (2017, August). Why modern open source projects fail. In *Proceedings of the 2017 11th Joint Meeting on Foundations of Software Engineering* (pp. 186–196). New York: ACM.
Cooper, J. R. (1998). A multidimensional approach to the adoption of innovation. *Management Decision, 36*(8), 493–502.
CORDIS. (2019). Retrieved September 5, 2019, from https://cordis.europa.eu/.

Cosgrove, L., Cristea, I. A., Shaughnessy, A. F., Mintzes, B., & Naudet, F. (2019). Digital aripiprazole or digital evergreening? A systematic review of the evidence and its dissemination in the scientific literature and in the media. BMJ evidence-based medicine.

D'Antoni, S. (2009). Open educational resources: Reviewing initiatives and issues. *Open Learning: The Journal of Open, Distance and e-Learning, 24*(1), 3–10. https://doi.org/10.1080/02680510802625443.

de la Fuente Valentín, L., Carrasco, A., Konya, K., & Solans, D. B. (2013). Emerging technologies landscape on education: A review. *IJIMAI, 2*(3), 55.

de Sousa Borges, S., Durelli, V. H., Reis, H. M., & Isotani, S. (2014, March). A systematic mapping on gamification applied to education. In *Proceedings of the 29th Annual ACM Symposium on Applied Computing* (pp. 216–222). New York: ACM.

Derntl, M., & Klamma, R. (2012, July). Social network analysis of european project consortia to reveal impact of technology-enhanced learning projects. In *2012 IEEE 12th International Conference on Advanced Learning Technologies* (pp. 746–747). IEEE.

Di Cosmo, R., & Zacchiroli, S. (2017). *September).* Software heritage: Why and how to preserve software source code.

Downes, S. (2007). Models for sustainable open educational resources. *Interdisciplinary Journal of Knowledge and Learning Objects, 3*. Retrieved from http://ijklo.org/Volume3/IJKLOv3p029-044Downes.pdf.

Easterby-Smith, M., Lyles, M. A., & Tsang, E. W. (2008). Inter-organizational knowledge transfer: Current themes and future prospects. *Journal of Management Studies, 45*(4), 677–690.

European Commission. (2015). Retrieved September 5, 2019, from https://www.kowi.de/Portaldata/2/Resources/fp7/FP7-ICT-report-ex-post-evaluation.pdf.

European Commission. (2016). Retrieved September 5, 2019, from http://europa.eu/rapid/press-release_MEMO-16-146_en.htm.

Evans, J. A. (2010). Industry collaboration, scientific sharing, and the dissemination of knowledge. *Social Studies of Science, 40*(5), 757–791.

Fecher, B., Friesike, S., & Hebing, M. (2015). What drives academic data sharing? *PLoS ONE, 10*(2), e0118053.

Feldman, M. P., & Lichtenberg, F. R. (2000). The impact and organization of publicly funded research and development in the European community. In *The Economics and Econometrics of Innovation* (pp. 177–200). Boston, MA: Springer.

Gómez-Miranda, M. E., & Román-Martínez, I. (2016). Las spin-off universitarias españolas: análisis económico-financiero y factores que condicionan su cifra de negocios. *Hacienda Pública Española, 217,* 131.

Goswami, S., & Mathew, M. (2005). Definition of innovation revisited: An empirical study on Indian information technology industry. *International Journal of Innovation Management, 9*(03), 371–383.

Hoekman, J., Scherngell, T., Frenken, K., & Tijssen, R. (2013). Acquisition of European research funds and its effect on international scientific collaboration. *Journal of Economic Geography, 13*(1), 23–52.

Hummel, H., Burgos, D., Tattersall, C., Brouns, F., Kurvers, H., & Koper, R. (2005). Encouraging contributions in Learning networks using incentive mechanisms. *Journal of Computer Assisted Learning (JCAL), 21,* 355–365.

IUNE. (2019). Retrieved September 8, 2019, from http://www.iune.es/es_ES/innovacion/spin-off/universidades-publicas-y-privadas.

Ivascu, L., Cirjaliu, B., & Draghici, A. (2016). Business model for the university-industry collaboration in open innovation. *Procedia Economics and Finance, 39,* 674–678.

Jahn, N., & Tullney, M. (2016). A study of institutional spending on open access publication fees in Germany. *PeerJ, 4,* e2323.

Joyce, C., Ochoa, T. T., Carroll, M. W., Leaffer, M. A., & Jaszi, P. (2016). *Copyright law* (Vol. 85). Durham, NC: Carolina Academic Press.

Karapanos, E., Teixeira, P., & Gouveia, R. (2016). Need fulfillment and experiences on social media: A case on Facebook and WhatsApp. *Computers in Human Behavior, 55,* 888–897.

Lerner, J., & Tirole, J. (2015). Standard-essential patents. *Journal of Political Economy, 123*(3), 547–586.

Mancini, M. (2019). Design-driven obsolescence. *The Design Journal, 22*(sup1), 2243–2246.

McAndrew, P. (2010). Defining openness: updating the concept of 'open' for a connected world. *Journal of Interactive Media in Education, 2010*(10), 1–13.

Mowery, D. C., Oxley, J. E., & Silverman, B. S. (1996). Strategic alliances and interfirm knowledge transfer. *Strategic Management Journal, 17*(S2), 77–91.

Nyberg, D. (1975). *The philosophy of open education.* London: Routledge and Kegan Paul.

Parlamento Europeo. (2017). Retrieved September 5, 2019, from http://www.europarl.europa.eu/doceo/document/A-8-2017-0209_ES.html..

Paulin, D., & Suneson, K. (2015). Knowledge transfer, knowledge sharing and knowledge barriers– three blurry terms in KM. *Leading Issues in Knowledge Management, 2*(2), 73.

Pilegaard, M., Moroz, P. W., & Neergaard, H. (2010). An auto-ethnographic perspective on academic entrepreneurship: Implications for research in the social sciences and humanities. *Academy of Management Perspectives, 24*(1), 46–61.

REDOTRI. (2017). Retrieved August 28, 2019, from http://www.redotriuniversidades.net/images/Articulos/Informe_Tecnico_EBTS.pdf.

Schimmer, R., Geschuhn, K. K., & Vogler, A. (2015). Disrupting the subscription journals' business model for the necessary large-scale transformation to open access.

Shapero, A., & Sokol, L. (1982). The social dimensions of entrepreneurship. In *Encyclopedia of entrepreneurship* (pp. 72–90).

Stokes, S. (2019). Digital copyright: law and practice. Bloomsbury Publishing. Google Book. Retrieved September 9, 2019, from https://books.google.co.uk/.

Tene, O., & Polonetsky, J. (2012). Big data for all: Privacy and user control in the age of analytics. *Northwestern Journal of Technology and Intellectual Property, 11,* xxvii.

Verhoeven, D., Bakker, J., & Veugelers, R. (2016). Measuring technological novelty with patent-based indicators. *Research Policy, 45*(3), 707–723.

Waldrop, M. M. (2016). More than Moore. *Nature, 530*(7589), 144–148.

Wong, E. Y. (2017). e-Print Archive: arXiv. org. *Technical Services Quarterly, 34*(1), 111–113.

Open Access This chapter is licensed under the terms of the Creative Commons Attribution 4.0 International License (http://creativecommons.org/licenses/by/4.0/), which permits use, sharing, adaptation, distribution and reproduction in any medium or format, as long as you give appropriate credit to the original author(s) and the source, provide a link to the Creative Commons license and indicate if changes were made.

The images or other third party material in this chapter are included in the chapter's Creative Commons license, unless indicated otherwise in a credit line to the material. If material is not included in the chapter's Creative Commons license and your intended use is not permitted by statutory regulation or exceeds the permitted use, you will need to obtain permission directly from the copyright holder.

Chapter 7
Prosumerism in Higher Education—Does It Meet the Disability Test?

Joe Cullen

7.1 Introduction: The Contribution of Prosumerism to Higher Education

'Prosumerism' was first coined by Alvin Toffler in his book 'The Third Wave' to denote people who produce some of the goods and services they then consume themselves—for example by making their own clothes, building their own cars, or cultivating vegetables for their kitchen (Toffler, 1980). Toffler envisaged a time when consumers would increasingly play a role as co-collaborators in production and supply chains, with the capacity to alter the design and the attributes of a product they wanted. A good contemporary example is recent trends in the fashion industry towards promoting more sustainable producer and consumer behaviours through new processes like 'mass customisation'—combining personalization with mass production; 'crowd design'—using crowdsourcing to create designs that can be customized into products; 'closet sharing'—the setup of a private or community-powered 'infinite wardrobe' so that customers don't own a clothing item but rent it for the time it's needed, and 'DIY fashion'—digital clothing models used by independent designers produced directly by customers using 3D printers.[1]

In the Higher Education sector, prosumerism has been associated with the shift towards 'learner-centred' teaching and learning activities, with the emphasis on student engagement and the co-production of knowledge. The argument is that greater student engagement in the teaching and learning process, and greater co-ownership of learning content, has a beneficial effect on learning outcomes (Bryson & Han, 2007; Barklay, 2010). A typical approach applied across a spectrum of learning settings, including higher education, is the application of a 'blended learning' pedagogy,

---

[1] https://issuu.com/tcbl/docs/sustainable_fashion_market.

J. Cullen (✉)
Arcola Research and Tavistock Institute, London, UK
e-mail: jcullen@arcola-research.co.uk

combining face to face teaching with a wide range of digital tools, with different tools being applied for different pedagogic purposes. For example, 'mind-mapping' tools aim to support students to link concepts and visualise them; simulations are applied to help students develop problem-solving and 'trouble-shooting' skills; wikis are applied to support collaborative learning and student blogs to disseminate the content created by students in their assignments. A recent development has been the migration of the 'flipped classroom' approach from K12 education to the higher education setting. Flipped classrooms replace educator-generated class content with student-generated content. Students are required to complete preparatory work and bring it to the classroom, where it is used to support greater interactivity between students as a group and between students and their teachers (Berrett, 2012). Adherents of the flipped classroom approach argue that it offers a number of advantages over conventional forms of teaching and learning. It allows students to learn at their own pace; it frees up class time for critical review and problem-solving; it provides students with more opportunities to learn 'twenty-first-century' skills that are more relevant with regard to subsequent job searching—and it fosters student ownership of their learning and their learning content. This, in turn, is linked to evidence of greater student engagement, improved peer learning and interaction, improved creativity and self-confidence, increased student performance and higher levels of student satisfaction (Wilson, 2014; Vasilchenko et al., 2017).

Equally, the increasing popularity of Personal Learning Environments (PLE's) in the educational field has been seen as evidence of the increasing adoption of a 'constructivist' pedagogy that emphasises a shift in the role of the educator from transmitter of information to facilitator of knowledge production. As Atwell (2007) argues, through PLEs, students—formerly consumers of knowledge—become producers, through creating and sharing content. Typically, PLEs bundle together different tools—including social media, wikis, blogs, multimedia and sharing platforms—in order to aggregate different learning services that, together enable learners to build and manage their own learning spaces, under their control, bring together different sources and contexts for learning and bridge educational institutional environments with the world outside. Other writers make an explicit connection between PLEs and prosumerism. PLE's enable students to choose the services and applications they need to generate or consume content. They actively participate in determining the aims and delivery of their learning experience. The diversity of tools embodied in a PLE supports a wide range of flexibility that learners can use to their advantage to customise the structure, content and delivery of educational services according to their own personal needs and 'learning styles'. In this way, the learner makes the transition from a passive recipient of information to the 'protagonist' of a learning experience. The processing of information can be managed by each learner using a set of tools that they choose, allowing each learner to tailor the learning process to their own needs and circumstances (Kompen et al., 2019).

A further indication of this increasing shift towards engaging students as more active co-creators and co-producers of their learning is the recent move towards equipping educators with the competences they need to work with students as co-collaborators. In November 2017, The European Commission's Joint Research Centre, JRC-Seville launched the European Competence Framework for the Digital Competence of Educators (DigCompEdu).[2] The Framework consists of 6 'competence areas', each of which covers a number of specific digital competences—making 22 competences in total. The competence areas that are most relevant to prosumerism are Area 3—Teaching and Learning; Area 5—Empowering Learners and Area 6—Facilitating Learners' Digital Competences. Within these areas, there are particular competence that have a significant bearing on the extent to which students in higher education institutions can be supported to play an active role in the co-production of knowledge. These cover the following. Competence 3.3—Collaborative Learning—requires educators in HE institutions to enable learners to use digital technologies as part of collaborative assignments; competence 3.4—self-regulated learning—requires them to use digital technologies to enable learners to plan, monitor and reflect on their own learning, share insights and come up with creative solutions; competence 5.1—Accessibility and inclusion—requires them to ensure accessibility to learning and resources for all learners, including those with special needs; competence 5.2—differentiation and personalization—requires them to use digital technologies to address diverse learners' needs, by allowing them to advance at different levels and speeds; competence 5.3—Actively engaging learners—requires them to use digital technologies to open up learning to new real-world contexts, which involve learners themselves in hands on activities, scientific investigation or complex problem-solving; competence 6.3—Digital Content Creation—requires them to use digital technologies to support learners to express themselves through digital means and to modify and create digital content in different formats, and, finally, competence 6.5—digital problem-solving—requires them to incorporate learning activities that help learners to transfer technical knowledge creatively to new situations. A key aim of this framework is to change the educator's role from a 'transmissive' communicator of knowledge to a role in which educators work with students to help them become 'creative, collaborative participants in a knowledge-based, interdependent world' (Caena & Redecker, 2019).

Because of the recency of this initiative, there is no available evidence to show either that educators currently have the necessary competences to support co-collaboration or that the application of these competences in the classroom leads to the learning outcomes attributed to co-produced learning, as cited above. A very small (unpublished) trial carried out by JRC-Seville with a group of English language teachers which assessed their digital competences according to the DigCompEdu framework suggested that overall the level of digital competences was relatively high. However, on a number of the digital competences linked to 'prosumerism'—like differentiation and personalization and self-regulated learning—scores were lower than average.[3]

---

[2] http://europa.eu/!gt63ch.
[3] Internal JRC-Seville Report, unpublished.

Work carried out by the author on further developing the DigCompEdu assessment tool—which included a review of state of the art in the use of digital technologies to support student collaboration, personalisation of learning, self-regulated learning, active engagement and digital content creation—suggested that the adoption of pedagogic approaches, including the use of digital tools, to support student–educator collaboration, co-design and co-production, is not widespread and the techniques and practices used across educational sectors, including higher education, varies considerably.[4] This conclusion chimes with other reviews carried out in the field. For example, a structured review of the use of the flipped classroom in higher education, which analysed 28 studies in the field, concluded that, whilst there is indirect evidence emerging of improved academic performance and student and staff satisfaction with the flipped approach, there is little conclusive evidence that it contributes to building lifelong learning and other twenty-first-century skills in undergraduate education and postgraduate education (O'Flaherty & Phillips, 2015).

7.2 The Growing Influence of Prosumerism on Higher Education

The debate over whether the use of co-production methods, techniques and practices in the learning environment leads to better teaching and learning outcomes reflects a much broader debate over prosumerism itself in the education landscape, and particularly in higher education. It has long been recognised that the shift from a conception of knowledge that is abstract, disciplinary based and valued for its own sake to an acknowledgement that experiential learning is also of value has been welcomed. The adoption of constructivism into academe has had a decentring effect, drawing on local and particularised knowledge to challenge dominant disciplinary discourses, structures and power relations. Knowledge is now seen to serve different purposes. One clearly discernible tendency relates to knowledge being valued for what Lyotard (1984) termed its 'performativity'. In terms of educational purposes, it represents a shift away from critical enquiry (enlightenment) and personal transformation towards learning experiences where knowledge utilisation is uppermost. This explains the increasing interest in the student learning experience, and a shift towards more student-centred teaching and learning. This has been driven by quality agendas, a greater responsiveness on the part of institutions to the changing demographic profile of students entering higher education, a recognition of the importance of informal learning processes, as well as the notion of the need to provide 'learning rich settings' (Knight, 2001).

However, there has been a strong thread in the literature that has been critical of this shift towards 'individuation'. Malcolm and Zukas (2001), for example, refer to what they see as the dominant psychological paradigm in teaching and learning

---

[4]Cullen (2019). Deliverable 2: Report on the content and structure of DigCompEduSAT (unpublished).

in HE, and the narrow way in which pedagogy has been conceived. They point to the way in which our understanding of the teaching and learning process has been dominated by the explicitly psychological visions of the learner and teacher. Thus, the research and practitioner literature on teaching and learning in higher education is highly individualistic in focus and preoccupied with the learning bit of the self. The model of the learner most strongly represented in the literature is a bundle of behaviours, attitudes and dispositions—often wrapped up in the concept of preferred 'learning style' or 'learner identity'. Failures in learning are readily attributed to deficits in learners, lack of appropriate abilities, skills dispositions of strategies; and occasionally deficits in individual teachers.

In turn, several analytic studies of higher education have observed the interiorisation into institutional values and purposes of external social and cultural forces. It is suggested that instrumentality, usefulness, adaptability and 'fit' for the existing system have become the dominant values in discourse about the aims of higher education (Brockbank & McGill, 1998). Whilst some commentators welcomed such responsiveness of the system to the changing society as enabling individuals and organisations to keep pace with cultural change and to advance themselves in the changing cultural context, a counter view has held that the university, as a key institution in the society, offers more value to the society if it can stand apart from it in some measure, adhering to cultural traditions of modern enlightenment rather than being captured by the utilitarian agenda (Barnett, 1994). Usher (2001) and Bagnell (2001) point to the lessening of the power of academics to define what constitutes worthwhile knowledge and serious learning in the face of the increasing trend towards the individuation of knowledge and the decentring of learning. Meanwhile, the shift towards participation in consumer markets, it has been argued, has created a cultural context in higher education in which social agendas are defined by the interests of individuals through their choices as consumers and producers, which results in the dominance of economic considerations in the cultural realm. Consumerist culture, and the commodification of knowledge has come to shape institutional and learner behaviour in the formal education system. The relationship between teacher and learner is reconstituted as a market relationship between producer and consumer.

Those responsible for the management of higher education have been more exposed to external environmental forces than academic staff at the front line of teaching and learning. The proximal forces having greatest impact on universities are mediated through political/channels—policy directives, accountability requirements and mechanisms. Such instruments convey the values of the new learning patrimony, fuelled by new economic and managerialist concerns. Successive waves of policy initiatives are expressions of governmental performativity agendas and the growing demand for greater accountability from the education system. This preoccupation with greater accountability, it has been argued, has led to the increasing dominance within higher education of three key discourses: 'assessment', 'employability' and 'managed learning environments'. Students are expected to acquire the capabilities and competences for managing knowledge as part of a lifelong learning or 'learning to learn' agenda, rather than being expected to assimilate knowledge. There has been a shift to operational criteria—what students are able to do, and their ability to apply knowledge. 'Employability'—a set of generic skills considered useful in employment contexts, is embodied in course documentation, module descriptors, and built into records of achievement or transcripts. The employability agenda is also reflected in a host of schemes and projects aimed at creating working relationships between higher education institutions and employers.

Curriculum planning has largely gone down the outcomes led path, within a rational planning model. The ingredients of such a model include a tight coupling between goals and objectives, curriculum and choice of instruction methods, and assessment of learning and evaluation—consistent with the view of the universe as determinate and linear. As Knight (2001) observes, rational curriculum planning has a commonsense quality about it that fits well with the managerialism of the public sector. Such a model, he suggests, is ill-suited to the complex learning with which higher education institutions are concerned. Complex learning is indeterminate and non-linear. It calls for attention to the quality of the learning environment and learning communities. Curriculum planning needs to be concerned with the spaces, interactions, experiences, opportunities and settings in which formal learning takes place. In such a process model, curriculum planning becomes mainly a matter of orchestrating good learning processes with each other, the content (the topics that subject/area experts identify as worth studying), the available learning time and other resources.

The concept of the managed learning environment, it is argued, has changed from a time and space bound setting—the lecture room, seminar or tutorial and the laboratory—to a much more fluid setting which includes combinations of real time learning and virtual learning; and formal learning in an institutional setting alongside other modes of learning in workplace, community or simulated settings, and which includes more fluid social relations between teacher and learners.

7.3 Critique of the Influence of Prosumerism in Higher Education

In recent years, this critical view of the increasing trend towards centralising the student experience as the key determinant of 'success' in higher education has been amplified to deliver a critique of 'prosumerism' itself. A major influence on this critique has been George Ritzer whose seminal book *The McDonaldisation of Society,* argued that principles of fast food restaurants have come to dominate virtually every aspect of society (Ritzer, 1996). Ritzer identified four main principles of McDonaldization—predictability, calculability, efficiency and control—that characterise how fast-food restaurants operate but which can also be applied to a wide spectrum of social structures and processes. In higher education, these four principles, it is argued, have converted universities into 'McBusinesses', turning students into consumers who buy degrees made up of bite-sized, credit-rated modules, enslaving universities into competing with each other to top national and global league tables and re-constructing lecturers as facilitators of the 'student experience' (Hayes & Wynyard, 2002). Ritzer later argued that the focus of capitalism has shifted from exploiting producers, to exploiting consumers, to exploiting prosumers. In the McDonalds case, Ritzer suggests, prosumers do unpaid work. Instead of having waiters in McDonald's, they have the prosumers carry their own food and clear their own tables. In the case of the new online global capitalists—like Amazon, Facebook and Google, the business model is supported by prosumers who not only consume products but who do all the advertising and product endorsement that formerly would have been done by expensive sub-contractors (Ritzer, 2015). Ritzer describes universities as 'the velvet cage of prosumption'. Students are increasingly seen, and see themselves, as consumers of education who are there to get their money's worth. Universities are set up to attract students (and their parents) to the university and then to keep them on campus to spend money. Yet fewer students have access to good teachers because of the high cost. Poorer students are now poorly educated. The wealthier students go to the most expensive universities and still have access to the best education, although they may not take full advantage of it (Ritzer, Jandrić, & Hayes, 2018).

What this suggests is that, rather than serving as an antidote to the entrenchment of traditional power structures, through the democratization of education, the prosumer's engagement mostly serves to reinforce the interests of the status quo. As Comor (2011) argues, 'the prosumer seems more likely to become, at the very least, the subject of ongoing exploitation and, quite possibly, an agent of increasingly complex forms of possessive individualism'. Alvesson (2013) refers to the 'massification' of higher education, as it is increasingly influenced by the principles of McDonaldisation, arguing that it raises fantasies about success in life, national greatness and a fast-track to top jobs that are unlikely to be fulfilled.

Cole and Bradley (2018) go further, arguing that the prosumer ethic in higher education serves to contribute to the dominance of global capitalism as a one-world system. They suggest that the marketing of prosumerism in education as 'personalisation of learning'—aimed ostensibly at providing opportunities for creative collaboration—is in fact a smokescreen for a more sinister agenda that aims to do two things: extend the culture of surveillance and commodify knowledge in order to make it more marketable. By encouraging students to increase their use of platforms like Facebook in their collaborative learning, the prosumer ethic makes them more vulnerable to exploitation of their personal data. By encouraging students to act as unpaid contributors to knowledge creation and affective capital—as a result of educational institutions exploiting their student experience—the prosumer ethic serves to contribute further to unpaid customer input into the production process.

An important question these critiques of prosumerism in higher education pose is what is the connection between prosumerism and social inclusion. Some studies suggest that, in order to be good prosumers, students need to have access to a wide range of content production resources. For example, students with access to a wide range of content production resources are likely to dominate in the world of social media. Access to social media has in turn been shown by a number of studies to be a key determinant of prosumer capability and success. But as long as content production resources are not evenly distributed, then not all prosumer voices will be heard (Ha & Yun, 2014).

A good test, therefore, of whether the current drive towards making higher education students more 'prosumerist' leads to improved learning outcomes is whether higher education provides opportunities for disadvantaged students to play a full role in the co-production of knowledge. Students with disabilities are arguably best placed to answer this question. The following sections of this chapter present the results of research carried out by the author on the extent to which higher education institutions in the EU are supporting the participation of students with disabilities in collaborative learning.[5]

7.4 Research Context and Methodology

The main objective of the research reported below was to assess the extent to which policies and practices in higher education within the EU at national and trans-national level enable disabled students to play an active role in collaborative learning. The methodology was based on 'scientific realist review' (Pawson, Greenhalgh, Harvey, & Walshe, 2005). This analysed policy and practice in the EU overall and in a selected range of member states: Greece, Italy, Slovenia, Poland and the UK. As Pawson puts it, doing a realist review entails 'feeling your way' through the available literature to find out how to do something that may involve many different ways. In practice, the review starts with a search of the literature, covering both bibliographic ('academic') databases and 'grey literature' (e.g. conference papers and online sources) to identify key policies and practices that support the integration of disabled students in collaborative learning. The longlist of items generated by the search process was then narrowed down to a shortlist of relevant material using 'inclusion-exclusion' criteria based on domain relevance, target group relevance, geographical relevance and quality of the evidence on impacts provided. Each item in the shortlist was then analysed using a content analysis procedure (Stemler, 2001; Neuendorf, 2002).

7.5 Research Results

Until the Amsterdam Treaty of 1996, the EU's approach to disability was based on a 'medical' understanding and a medical model. This supported the view that disability was the result of physical or mental impairments that affect the individual. The 1996 treaty—particularly Article 13—offered an alternative perspective on disability—the 'social model'—that incorporated references to the effects of environment, culture and surroundings. A subsequent Council of Europe Directive, also in 1996,

---

[5]This research was partly supported by a grant from the European Commission's 'Tempus' programme.

reinforced this shift in understanding and policy orientation, asserting that 'The core value of equality—rendered here as equal opportunities—is now seen as the central benchmark against which economic and social structures must be assessed'. The EU Fundamental Rights Agency, established in 2007, provided the EU and member states with expertise on courses of action in human rights—including the rights of people with disability (although not expressly mentioned in the legislation). At the trans-national level, and across virtually all member states, there is a legislative framework in place which in principle supports the integration of students with disabilities within the higher education system. This has as its foundation the United Nations Convention on the Rights of People with Disabilities (UNCRPD).

Accessibility, equal opportunities and social inclusion for people with disabilities are also referenced in the EU general budget, for example, in areas relating to: Employment and Social Affairs, Energy and Transport, Environment, Regional Policy, Education and Culture, Communication, External Relations, Enlargement, Commission's Administration, Statistics, European Personnel Selection Office and Administrative Expenditure related to Policy Areas. Disability is also highlighted in the key over-arching policy 'EU2020'.[6] This provides a 'new strategy for jobs and smart, sustainable and inclusive growth'. To achieve the objectives outlined in the Strategy, the European Council agreed to set EU headline targets, which serves as a benchmark for the national targets that the Member States will need to submit to the Commission. EU2020 includes seven 'flagship initiatives', some of which have direct relevance for people with disabilities, for example, the 'Platform against poverty', 'Youth on the move', 'An agenda for new skills and jobs' and the 'Digital Agenda'. These key policy instruments have been supported by a number of additional communications, and mandates, notably the Communication on eAccessibility, focusing on improving the consistency of eAccessibility requirements in Public Procurement; the Single Market review, focusing on Consumer Empowerment and the promotion of accessibility standards, Mandate 420, focusing on accessibility of the Built Environment and Mandate M 376, focusing on accessibility issues in ICT products and services for public procurement.

Within the higher education sphere, the over-arching legal and policy background for the EU has been shaped by the European Disability Action Plan 2003–2010 aimed at mainstreaming disability issues within all relevant EU policies and the EU Disability Strategy 2010–2020 which emphasises equal access to quality education and lifelong learning as key factors in enabling full participation in society. Against this background, accessibility of education and lifelong learning to persons with disabilities has gradually become a more prominent issue on the agenda of EU policymakers. Shared objectives and a framework for co-operation between countries were agreed by education ministers under 'ET2020', which included a commitment to ensure that European Union's education and training systems became 'accessible to all'.

However, a realistic picture of disability in higher education is difficult to establish, since comprehensive European Commission statistics are only available from

---

[6]Commission Communication 'Europe 2020: a strategy for smart, sustainable and inclusive growth'.

2011.[7] These show that disability is a key factor in shaping inequalities within education, with 63% of the EU 16–18 age group reporting some form of physical or mental restrictions in education, compared 83% reporting no restriction and in higher education 48% reporting some form of physical or mental restrictions in education, compared with 85% reporting no restriction.

The literature shows a number of commonalities with regard to the situation and needs of students with disabilities in EU countries. In general, young disabled people have less chance to access higher education than their non-disabled peers. For example, in Norway, 9% of young disabled people entered higher education compared to 21% of the general population of this age. In Malta, 4.4% of disabled people reached higher education against 10% of non-disabled people, whilst in Spain, only 5.4% of disabled people had a university education compared to 19.1% for non-disabled people. In the UK, only 28% of disabled young people enter higher education by the age of 19 compared to 41% of non-disabled young people, yet amongst those students who declare disability and complete their first degree (Bachelor), 56% attain at least an 'upper second' class degree, almost the same as for non-disabled students (59%).[8]

Young disabled people are also more likely than non-disabled youth to experience disruption to their studies. According to the OECD, disabled students tend to be more likely to follow part-time courses than non-disabled students, to drop out after the first year and are less likely to graduate (OECD, 2016). The OECD research on young disabled people' transition to tertiary education and employment also shows that disabled young adults are less likely than their non-disabled peers to access the most professionally promising courses. The ANED report shows that, in Germany, disabled students tend to have more erratic pathways during their studies; need more time for their studies, are more likely than non-disabled students to change their courses and/or university and are less likely to gain a university degree. In the absence of appropriate support systems, such difficulties impact more greatly on students with more severe or complex impairments.

Because education systems have largely remained subject to the particular legal norms and practices of member states, rather than dictated by trans-national institutions, support for disabled students varies significantly across the EU. Some countries implement preferential enrolment procedures. Portugal imposes an admissions quota for disabled students; in Germany disabled applicants may be granted a privileged access by the national authority responsible for the allocation of university places; in Greece, 5% of all places are reserved for disabled students; in Hungary, disabled students are given 50 points more for their entry exam; in Norway disabled young adults who do not have an upper secondary school diploma can access tertiary education, on condition that they obtain this diploma during the first semester of university studies; in the UK further education Colleges and Universities may also provide 'access

---

[7] Directorate General Employment, Social affairs and equal opportunities, Unit Integration of People with Disabilities (2010).

[8] Source: ANED, 2011.

courses' to students who have not gained entry level at school, which may be targeted to social groups with low participation rates, including those with disabilities. However, these incentives are not universal across all member states.

Similarly, provision of support to students with disabilities once they have enrolled varies from country to country. In Ireland, for example, there is a fund for disabled students which pays for adapted learning aids (e.g. computers, printers, scanners, dictaphones), human support (e.g. personal assistant, note taker, educational support, specific courses) and transportation costs. In Denmark, youth eligible for special education support (SPS) are entitled to assistance and counselling for needs assessment, technological aids, interpreters, and note takers. This variability in provision reflects the fact that in most countries it is the responsibility of universities, rather than the public authorities, to provide disabled students with support. This pattern also extends to financial support in general, where the EU situation is characterised once again by varying practices. These appear to be broadly linked to the cost of fees. In the Nordic countries, where costs tend to be relatively high, financial support is more likely to be linked to contingencies. In Norway, for example, students can apply for a state-funded study loan from the State Bank (statens lanekasse), which will be partially transformed into a grant if they successfully pass their examinations. In Denmark, the 'handicap supplement' compensates for the loss of income due to difficulties in accessing to employment during university studies for students eligible for the special education allowance, as such income would normally be necessary to pay the interest on a student's loan. In other countries where tuition fees are not very high, young disabled people may have free or reduced tuition fees as in Germany, Iceland and Spain.

A key determinant of the extent to which disabled students can play the role of 'prosumers' in the higher education sphere is the extent to which they have access to the digital tools, and supporting pedagogies, that enable them to learn at their own pace, build, manage and control their own learning spaces, bring together different sources and contexts for learning and bridge educational institutional environments with the world outside. In this context, the research shows there is no strategic, holistic and integrated system in place either at trans-national nor national level to embed assistive technologies, for example, that support better choice and control of disabled students over their learning experience. Whilst some anecdotal examples of innovation in assistive technologies and assistive pedagogies could be identified, there is no strong evidence base that prosumerism is making a positive contribution to the learning experience and the learning outcomes of students with disabilities. Some examples of good practices highlighted include:

- London University—the Institute of Education and University College—have dedicated Disability Assistive Technology rooms which provides a range of facilities and tools including: specialized software (e.g. Text Help Read & Write; Inspiration); ergonomic aids (foot rests; adjustable seating; tracker ball mice); a Student Enabling IT Suite, which includes tools like: Dragon Naturally Speaking (a speech

recognition programme which enables voice-activated typing); Inspiration (software to convert a visual idea into an essay template); Texthelp (text-to-speech technology); Zoomtext (enlarges all that is seen on the screen)
- Thinking about Dyslexia—a UK HEI web-based service on dyslexia which includes video interviews linked to resources on inclusive teaching methods; mind-mapping, podcasting, webCT and students tape-recording lectures and meetings
- Active Learning in Computing (ALiC)—a UK initiative on improving teacher sensitivity to specific impairments in e-learning delivery. This includes simulations of visual, motor, hearing and cognitive impairments, which illustrate the implications for disabled students of taught material, and of how e-assessment might cause problems.
- WISE (Wiring Individualized Special Education)—an Italian initiative aimed at supporting homebound students. Centred on a dedicated portal, WISE supports a community of practice to disseminate resources, good practices and expertise to support the integration of home-bound students within a more active student community.
- University of Macerata (Italy) provides support to students with disabilities through the work of the University Centre of Orientation (CAO), which provides specialist services for students with disabilities, including a 'front office' to support 'drop-in' services; physical support; specialised tutoring; counselling; organisational support; assistive technology; use of the Learning Management System; personalised exams; tuition exemption; specially equipped rooms
- Warsaw University, Office for Persons with Disabilities (OPD)—is the centralizing agency set up to implement the provisions of the Act on Higher Education. It provides: on-going assistance for students and university applicants who have disabilities or chronic illnesses; support for university staff who teach students with disabilities; mobility adaptation of University premises; transportation provision; ICT solutions—including adapted keyboards: trackball devices, Magic Wand Keyboard, 'HeadMouse', text magnification software, portable transmitter–receiver sets; digital library.

As these examples show, turning legislation and policy into practice has proved problematic, and support for disabled students varies significantly across the EU. This is because in most countries, unlike in the school sector, provision of support in the Higher Education sector is not obligatory, and is largely left to individual institutions to make their own interpretations on what is adequate provision. Most of the effort to support the needs of disabled students has been focused on providing support for students with disabilities whilst they are studying. This support has been concentrated in three main areas: Financial support—for example, block grants to HEIs and 'tailored' support for individual students; Access and mobility—for example, providing ramps; wheelchair access and transport; and Technical/Pedagogic support—for example, providing photocopies; tape recordings; transcriptions; braille documents; e-exams; note-takers; signing facilities.

Less effort has been devoted to other key areas of need for students who are studying in HEI's, in particular: raising awareness amongst student peers and teaching

Table 7.1 Summary of provision of support for disabled students in the EU and selected countries

Policy	EU	UK	SI	IT	GR	PL
Endorsement of UNCRDP						
Endorsement of EU Disability Action Plan and Disability Strategy						
Provision of national policies						
Implementation						
Pre-study (improving access)						
Financial support						
Accessibility (built environment)						
Accommodation						
Use of ICTs and assistive technologies						
Adapted content (e.g. digital libraries)						
Organisational support and governance (e.g. dedicated support staff)						
Awareness-raising and training for staff and students						
Post-qualification support measures						
Outcomes and Impacts						
Level and quality of data						
Level and quality of monitoring and evaluation of impacts						

and support staff of the issues faced by disabled students and how to address them; providing training for staff in order to improve the level and quality of support; developing dedicated services for students with disabilities—for example, Disability Officers and Student Counselling Services. The areas that have remained particularly under-developed, and where the main gaps in support are highlighted, are in the 'pre-study' and 'post-study' phases of student life.

To summarise, Table 7.1 provides an analytical summary of state of the art in the EU and in the selected countries in terms of three dimensions:

- The policy context—the extent to which UNCRDP principles are endorsed; the extent to which EU policy actions are incorporated and the level and comprehensiveness of national policies to support disabled students in HEI's
- The level of implementation of these key policy instruments and their objectives, in relation to pre-study; financial; accessibility; accommodation; use of ICTs

and assistive technology; use of adapted content; organisational and governance support; awareness-raising and training; post-qualification support
- Outcomes and impacts—the level and quality of available profiling and evaluation data on disabled students; their needs, and the effects of policy and practice.

Each aspect is assessed on the basis of the evidence, on the following scale:

Level	
	1 – Not covered or very low
	2 – Variable
	3 – High

Table 7.1 shows:

- In terms of policy, on the whole, the provisions of the UNCRDP have been, in principle ratified and endorsed. However, there is much less evidence that key EU policy instruments on disability and education are being addressed. In turn, national policy aimed at promoting support for disabled students has been relatively well-developed in the UK, Greece and Italy.
- In terms of implementation, the least-developed areas here are in the phases of the study course that come before and after studying itself, that is, the pre-study phase (focusing on helping disabled young people to apply for HEI places) and the post-qualification phase (focusing on preparing disabled graduates for the job market). Measures to provide financial support for disabled students have been relatively well-developed, with the exception of Slovenia. Similarly, measures and practices for study support are relatively well-developed, though provision is variable between and within EU countries. Most countries and many HEIs are now routinely using ICTs to support study for disabled students, through digitisation of teaching material, online digital libraries and the use of assistive technologies.
- Adaptations to the built environment and to accommodation facilities are two areas that are relatively well-developed across the EU, although again the level and quality of provision is uneven, and depends on a number of factors, including the length of time the HEI has been established; the interpretation of the UN and EU directives in national legislation; the spatial configuration of the HEI.
- Conversely, awareness-raising and staff and student training in providing support for students with disabilities rates relatively poorly.
- With the exception of a small number of initiatives operating at the transnational level—for example, the ANED (Academic Network of European Disability Experts)—and ad hoc research operating at the national level (e.g. the UK HEFCE survey of universities) there is very little systematic data collected at transversal or national levels on the profiles and needs of disabled students—particularly 'prospective' students—and even less on the effects of the implementation of policy and practices aimed at supporting their integration and active engagement.

7.6 Conclusions

This Chapter has looked at the 'prosumer' trend in higher education in the EU, considering, on the one hand, the alleged benefits associated with supporting greater control by students over the design of their courses; its content; assessment of course outcomes and contribution to the 'student experience'. This is set against a counter-argument that prosumerism is turning higher education institutions into so-called 'McBusinesses', in which student data are used to increase surveillance of students and monetise the student experience, whilst the knowledge produced by students, acting in co-production mode as unpaid workers, is harvested to increase the profit margin of educational enterprises.

It was suggested that a good test of prosumerism is the extent to which it supports social inclusion—in terms of better integration of marginalised and vulnerable groups into the educational institution and in terms of supporting them to play a more active role as co-producers of knowledge. An appropriate test case, it was suggested, is the position of students with disabilities. Research was then presented to provide an overview of the extent to which policy and practice in higher education in the EU generally and in five selected countries is enabling students with disabilities to learn at their own pace, build, manage and control their own learning spaces, bring together different sources and contexts for learning and bridge educational institutional environments with the world outside. The research shows that turning legislation and policy into practice has proved problematic, and support for disabled students varies significantly across the EU. Whilst some anecdotal evidence of good practices, for example, involving assistive technologies and pedagogic practices that support better choice and control of disabled students over their learning experience, there is no strategic, holistic and integrated system in place either at trans-national or national level that supports better integration of disabled students and supports disabled students to play a more active role as co-producers of knowledge.

The evidence base on the positive effects of prosumerism in higher education is therefore not enhanced by the research. The jury is still out on whether prosumerism has a beneficial effect on learning outcomes or whether it represents an increasingly pervasive threat to traditional, 'liberal' values of academe.

References

Alvesson, M. (2013). The triumph of emptiness: Consumption, higher Education and work organisation. Oxford: OUP.
Atwell, G. (2007). Personal learning environments—The future of eLearning?. Elearning papers.
Bagnall, R. (2001). Locating lifelong learning and education in contemporary currents of thought and culture. In D. Aspin, J. Chapman, M. Hatton & Y. Ball, S 'Performativities and fabrications.
Barkley, E. (2010). *Student engagement techniques: A handbook for college faculty.* SanFrancisco: Jossey-Bass.
Barnett, R. (1994). *The limits of competence.* Buckingham: Open University Press/SRHE.

Berrett, D. (2012). How 'flipping' the classroom can improve the traditional lecture. *The Chronicle of Higher Education, 19*, 2012.

Brockbank, A., & McGill, I. (1998). *Facilitating reflective learning in higher education*. Buckingham: SRHE/Open University Press.

Bryson, C., & Hand, L. (2007). The role of engagement in inspiring teaching and learning. *Innovations in Education and Teaching International, 44*(4), 349–362. http://dx.doi.org/10.1080/14703290701602748.

Caena, F., & Redecker, C. (2019). Aligning teacher competence frameworks to 21st century challenges: The case for the European digital competence framework for educators (Digcompedu). *European Journal of Education, Research and Policy, 54*, 356–369.

Cole, D., & Bradley, J. (Eds.). (2018). *Principles of transversality in globalization and education*. Singapore: Springer.

Comor, E. (2011). Contextualizing and critiquing the fantastic prosumer: Power, alienation and hegemony. *Critical Sociology, 37*, 309–327.

Cullen, J. (2019). Fixing what's broken' – an action research approach to working with young people on the margins. *Proceedings of the Children and Childhoods Conference*. University of Suffolk, 16–17th July 2019.

Ha, L., & Yun, G. W. (2014). Digital divide in social media prosumption: Proclivity, production intensity, and prosumertypology among college students and general population. *School of Media and Communication Faculty Publications, 10*. https://scholarworks.bgsu.edu/smc_pub/10.

Hayes, D., & Wynyard, R. (Eds.). (2002). *The McDonaldization of higher education*. New York, NY: Praeger.

Knight, P. (2001). Complexity and curriculum: a process approach to curriculum-making. *Teaching inn Higher Education, 6*(3), 369–381.

Kompen, R., Edirisingha, P., Canaleta, X., Alsina, M., & Monguet, J. (2019). Personal learning environments based on Web 2.0 services in higher education. *Telematics and Informatics, 38*, 194–206.

Lyotard, J. F. (1984). *La condition postmoderne: rapport sur le savoir*. English translation by Geoffrey Bennington and Brian Massumi, University of Minnesota Press.

Malcolm, J., & Zukas, M. (2001). Bridging pedagogic gaps: Conceptual discontinuities in higher education. *Teaching in Higher Education, 6*(1), 33–42.

Neuendorf, A. (2002). *The content analysis guidebook*. London: Sage.

OECD. (2016). *OECD science, technology and innovation outlook 2016*. Paris: OECD Publishing, https://doi.org/10.1787/sti_in_outlook-2016-en.

O'Flaherty, J., & Phillips, C. (2015). The use of flipped classrooms in higher education: A scoping review. *Internet and Higher Education, 25*, 85–95.

Pawson, R., Greenhalgh, T., Harvey, G., Walshe K. (2005). Realist review—A new method of systematic review designed for complex policy interventions. *Journal of Health Services Research & Policy, 10*(Suppl 1), 21–34.

Ritzer, G. (1996). *The McDonaldization of society: An investigation into the changing character of contemporary social life*. Thousand Oaks, California: Pine Forge Press.

Ritzer, G., Jandrić, P., & Hayes, S. (2018). The velvet cage of educational con(pro)sumption. *Open Review of Educational Research, 5*(1), 113–129.

Ritzer, G. (2015). Prosumer capitalism. *The Sociological Quarterly, 56*(3), 413–445.

Stemler, S. (2001). An overview of content analysis. *Practical Assessment, Research & Evaluation, 7*(17).

Toffler, Alvin. (1980). *The third wave: The classic study of tomorrow*. New York, NY: Bantam.

Usher, R. (2001). Lifelong learning in the postmodern. In D. Aspin, J. Chapman, M. Hatton and Y. Sawano (Eds.), *International handbook of lifelong learning* (35–52). London: Kluwer Academic Publishers.

Vasilchenko, A., Green, D. P., Qarabash, H., Preston, A., Bartindale, T., & Balaam, M. (2017, June). Media literacy as a by—product of collaborative video production by CS students. In

Proceedings of the 2017 ACM Conference on Innovation and Technology in Computer Science Education (pp. 58–63). ACM.

Wilson, S. (2014). The flipped class: A method to address the challenges of an undergraduate statistics course. *Teaching of Psychology, 40*(3), 193–199.

Open Access This chapter is licensed under the terms of the Creative Commons Attribution 4.0 International License (http://creativecommons.org/licenses/by/4.0/), which permits use, sharing, adaptation, distribution and reproduction in any medium or format, as long as you give appropriate credit to the original author(s) and the source, provide a link to the Creative Commons license and indicate if changes were made.

The images or other third party material in this chapter are included in the chapter's Creative Commons license, unless indicated otherwise in a credit line to the material. If material is not included in the chapter's Creative Commons license and your intended use is not permitted by statutory regulation or exceeds the permitted use, you will need to obtain permission directly from the copyright holder.

Chapter 8
Empowering University Educators for Contemporary Open and Networked Teaching

Fabio Nascimbeni

Abstract The chapter explores the competences that university educators should master in our increasingly digital, open and connected societies in order to fill their role effectively and responsibly. Starting from a brief analysis of the concepts of collaborative learning and open education, we analyse three teachers' competencies frameworks, focusing on the digital, collaboration and openness aspects of contemporary teaching. We conclude that educators should not build radically new competences but should rather update their competences in line with emerging needs. Also, we notice that some additional competence areas should be developed by educators, if we want them to be able to bridge the work of students in formal and informal settings. We propose six competences areas in this sense: personal data management, capacity to leverage the open web, intercultural digital dialogues, critical view on media, digital ethical issues, accessibility. These areas are becoming increasingly important for educators to be able to critically engage learners in the core issues of our digital, networked and open societies, guiding them—in open and collaborative ways—towards solutions to the newly emerging problems of our times.

Keywords Open and networked teaching · Higher education · Teachers training · Collaborative learning · Teaching innovation · Open education

8.1 Introduction: A New Role for Educators in Contemporary Societies

We are living in an increasingly open and participatory society, characterised by developments such as a growing importance of informal learning, new understandings of intellectual property, mixed modes of cultural expressions and a more proactive conception of citizenship (Jenkins, Ito, & boyd, 2015). The impact of these developments on the way people learn is twofold. On the one hand, the pervasive and seamless presence of Information and Communication Technology (ICT) has

---

F. Nascimbeni (✉)
Research Institute for Innovation & Technology in Education (UNIR iTED),
Universidad Internacional de La Rioja (UNIR), Logroño, La Rioja, Spain
e-mail: fabio.nascimbeni@unir.net

© The Author(s) 2020
D. Burgos (ed.), *Radical Solutions and Open Science*, Lecture Notes
in Educational Technology, https://doi.org/10.1007/978-981-15-4276-3_8

made a number of processes typical of the learning value chain more efficient, thanks to approaches such as mobile learning, learning analytics or personalised learning (Bates, 2015). On the other hand, new developments such as the emergence of Open Educational Resources (OER) or the use of social networks for teaching are fostering pedagogic innovation, moving away from traditional lecture-based dynamics towards open and networked teaching practices (Kyndt et al., 2013; Van Leeuwen, Janssen, Erkens, & Brekelmans, 2013).

In order for universities to adapt to these changes and to be able to maintain their relevance within society, many aspects of higher education need to be restructured (Sledge & Dovey Fishman, 2014), starting with the role of educators (Pearce, Weller, Scanlon, & Kinsley, 2010). "The three key elements of digital, networked and open converge most significantly around the production, pedagogy and delivery of education" (Weller, 2012, p. 85). The role of educators, traditionally considered as the *experts* tasked with communicating the necessary bodies of knowledge to students, is being questioned by educational researchers, who tend to increasingly define educators as *co-travellers*, *mediators* or *facilitators*. Connectivism emerged as a new educational theory supporting these claims. This theory considers that the spread of ICT and the deriving open and networked pedagogic approaches are challenging traditional schemes within education systems, and, in particular, the idea that educators are the only ones entitled to produce and deliver knowledge (Siemens, 2004; Downes, 2012; Rivoltella & Rossi, 2012). "Since the distributed and networked structure of knowledge in the digital age challenges the traditional view of education delivered within the borders of school, strict time periods and content, the role of the teacher has been redefined in the context of the connectivist paradigm to include networked learning environments" (Ozturk, 2015, p. 6).

8.2 Setting the Target: Collaborative and Open Teaching

In order to better understand the new role of university educators as well as to start defining the competences that they should master to fill their function effectively and responsibly, we will start from two educational approaches: collaborative learning and open education. These approaches have been existing since human beings started to reflect on teaching and learning, and are increasingly gaining ground in contemporary open and networked societies. *Collaborative learning* is about learners working together to understand concepts, to develop projects, to solve problems and ultimately to create knowledge. If properly managed, collaborative learning has the potential to foster the strengths of individual students while building fundamental skills such as teamwork, problem-solving and empathy (Kyndt et al., 2013). Within this approach, peer–to-peer learning is particularly important, since it engages learners in the same working processes providing them with opportunities to teach and be taught by one another (Williams et al., 2011). *Open education* deals with opening up the different components of the educational process (Weller, 2014), making sure that all necessary barriers to learning are removed. The change brought by open education touches upon all aspects of educators' work: learning design, for example, through sharing course design ideas with fellow teachers and with students, teaching content, by using and allowing the reuse of OER, and pedagogical approaches, for instance, by fostering participation of non-enrolled students and of other stakeholders in the learning process (Nascimbeni & Burgos, 2016).

While in formal educational contexts the change process towards open and networked learning is happening at a relatively slow pace (OECD, 2016), in informal learning settings collaboration and openness are often the norm. Think, for example, of a person openly sharing a video on a specific theme (from music to carpentry to physics) to explain a concept to a community. This simple act, translated into formal learning settings such as within a university course, is fully in line with Conole's five principles of open learning: collaboration and sharing of information, connected communication about learning and teaching, collectivity to grow knowledge and resources, critique for the promotion of scholarship and serendipitous innovation (Conole, 2013). Successful collaborative and open learning is indeed the key to build active learning environments, encouraging students to give and receive feedback and to evaluate each other's learning, and can have a tremendous impact on the development of twenty-first-century skills such as intercultural communication and critical thinking (Dede, 2010).

8.3 Competence Frameworks for Open and Networked Teaching

Adapting the work of Stacey (2013) and Reynolds (2015), we can ascertain three key characteristics that open and networked educators should have. First, they should nurture learners' connections and dialogues for the purpose of sharing ideas and solving problems, considering their classroom as a learning network where each link represents a possibility for new learning. Second, educators should be able to work in the open, engaging learners in a collaborative process of knowledge co-creation and open sharing, instead of just letting them use a pre-defined set of learning resources. Third, they should consider learners as autonomous agents within the learning process, allowing them to operate independently and learn at their own pace, in their own direction, and using their own connections.

The transition process of educators along these lines entails not only changing the way teachers design their courses, license their materials, support knowledge creation among students, but also supporting a reflection on their professional identity, and is therefore an extremely challenging process. The introduction of collaborative and open practices brings in fact a major cultural shift within educators' self-perception, related to the need of rethinking and reshaping the roles played by teachers and students within the learning process and the underpinning knowledge production process (Rivoltella & Rossi, 2012). This process is made more complex by the fact that in general terms educators do not feel competent in implementing innovative and collaborative approaches in their teaching (Gillies & Boyle, 2010; Ruys, Van Keer, & Aelterman, 2011).

Given the complexity of the task, a first important step is to define which competences should be mastered by educators to be able to meaningfully and responsibly teach through open and networked practices. A good place to start looking for these competences are the existing competence frameworks that aim to define the competences of educators in contemporary societies. An important recent development in this domain is the DigCompEdu framework by the Joint Research Centre of the European Commission, that aims to inspire digital literacy initiatives in European countries targeted to educators (Kluzer & Pujol, 2018) (Fig. 8.1).

DigCompEdu is advocating for a rather holistic understanding of digital literacy, that considers the needed digital competences of twenty-first-century educators, in the centre of the above figure, together with their professional engagement activities, on the left side, and with the impact that teachers can have on their learner's digital literacy, on the right side (Nascimbeni, 2018). The framework operationalises this approach through six competencies areas: (1) work effectively in an ICT-rich professional environment, (2) find, create and share digital resources, (3) effectively use digital tools for teaching and learning, (4) enhance learning assessment through ICT, (5) empower learners and foster learners-centred strategies through the use of digital tools and (6) create digital literacy among learners, in terms of active citizenship and media literacy. These areas are then detailed along 23 competences, with exhaustive proficiency descriptors. By looking at the way these competences are described, we find that collaboration (among teachers, with students and with other stakeholders) inspires the whole framework, and that openness is definitely present, both in terms of use of OER and of stakeholders' engagement and collaboration. The DigCompEdu framework does indeed advocate for a change in the role of teachers, by introducing

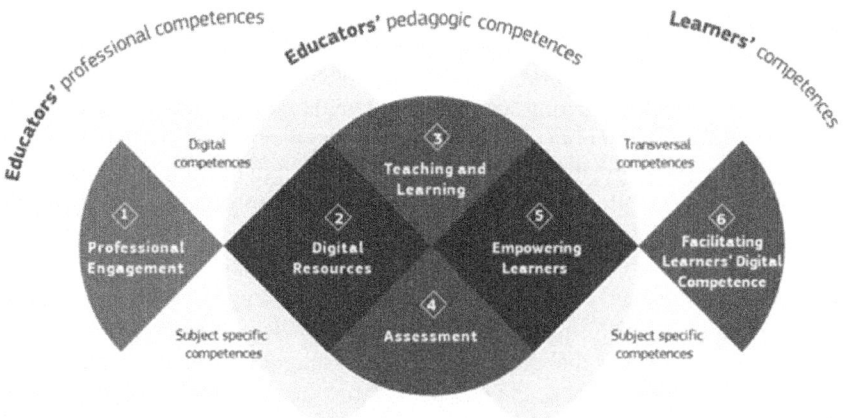

Fig. 8.1 The DigComp Edu framework (Kluzer & Priego, 2018)

meta-cognitive and self-development teachers' competences, getting them ready for open and networked learning settings (Loeckx, 2016).

To complement the DigCompEdu framework, that addresses collaboration and openness through the lens of digital literacy, it is important to consider also educators competencies frameworks that target specifically collaborative learning and open education.

An attempt to capture the competencies categories that educators would need to acquire to successfully implement collaborative learning in the classroom has been done with the Implementing Collaborative Learning in the Classroom (ICLC) framework (Kaendler, Wiedmann, & Rummel, 2015). The proposed competences areas identified within ICLC are: planning, connected to the course preparation phase; monitoring, supporting and consolidating, connected to the course interactive phase; and reflecting, for the post-course phase. These should be accompanied by subject-specific knowledge and by teachers' beliefs and attitudes, two important elements that influence the selected collaborative learning strategies (Fig. 8.2).

The most interesting feature of the framework is that it stresses the fact that—in order to successfully adopt collaborative learning practices—educators do not need to acquire new competences, but they rather require to adapt their teaching strategies to collaborative learning settings. The proposed competences areas are indeed typical of teaching cycles and are declined in such a way to support collaborative learning. The pre-active phase deals with lessons preparation and with setting up the collaborative learning system before students start working in groups. In the inter-active phase, educators support students to find solutions to the problem they are working on and to facilitate review of the work by other students. Finally, the post-active phase takes deals with the capacity of facilitating learners' reflection on the previous phases.

In the area of open education, the eight attributes presented in Fig. 8.3 (Hegarty, 2015) do represent quite well what are the key competences that educators needs to master in order to work openly with their students.

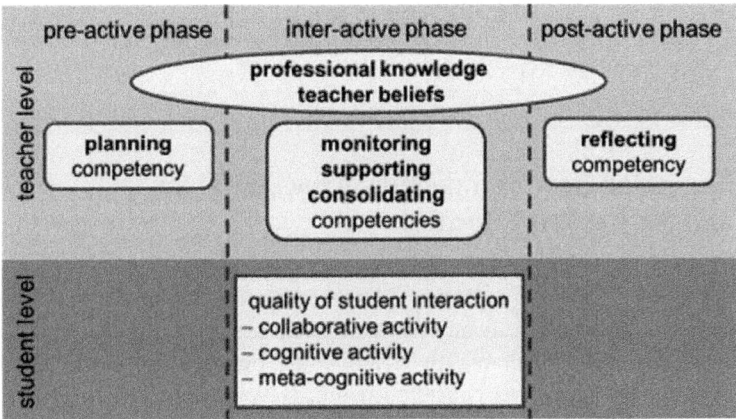

Fig. 8.2 The ICLC framework (Kaendler et al., 2015)

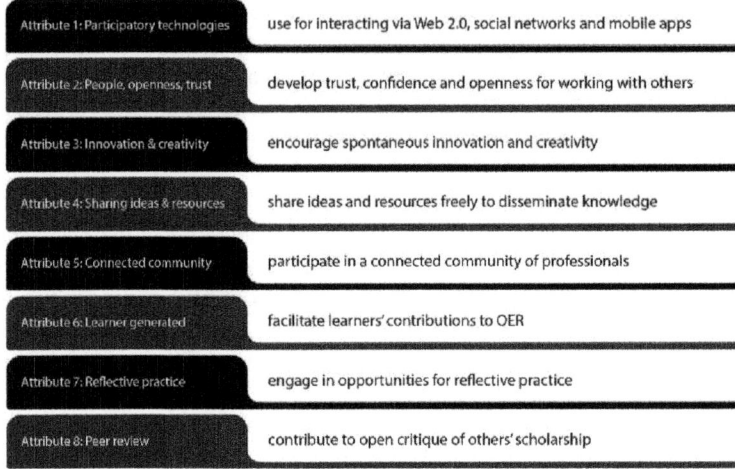

Fig. 8.3 Eight attributes of open pedagogy (Hegarty, 2015)

Also in this case, the majority of competences are actually *open declinations* of typical educators' competences. As noted by a recent JRC report, academics need to start from their teaching practices in order to find ways in which they can share and collaborate openly, and this must be accompanied not so much by new competencies but rather by a mindset shift (Inamorato dos Santos, 2019). It must be noted that, as given openness is strongly connected with personal attitudes and preferences (Cronin, 2017), it is almost impossible to split the components of open education into clearly distinct dimensions. The components of the eight dimensions indeed overlap in many ways and are all part of a new way of teaching, that fosters trust, sharing, collaboration, connectedness, peer interaction and review. As we have seen before when analysing the competences needed to support collaborative learning, also in the realm of openness it is fundamental to let students be in control of their work, for example, by letting them chose the open licenses they prefer or what parts of their work they want to publish openly (Ward, 2017).

8.4 Suggested New Competency Areas for Open and Networked Educators

Our analysis of the three competence frameworks presented above concludes that educators should not build radically new competences but should rather update their competences in terms of collaborative learning and open education, at least as long as we stay within the formal education realm. Nevertheless, one key capacity of contemporary educators—not only in higher education—is to be able to meaningfully bridge formal and informal learning, connecting the work that happens in the classroom with the many knowledge-rich activities that take place outside learning institutions. In this perspective, some additional competences should be acquired by teachers to actively manage the knowledge they produce and to make use of knowledge produced by their students, in a collaborative, engaging and open way.

We propose six competences areas that should be explored to align the capacities of educators with the needs of contemporary open and networked societies, at the same time bridging formal and informal learning (Fig. 8.4).

First, *personal data management*. In a data-driven society, being able to understand the issues and criticalities connected to the use of personal data is fundamental. This has to do with comprehending the terms of use of online platforms as well as with behaving in line with legal and technological developments, but also with using learners' data properly when applying learning analytics techniques (Slade and Prinsloo, 2013). This is particularly important given the raise of online business models, also within educational settings, that involve tracking and profiling of users, whose data can potentially be misused in many ways (O'Neil, 2016). A possible source to define the detailed competences that should be included in this area is the *My Data* model, a rather advanced approach that aims to move from the current organization centric models to human centric systems where personal data are treated as a resource that the individuals can easily access and decide upon (Poikola, Kuikkaniemi, & Honko, 2014).

Second, the *capacity to leverage the open web*. In a society where openly sharing knowledge is becoming in many cases the norm, a fundamental component of educators' literacy should be the capacity to both share the knowledge they produce and to make use of knowledge produced by others in a responsible, transparent and traceable way (Villar, 2019). Learning how to teach through open communities and with open and networked practices implies both a set of technical skills, related, for example, to copyright understanding, and a fundamental change in daily practices of course design, content production, teaching and assessment (Nascimbeni & Burgos, 2016). By relying on the open web, educators should be able to work through open

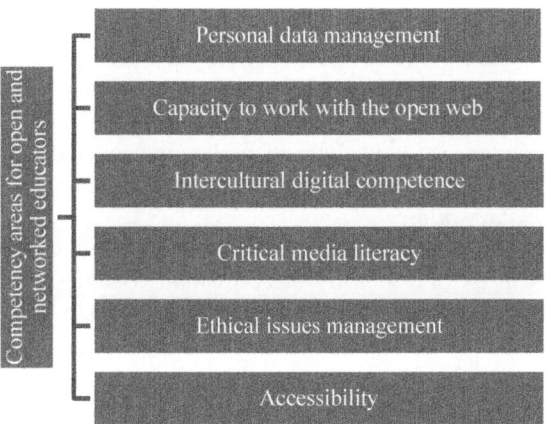

Fig. 8.4 Six competence areas for open and networked teaching

and connected online identities, meaning that they should adopt a transparent and consistent attitude in online spaces related to their teaching work (Ross, Sinclair, Knox, Bayne, & Macleod, 2014) and should rely on social networks to enrich their teaching by setting up and nurturing their personal learning network (Tour, 2017).

With the *ability to engage in intercultural digital dialogues* we mean that educators should use digital technologies to move from a reactive and defensive position with respect to the increased multiculturality of our societies—and of our students' cohorts—towards an active approach able to add value to learning experiences thanks to the existence of multiple cultural perspectives. Apart from developing intercultural communication skills, engaging in intercultural digital dialogues bears the capacity to move across diverse online communities, grasping and following alternative norms and respecting multiple perspectives. This in turn can influence the possibility of learners with different backgrounds to identify with and relate to teaching resources, avoiding biases and stereotypes (Elder, 2019).

Fourth, having a *critical view on media* means being able to deconstruct, question and challenge online and offline media content. In a world where 40% of young people seem to prefer to get their news from social media (Common Sense Media, 2018), educators must be able to support students in understanding the implications of the current *cognitive war* (Trinchero, 2018), including the difference between real and fake news. In more general terms, they shall guide students on how to consume, understand and create media that corresponds to fact-checking standards. Already in 2008, before the massive advent of social media, UNESCO had identified five broad competencies for media and information literacy: understanding, critical thinking, creativity, cultural awareness and citizenship (UNESCO, 2008). Since then, a number of efforts have tried to detail what being *media literate* today should mean (see e.g. Richardson, Milovidov, & Schmalzried, 2017), but to our knowledge educators' competences have not yet been targeted deeply enough by the media literacy movements.

Fifth, the *capacity to deal with digital ethical issues*. Already recognised as one of the three fundamental dimension of teachers' digital literacy more than a decade ago (Calvani et al., 2008), ethical issues have been gaining importance in the era of social media. Educators shall know when and at what conditions information can be shared, or whether or not they can use openly available knowledge, or how to deal with issues such as Artificial Intelligence or the scarcity of learners' attention (Farrow 2016). The problem is that most of these questions lie in grey areas where solutions are being debated at the moment, and are connected with the need to be able to apply traditional ethical frameworks to problems that are emerging in the digital world.

Sixth, educators should be able to deal with *accessibility issues*. First, they should be aware of technical web accessibility issues, so to allow students with access limitations to understand, navigate and contribute to the web. Second, they should be able to make their courses more accessible to all student categories, including disabled students. One way to do this is to follow the Universal Design for Learning (UDL) framework, which provides multiple ways of engaging with a course content, for example, representing ideas from different angles and in different media types, providing support for students to express their understanding of concepts in different ways, or allowing students to engage through a variety of different activities depending on their capacity (Rose & Meyer, 2007).

Two considerations must be made about these areas of competency. First, this does not want to be an exhaustive list, since new important competences are continuously being codified. To make an example, *computational thinking* could probably be added to the list, given its role in facilitating the understanding of how and why certain elements of our digital world are framed in specific ways, including the way big data and related algorithms work. Second, these competencies, some of which were not even grouped as such just a few years ago, dynamically evolve over time, influencing and being influenced by technological and societal developments. To make an example, being capable of collaborating online some 15 years ago, before the boom of social media, meant a completely different thing with respect to being able to collaborate online today. These competences are therefore inherently difficult to be documented and framed in a capacity building process, and because of this they should be developed through experiential approaches, making sure that enough attention is put on all the sociocultural nuances of what it means to live—and teach—in contemporary open and collaborative societies.

8.5 Conclusions

Contemporary educators must be able to prepare students to be active and responsible citizens in increasingly knowledge-based and knowledge-sharing society, managing their emerging collective intelligence dynamics in an open and transparent way (Recker, Yuan & Ye, 2014). In order to do so, they need to be capable of engaging learners in digital dialogues based on shared ethical, multicultural and equity strategies and to foster the role of students as knowledge producers and not just as consumers (Alexander, Adams Becker, & Cummins, 2016). Such an engagement capacity would also help bridging formal and informal learning settings, since research shows that students are not always comfortable with collaborative teaching approaches within formal learning settings, despite their daily use of social networks (Schleicher, 2014).

If we want our students to develop a curios and critical mindset and to become independent, resilient and self-regulated citizens, we need educators that can critically discuss with them the core issues of our increasingly digital, networked and open societies, guiding them towards solutions to the newly emerging problems of our times. For this to happen, we must make sure that educators develop the capacity to adapt their experience to open and networked settings, at the same time acquiring a set of new competences. Only by building on teachers experience and at the same time enriching this with new skills, educators can transform into actors able both to teach competently in digital, open and networked settings and to co-shape with their learners existing practices in an active ad critical way.

References

Alexander, B., Adams Becker, S., & Cummins, M. (2016). *Digital literacy: An NMC horizon project strategic brief* (Vol. 3.3). New Media Consortium.

Bates, T. (2015). *Teaching in the digital age*. BC Open Textbooks.

Calvani, A., Cartelli, A., Fini, A. & Ranieri, M. (2008). Models and instruments for assessing: Digital competence at school. *Journal of e-Learning and Knowledge Society, 4*(3), 183–193. Italian e-Learning Association.

Common Sense Media. (2018). *The common sense census: Media use by kids age zero to eight 2017*. Retrieved from https://www.commonsensemedia.org/research/the-common-sense-census-media-use-by-kids-age-zero-to-eight-2017.

Conole, G. (2013). *Designing for learning in an open world*. New York: Springer.

Cronin, C. (2017). Openness and Praxis: Exploring the use of open educational practices in higher education. *The International Review of Research in Open and Distributed Learning, 18*(5).

Dede, C. (2010). Comparing frameworks for 21st century skills. In J. Bellance & R. Brandt (Eds.), *21st century skills: Rethinking how students learn* (pp. 51–76). Bloomington: Solution Tree.

Downes, S. (2012). *Connectivism and connective knowledge: Essays on meaning and learning networks*. Ottawa: National Research Council Canada.

Elder, A. K. (2019). *The OER starter kit*. Ames: Iowa State University Digital Press.

Farrow, R. (2016). A framework for the ethics of open education. *Open Praxis, 8*(2), 93–109.

Gillies, R. M., & Boyle, M. (2010). Teachers' reflections on cooperative learning: Issues of implementation. *Teaching and Teacher Education, 26,* 933–940.

Hegarty, B. (2015). Attributes of Open pedagogy: A model for using open educational resources. *Educational Technology*.

Inamorato dos Santos, A. (2019). *Practical guidelines on open education for academics: Modernising higher education via open educational practices* (based on the OpenEdu Framework), EUR 29672 EN, Publications Office of the European Union, Luxembourg, 2019, ISBN 978-92-76-00194-2, https://doi.org/10.2760/55923, JRC115663.

Jenkins, H., Ito, M. & Boyd, D. (2015). *Participatory culture in a networked Era: A conversation on youth, learning, commerce, and politics*. Cambridge: Polity Press.

Kaendler, C., Wiedmann, M., Rummel, N., et al. (2015). Teacher competencies for the implementation of collaborative learning in the classroom: A framework and research review. *Education Psychology Review, 27,* 505.

Kluzer, S., & Pujol, P. L. (2018). *DigComp into action—Get inspired, make it happen*. Luxembourg: Publications Office of the European Union.

Kyndt, E., Raes, E., Lismont, B., Timmers, F., Cascallar, E., & Dochy, F. (2013). A meta-analysis of the effects of face-to-face cooperative learning. Do recent studies falsify or verify earlier findings? *Educational Research Review, 10,* 133–149.

Loeckx, J. (2016). Blurring boundaries in education: Context and impact of MOOCs. *The International Review Of Research In Open And Distributed Learning, 17*(3).

Nascimbeni, F. (2018). Rethinking digital literacy for teachers in open and participatory societies. *International Journal of Digital Literacy and Digital Competence (IJDLDC), 9*(3), 1–11.

Nascimbeni, F. & Burgos, D. (2016). In search for the open educator: Proposal of a definition and a framework to increase openness adoption among University Educators. *The International Review of Research in Open and Distributed Learning, 17*(6).

OECD. (2016). *Innovating education and educating for innovation: The power of digital technologies and skills*. Paris: OECD.

O'Neil, C. (2016). *Weapons of math destruction: How big data increases inequality and threatens democracy*. New York: Crown.

Ozturk, H. T. (2015). Examining value change in MOOCs in the scope of connectivism and open educational resources movement. *International Review of Research in Open and Distributed Learning, 16*(5).

Pearce, N., Weller, M., Scanlon, E. & Kinsley, S. (2010). Digital scholarship considered: How new technologies could transform academic work. *Education, 16*(1).

Poikola, A., Kuikkaniemi, K., & Honko, H. (2014). *MyData a Nordic model for human-centered personal data management and processing*. Helsinki: Finnish Ministry of Transport and Communication.

Recker, M., Yuan, M., & Ye, L. (2014). Crowdteaching: Supporting teaching as designing in collective intelligence communities. *International Review of Research in Open and Distributed Learning, 15*(4).

Reynolds, R. (2015). *Eight qualities of open pedagogies*. Retrieved Oct 9, 2019 from https://nextthought.com/thoughts/2015/02/ten-qualities-of-open-pedagogy.

Richardson, J., Milovidov, E., & Schmalzried, M. (2017). *Internet literacy handbook*. Strasbourg: Council of Europe.

Rivoltella, P. C., & Rossi, P. G. (Eds.). (2012). *L'agire didattico*. Brescia: Editrice La Scuola.

Rose, D. H., & Meyer, A. (2007). Teaching Every student in the digital age: Universal design for learning. *Education Technology Research and Development, 55*, 521–525.

Ross, J., Sinclair, C., Knox, J., Bayne, S., & Macleod, H. (2014). Teacher experiences and academic identity: The missing components of MOOC pedagogy. *Journal of Online Learning and Teaching, 10*(1), 57–69.

Ruys, I., Van Keer, H., & Aelterman, A. (2011). Student teachers' skills in the implementation of collaborative learning: A multilevel approach. *Teaching and Teacher Education, 27*, 1090–1100.

Schleicher, A. (2014). *Equity, excellence and inclusiveness in education: Policy lessons from around the world*. In International summit on the teaching profession. Paris: OECD.

Siemens, G. (2004). Connectivism: A learning theory for the digital age. *International Journal of Instructional Technology and Distance Learning, 2*(1), 3–10.

Slade, S., & Prinsloo, P. (2013). Learning analytics: Ethical issues and dilemmas. *American Behavioral Scientist, 57*(10), 1510–1529.

Sledge, L., & Dovey Fishman, T. (2014). *Reimagining higher education*. Westlake: Deloitte University Press.

Stacey, P. (2013). *The pedagogy of MOOCs*. Retrieved Oct 9, 2019 from http://edtechfrontier.com/2013/05/11/the-pedagogy-of-moocs.

Tour, E. (2017). Teachers' self-initiated professional learning through personal learning networks. *Technology, Pedagogy and Education, 26*(2), 17–192.

Trinchero, R. (2018). Against the cognitive war. Promoting active skepticism. *Media Education. 9*(1), 17–36.

UNESCO. (2008). *Teacher training curricula for media and information literacy*. In Report of the International Expert Group Meeting. Paris: UNESCO.

Van Leeuwen, A., Janssen, J., Erkens, G., & Brekelmans, M. (2013). Multidimensional teacher behavior in CSCL. In N. Rummel, M. Kapur, M. Nathan & S. Puntambekar (Eds.), *To see the world and a grain of sand: Learning across levels of space, time, and scale: CSCL 2013 Conference Proceedings*, International Society of the Learning Sciences.

Villar, D. (2019). *Celebrating the open web as a route towards a (more) critical digital education*. Retrieved Oct 9, 2019 from https://education.okfn.org/celebrating-the-open-web-as-a-route-towards-a-more-critical-digital-education/.

Ward, D. (2017). *Turning open education into a social movement*. Centre for Teaching and Excellence blog: University of Kansas.

Weller, M. (2012). *The digital scholar*. London: Bloomsbury Academic.

Weller, M. (2014). *The battle for open*. London: Ubiquity Press.

Williams, R., Karousou, R. & Mackness, J. (2011). Emergent learning and learning ecologies in Web 2.0. *International Review of Research in Open and Distance Learning. 12*(3).

Fabio Nascimbeni works as Assistant Professor at the Universidad Internacional de la Rioja (UNIR), where he holds the Telefonica Chair on Digital Society and Education. He is a Senior Fellow of the European Distance and eLearning Network (EDEN), a member of the Advisory Board of the Open Education Working of the Open Knowledge Foundation, a fellow at the Centro de Estudos sobre Tecnologia e Sociedade of the University of Sao Paulo (USP) in Brazil and the Nexa Centre of the Politecnico di Torino. He has been active in the field of learning innovation and ICT for learning since 1998, by designing and coordinating more than 40 research and innovation projects and promoting European and international collaboration in different areas, from school education to higher education, to lifelong learning, to ICT research. He has been working across Europe as well as in Latin America, the Caribbean, the South Mediterranean and Southeast Asia. His main research interests are open education, learning innovation, digital literacy, social and digital inclusion.

Open Access This chapter is licensed under the terms of the Creative Commons Attribution 4.0 International License (http://creativecommons.org/licenses/by/4.0/), which permits use, sharing, adaptation, distribution and reproduction in any medium or format, as long as you give appropriate credit to the original author(s) and the source, provide a link to the Creative Commons license and indicate if changes were made.

The images or other third party material in this chapter are included in the chapter's Creative Commons license, unless indicated otherwise in a credit line to the material. If material is not included in the chapter's Creative Commons license and your intended use is not permitted by statutory regulation or exceeds the permitted use, you will need to obtain permission directly from the copyright holder.

Chapter 9
Integration of Formal, Non-formal and Informal Learning Through MOOCs

Hyunjin Cha and Hyo-Jeong So

Abstract Since the first appearance of MOOCs in the higher education context, MOOCs have been integrated and transformed into several learning variations. In particular, by integrating formal traditional courses with informal learning approaches, MOOCs have been expanding the position as a learning platform to provide students with diverse learning experiences delivered through blended learning modalities. This chapter aims to discuss how MOOCs have been integrated into higher education contexts to blend formal, non-formal and informal learning experiences. An integration framework suggested in this chapter is based on two factors, namely credit recognition and online learning that lead to three types of MOOC-integrated learning experiences: Type I—formal MOOC learning, Type II—formal blended MOOC learning, and Type III—non-formal/informal MOOC learning. Based on this framework, we mainly illustrate three integration approaches, namely blended learning, flipped learning, and non-formal/informal learning experiences, with relevant research studies. The chapter concludes with some suggestions for research directions that can inform future research on integrating formal and non-formal/informal learning experiences through MOOCs in higher education.

Keywords MOOCs · Flipped learning · Blended learning · Formal learning · Informal learning · Non-formal learning

---

H. Cha
SoonChunHyang University, #6524, 22 Soonchunhyang-ro, Shinchang-myeon, Asan-si, Chungcheongnam-do 31538, Republic of Korea
e-mail: lois6934@hanmail.net

H.-J. So (✉)
Ewha Womans University, Education Building A #405, 52, Ewhayeodae-gil, Seodaemun-gu, Seoul 03760, Republic of Korea
e-mail: hyojeongso@ewha.ac.kr

9.1 Introduction

Scholars have pointed out the problems of a knowledge-transmission paradigm of education rooted in industrialism, such as uniform teaching and learning, teacher-centric methods, standardized assessment, and learning by acquisition (Halverson & Collins, 2009). Higher education intuitions have explored new methods of teaching and learning with the integration of technologies to move away from knowledge-transmission to knowledge creation, and to provide students with more flexible learning opportunities through online technologies. The growth of online learning in the higher education sector has occurred through blending various learning approaches. Massive Open Online Course (MOOC) is one of the emerging approaches in higher education that leverages the openness of learning content for massive learners for the delivery of content and instruction. For the past decade, MOOCs have been transformed into several variations since the first appearance in the higher education sector. Brown (2018) suggests that MOOCs have gone through three waves. During the first wave, MOOCs were mainly used for marketing purposes to increase the institution's visibility and to recruit more students. The second wave is to use MOOCs for lifelong learning, propelled by large-scale MOOC projects at a national level and a cross-institutional level. The third wave is to use MOOCs for credit recognition and continuing professional development pathways.

Despite such increasing variations of MOOCs in the higher education landscape, a little framework is available to unpack mechanisms that blend various learning experiences. In MOOCs, as portions of learning experiences are delivered partly through online modalities, various integrations can happen, affecting what students learn online and face-to-face. Further, MOOCs have been increasingly positioned as a platform to integrate formal traditional courses with informal learning experiences. Given this nature of variations in MOOCs, this chapter aims to present and discuss various ways of integrating formal and informal learning experiences through MOOCs. This chapter is structured to firstly provide theoretical understandings of various MOOCs in the higher education sector, and then to present the integration framework with discussions of respective research studies. In the integration framework, we mainly discuss three approaches: blended learning, flipped learning, and non-formal/informal learning. The chapter concludes with some suggestions for research directions that can inform future research on integrating formal and informal learning experiences through MOOCs in higher education.

9.2 Theoretical Foundation

9.2.1 *MOOCs: Concepts and Features*

MOOCs have provided innovative open learning environments since the term was first introduced in 2008 (Akgül, 2018; Littlejohn & Milligan, 2015). MOOCs have been derived from distance education but have more distinctive features as courses are completely online, free and open to anyone, and available to massive audiences (Atiaja & Gueerero, 2016; Iniesto, McAndrew, Minocha, & Coughlan, 2017). MOOCs were originated from the Open Educational Resources (OER) movement, which is a philosophy to offer educational opportunities to all through free content and courses (Atiaja & Guerrero, 2016). The original notion of this innovative approach is for open access to learning. Moreover, the socio-cultural trends accelerated through the development of web 2.0 technology and social networks promoted the emergence of connectivism as a new pedagogical phenomenon that emphasizes participating and interacting, sharing ideas, and developing new knowledge through the continual improvement of knowledge among learners on the open learning platforms.

MOOCs as the innovative educational stream have attracted much public attention since diverse groups of learners can benefit from open access with a formal educational structure, free or low cost, flexible learning process with preferred pace and place, social learning opportunities, and even earning certificates and credits from prestigious universities (Iniesto et al., 2017). From learners' perspectives, there are a variety of motivations to take MOOC courses: to gain better understanding about a certain subject or topic, to explore a specific field of interest, to participate in social interactions, and to have fun and enjoyable experiences without any expectation of achievement and completion (Belanger & Thornton, 2013).

MOOCs have many advantages over traditional brick-and-mortar university models. First, MOOCs provide massive and diverse learners from all over the world with an opportunity to access open, free, and high-quality learning content (Abdelrahman, 2016). Second, MOOCs provide individual learners with an opportunity to personalize their learning in terms of topics, time, place, and methods (Morris, 2014). MOOC learners have different learning objectives and plan to utilize online courses according to their personal needs. In MOOCs, while some students aim to achieve a certificate by studying the entire weeks of content with assignments, other students plan to study a specific element and content that they are interested in. To support such different student needs, MOOCs have taken an open approach to increase the availability of on-demand course videos and flexible schedules (Lapworth, 2018). Third, at an institutional level, MOOCs can be a strategic driver to increase student recruitments through the increased visibility of institutions and can promote the accessibility of lifelong learning opportunities with flexible pathways to international alliances (Brown, 2018). Universities can expand curriculums and opportunities with cross-cultural knowledge and friendship around the globe for their students. Finally, MOOCs have recently evolved to use learning analytics to better identify student profiles and learning paths. As big data and intelligent technologies are advancing, learners' self-regulation can be promoted through the automatic tracking of the frequency and patterns of learner engagement in MOOCs (Cha & Park, 2019).

9.2.2 Comparison of Traditional, Blended, and Flipped Learning

For a clear conceptualization of integrating MOOCs in higher education, we firstly contrast the characteristics (a) traditional instruction, (b) blended learning, and (c) flipped learning. First, traditional instruction can be described as a direct instruction approach, where an instructor mainly delivers a face-to-face lecture in a classroom. Students learn mainly through textbooks, lectures, and assignments in the classroom setting. It is important to acknowledge that direct instruction or an instructor-led lecture is not in itself good or bad. There is sufficient evidence that direct instruction is effective for delivering declarative knowledge to learners and for reducing cognitive load (Kirschner, Sweller, & Clark, 2006). Rather, the critics of direct instruction are associated with the lack of time devoted to high-order cognitive skills, such as applying, analyzing, and evaluating, since most of the class time is devoted to transmitting content knowledge in an instructor-centric mode (Kuhn, 2007).

Second, blended learning refers to the combination of face-to-face instruction and computer-mediated instruction (Graham, 2006). The term blended learning is widely used both in research and practices. Howecer, it is challenging to distinguish flipped learning and blended learning since both approaches involve online and face-to-face (F2F) learning activities. Although flipped learning is perceived as a form of blending online and offline learning (Strayer, 2012), some scholars have argued that flipped learning differs from blended learning by clearly separating online and offline activities (Hwang & Lai, 2017). For instance, Thai, Wever, and Valcke (2017) compare a flipped classroom with other similar learning approaches that combine face-to-face and online learning components. Table 9.1 shows that the key difference between blended learning and the flipped classroom is reversing the order of online and face-to-face settings in presenting lectures and guiding questions, as well as in the immediacy of a feedback loop. That is, in the flipped classroom, lectures are delivered online, and guiding questions that scaffold students' deeper understanding about knowledge acquired from the lecture videos occur in a face-to-face mode with immediate feedback.

Lastly, it is possible that in-class teaching of flipped learning remains an instructor-centered approach when instructors focus mainly on reviewing the content that learners have already learned through lecture videos before class. With that, the Flipped

Table 9.1 Comparison of the main characteristics of various learning approaches (Thai et al., 2017)

	Traditional learning	e-learning	Blended learning conditions	
			Blended learning	Flipped classroom
Lecture	F2F	Online	F2F	Online
Guiding questions	F2F	Online	Online	F2F
Feedback	F2F immediate	Online delayed	Online delayed	F2F immediate

Learning Network (FLN) differentiates the concepts of flipped classroom and flipped learning. Flipping a class is a method of presenting lectures and supplementary materials in advance before class, as some instructors have already done in the past. The FLN suggests that although flipping a class can lead to flipped learning, it does not necessarily do so. For the proper implementation of flipped learning, the FLN suggests that instructors must incorporate the four pillars of F-L-I-P™, namely flexible environment, learning culture, intentional content, and a professional educator (Bergmann & Sams, 2014). In this study, we use the term flipped learning, following the definition by FLN, to refer to "a pedagogical approach in which direct instruction moves from the group learning space to the individual learning space, and the resulting group space is transformed into a dynamic, interactive learning environment where the educator guides students as they apply concepts and engage creatively in the subject matter" (Flipped Learning Network, 2014, p. 1). Flipped learning advocates learning experiences that engage learners in cognitive processes demanded in the real-world context. By moving much of the abstract learning outside of class and bringing in more practical activities into the class, this sequence of learning can better facilitate student engagement in high-level cognitive activities and knowledge integration.

9.3 Integration Framework

Credit recognition is an important consideration of MOOCs in higher education. Sandeen (2013) suggests that higher education institutions are entering the era of the hybrid MOOC called "MOOC 3.0 or hMOOC", which indicates the increasing trend of integrating MOOCs into traditional academic programs or courses for academic credits. However, Chamberlin and Parish (2011) contend that students who receive credits from MOOCs tend to receive more benefits such as additional meetings and activities with the facilitator than non-credit students. If students choose to enroll in MOOCs due to the advantage of the flexible learning environment to earn academic credits, their behavior may not be fully encouraged by intrinsic motivation, but by external incentives to some extent. Hence, it is necessary to distinguish two types of MOOCs: (a) formal, certification-oriented participation in MOOCs where learning is primarily centered on receiving credits from MOOCs and (b) non-formal, professional development-oriented participation in MOOCs where learning is centered on the utilization of knowledge in real-world contexts.

Based on the understanding of different learning approaches, we propose a framework that integrates formal and informal learning experiences through MOOCs. While there are various ways to conceptualize formal, non-formal and informal learning, we adopt the definitions by OECD (2010):

- *Formal learning*: learning that occurs in an organized structured environment and is explicitly designated as learning in terms of learning objectives, time, or learning support.

- *Informal learning*: learning that results from daily activities related to work, family, or leisure. It is not organized or structured in terms of learning objectives, time, or learning support.
- *Non-formal learning*: learning which is embedded in planned activities not explicitly designated as learning in terms of learning objectives, time, or learning support.

Our proposed MOOC integration framework is based on two factors, namely credit recognition and online learning. As shown in Fig. 9.1, this leads to three types of MOOC-integrated learning experiences. Type I is formal MOOC learning that refers to a learning approach where learners take a MOOC without any face-to-face instruction and receive academic credits. Type I is formal learning since learning experiences tend to be structured with an explicit goal to earn credits or certificates. Type II is formal blended MOOC learning where MOOCs are used to supplement or replace some portions of formal courses. Under this type, two combinations are possible depending on how and when MOOCs are used in the course structure: blended learning and flipped learning. As shown in Table 9.2, we adopt the framework by Thai et al. (2017) to differentiate blended learning and flipped learning. In blended learning, a lecture is delivered by instructors in a classroom in a face-to-face mode, and MOOCs are typically used as part of learning activities after F2F lectures. Flipped learning is a special form of blended learning where the primary delivery of instructional content is online via MOOCs and occurs in a remote location before classroom sessions. F2F in-class time is devoted to learning activities that aim to enhance the understanding of lecture content. Type III is non-formal or informal MOOC learning where learners use a MOOC without an intention to earn credits or certificates. The degree of structuring learning experiences determines non-formal

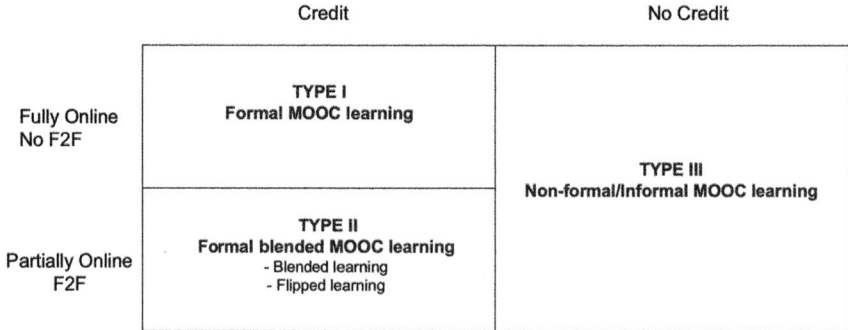

Fig. 9.1 MOOC integration framework

Table 9.2 Blended learning versus flipped learning

	Lecture	Activities
Flipped learning	Online	Face-to-face
Blended learning	Face-to-face	Online

or informal learning experiences. Non-formal learning tends to be a more structured use of MOOCs, whereas informal learning with MOOCs can take place in a less structured way.

In the following section, we review and discuss how MOOCs have been used in various integration approaches. Type 1 (fully online MOOC) is not discussed here since this chapter is interested in incorporating different learning components such as the combination of online and offline learning or formal and informal learning experiences. Our review of the existing literature reveals that three integration approaches are often used in the higher education contexts: (1) integrating MOOCs in blended learning, (2) integrating MOOCs in flipped learning, and (3) integrating MOOCs in non-formal and informal learning.

9.3.1 Integration Approach I: Integrating MOOCs in Blended Learning

The first integration approach is to utilize MOOCs in blended learning to supplement and/or replace some segments of courses and learning contents in traditional formal learning (Bralić & Divjak, 2016; National Research Council, 2012). Blended learning varies in concepts and models, depending on what form and mode are blended (Bryan & Volchenkova, 2016). In this chapter, blended learning is defined as a hybrid form of learning that integrates MOOCs into traditional brick-and-mortar classrooms by taking the benefits of MOOCs in flexible ways. While some researchers (e.g., Bergmann & Sams, 2012; Hung, Sun, & Liu, 2018) used flipped learning in the same sense as blended learning, flipped learning has been studied with its own specific purposes and characteristics. Therefore, we classify flipped learning as a separate integration approach rather than blended learning. In this section, we discuss how MOOCs have been used in blended learning, which combines different learning modes (e.g., integration of online and offline, integration of MOOCs, and traditional classrooms).

Table 9.3 presents the summary of previous studies in the integration approach I. First, Griffiths, Mulhern, Spies, and Chingos (2015) conducted 10 case studies to address the issues of using MOOCs as a blended learning approach in traditional formal education. Faculty members from ten cases who voluntarily participated in the research were asked to integrate MOOCs into a variety of small, single-section courses. Depending on the case, instructors utilized MOOCs for replacing some segments of courses or enhancing the existing course materials. Their study found that there were no statistically significant differences in learning outcomes between the blended learning group and the traditional learning group. However, it was revealed that student satisfaction in the blended learning group was significantly lower than the traditional group since students preferred face-to-face interaction with instructors. In spite of low student satisfaction, Griffiths et al. (2015) found that faculty

Table 9.3 Summary of previous studies in the integration approach I

Reference	Methods	Subjects	Students	MOOCs platform and purpose	Major findings
Griffiths et al. (2015)	– Case study – Quantitative and qualitative data	– Art – Poetry – Genetics – Psychology learning community – Information technology – Political science – English learning community A – Philosophy – Literature – English learning community B	– Undergraduates – Sizes ranged from 6 to 60	Platform: Coursera – Content portion – Live public offering – Replace some lectures – Replace some content – Replace some of the course – Supplemental – As a common experience – Entirely online – Provide greater insight into subject – Provide context to the literature	– Faculty members identified six benefits of using MOOCs in blended learning – Student satisfaction in the blended learning group was significantly lower. They preferred face-to-face interaction with instructors
Bralić and Divjak (2016, 2017)	– Case study – Quantitative and qualitative data	Discrete Mathematics with Graph Theory (DMGT)	– First-year masters students – Sizes differ in each term: 107 in 14/15 88 in 15/16 83 in 16/17	Platform: Coursera – To give students more online learning experiences – To help part-time students who are not able to fully participate in campus-based courses	Positive – Provide regular knowledge assessment – Positive experience in online learning – Helpful for part-time students Negative – Student workload – Language barriers
Cornelius (2019)	– Case study – Quantitative and qualitative data	Africa: sustainable development for all	Undergraduates 88 students	Platform: FutureLearn – To provide an interdisciplinary opportunity for curriculum enhancement for first- and second-year on-campus undergraduates	Compared with the general undergraduate cohort, the blended learning cohort was more engaged in some items in learning with others, reflecting and connecting, staff-student partnership, etc., but less engaged in critical thinking and course challenge

members identified six benefits of using MOOCs in blended learning: replacing lectures, augmenting secondary materials, filling gaps in expertise, exposing other types of teaching, reinforcing critical thinking, and improving how to learn online.

As another blended learning example, Bralić and Divajak (2016) conducted a case study about integrating MOOCs into a traditional course in a higher education context to demonstrate the qualitative effects on learning experiences of MOOCs as well as on learning achievements among part-time students through student's learning diary. The learning diary consisted of eight open questions to identify the benefits of learning experiences, effects on learning achievement for the part-time students, students' workload, and main challenges. The study revealed that the qualitative feedback and reflections from students were positive, especially in terms of self-paced learning and knowledge assessment on a regular basis. In particular, students recognized blended learning as a good approach taking the best of two modes since online learning was not highly motivating compared to face-to-face learning. However, they claimed that the main challenges were related to language problems and more time required to complete online MOOC contents.

Bralić and Divajak (2017) extended the study to trace student changes through three consecutive academic years and to see the effects of blended learning with MOOCs. They found that students who experienced blended learning wanted to take more MOOCs when they were given an option to choose either MOOCs or offline projects as assignments. Furthermore, they also reported that the former group who selected MOOCs as assignments achieved higher than those who selected an offline project as assignments. From the qualitative analysis, it was reported that most of the students had highly positive learning experiences with MOOCs such as opportunities with frequent evaluation and complementary learning experiences of what was taught in the offline class. The blended learning approach made students complete the online MOOC course and improved their self-efficacy. In addition, part-time students indicated that MOOCs helped them to adopt self-paced learning and met their individual needs.

Recently, Cornelius (2019) used a blended learning approach that replaced 6-week MOOC lectures, combining tutor-led tutorials and an independent study with additional materials. Quantitative and qualitative data were collected to analyze factors that might impact learner's engagement through MOOCs. The survey results showed that students from the blended learning approach were more engaged in the aspects of learning with others, reflecting and connecting, research and inquiry, staff–student partnership, and skills development compared to those in the offline campus approach.

In addition, the qualitative results demonstrated that students considered MOOCs as a flexible way of learning with a variety of resources. In particular, active and social learning was achieved through authentic contents and examples shared by peers in the discussions forum. Overall, incorporating MOOCs into traditional classrooms as a blended learning approach has many advantages: enhancing learning by making learners engaged in varied expertise and other styles of teaching and learning activities as well as enriching teaching and learning resources. The blended learning approach can also reinforce learning experience by providing the flexibility of teaching and learning, supporting diversity, and improving efficiency (Sharpe, Benfield, Roberts & Francis, 2006). Indeed, students in the previous studies described self-control, flexibility, and diversity as positive features of the blended approach. However, as seen in low student satisfaction in some studies (e.g., Griffiths et al., 2015), it is crucial to consider how to employ MOOC contents in a blended context. That is, instructors should first consider how to integrate MOOCs into their formal education contexts since there are varied blended learning concepts and approaches.

9.3.2 Integration Approach II: Integrating MOOCs in Flipped Learning

The second and most prevalent integration is a flipped learning approach that integrates MOOCs into pre-class activities to promote student-centered learning during face-to-face in-class sessions (Hung et al., 2018). In general, flipped learning consists of pre-class, in-class, and after-class activities. Flipped learning originated from the idea of how instructors better utilize in-class time (Tucker, 2012). During the in-class time in flipped learning, it is crucial to have more interactions between peers and instructors through student-centered activities. To make the in-class time more interactive and student-centered, instructional video lectures are considered a powerful tool to replace teacher-led passive lectures. The concept behind flipped learning is to make students more actively engaged in learning, rather than passive participants in teacher-led lectures during the face-to-face in-class time (Bishop & Verleger, 2013). In this respect, MOOCs courses and videos can also play an important role in helping instructors transform such instructor-centric lectures to student-centric learning experiences.

In this section, we consider previous studies that used MOOCs as a flipped learning approach in traditional brick-and-mortar university contexts. Table 9.4 presents the summary of previous studies in the integration approach II. Bruff, Fisher, McEwen, and Smith (2013) designed a course as a flipped learning approach by combining MOOC lectures and in-class activities such as supplementary reading and seminar in a traditional formal education setting. Ten weeks during the 14-week semester included MOOCs components so that the instructor was able to focus on in-class activities with interactive discussion and challenging materials. In this case study, students described the MOOC contents as effective, informative, and useful for self-paced learning and thought that online lectures opened up a space for productive in-class discussions. The most obvious change was that students recognized the role of the instructor as a facilitator for in-class activities. However, they also pointed out some challenges such as the misalignment between online lectures and in-class components.

Ghadiri, Qayoumi, Junn, Hsu, and Sujitparapitaya (2013) conducted a pilot study that adopted flipped learning with three distinct activity phases: online outside-of-the class with edX contents, in-class team-based learning, and after-class activities as described in Table 9.5. In the pilot study, despite student complaints about

Table 9.4 Summary of previous studies in the integration approach II

Reference	Methods	Subjects	Students	MOOCs platform and purpose	Major findings
Bruff et al. (2013)	– Quantitative: survey – Qualitative: focused group interview	– Machine learning	– Graduate-level – 10 students in the focus group	Platform: Coursera – Purpose: to use it as part of the course – Design of flipped learning (1) Pre-class: MOOC lecture (10 weeks) (2) In-class: reading, seminar, discussion (3) Final 4 weeks: project	– Positive: as effective, informative, useful for self-paced learning, productive in-class discussions – Negative: misalignment between online and offline class
Ghadiri et al. (2013)	Case study – Quantitative: exam – Qualitative: student's reaction	– Introduction to circuit analysis	Undergraduates	Platform: edX – Purpose (1) To improve students' passage rate (2) To shorten time-to-degree – Design of flipped learning (1) Pre-class: outside-of-class e-learning (2) In-class: F2F, team-based learning (3) After-class: follow-up activities	– Positive: supplementary materials, self-paced learning, and productive in-class activities – Negative: materials not corresponding to in-class materials, time-consuming, difficult online homework

(continued)

Table 9.4 (continued)

Reference	Methods	Subjects	Students	MOOCs platform and purpose	Major findings
Holotescu et al. (2014)	Case study – Quantitative: analysis of student's behaviors – Qualitative: open comments on pedagogical benefits of MOOCs	– Web programming	70 undergraduates students	Platform: Cirip.eu and various MOOCs – Purpose (1) To allow students to be familiar with and analyze the MOOC trends (2) To enlarge knowledge of the course – Design of flipped learning (1) Pre-class: 10% of MOOC activities (2) In-class: discussions (3) After-class: portfolio development	– Positive: learner-centric teaching, self-paced learning with enhanced attention, openness, collaboration with peers, active learning, – Challenging: new tasks and skills required for instructors
Dunn (2015)	– Qualitative: survey of students' responses	– Statistics for engineering	99 undergraduates students	Platform: Coursera – Purpose (1) Final-year students: maintain relevant skills with life-long learning (2) Cost-effective approach – Design of flipped learning (1) Pre-class: reading, video, quizzes (2) In-class: recap of concepts, worksheet, online submission and feedbacks	– Positive: supplementing traditional lectures and promoting self-directed learning – Negative: misaligned and irrelevant videos and assignments

Table 9.5 Three distinct phases for the flipped learning approach (Ghadiri et al., 2013)

Step 1. online outside-of-the class	Step 2. in-class team-based learning	Step 3. after-class activities
edX topical mini-lecture videos	Mental ramp-up period	Professor emails absent students with class materials
edX online textbook	In-class mini-review lecture	Optional, friday, one-hour, F2F walk-in session
edX problem sets	Group quiz	
edX online lab experiments	Solution of group quiz	
SJSU virtual discussion board	Individual quiz	
Assessment handout for the next class session	Solution to the individual quiz	
	Preview for next class session	

the extensive time and efforts required weekly with constant tests, the success rate of the course increased from 65% to 91%. Qualitative data revealed that students perceived both positive and negative aspects. The positive aspects include accessing supplementary materials, self-paced learning, and productive in-class activities, whereas negative aspects include materials not corresponding to in-class materials, time-consuming activities, and online homework that is difficult, irrelevant, and too frequent.

Holotescu, Cretu, Grosseck, and Antoanela (2014) integrated different MOOCs, and the in-class time was devoted to discussion, exercise practices, and feedback on assignments. As the study was designed as a flipped learning approach, they evaluated MOOC participation and the pedagogical benefits of the flipped learning approach. The pedagogical benefits include learner-centric teaching, self-paced learning with enhanced attention, openness, collaboration with peers, active learning, etc. However, they emphasized that instructors must be equipped with new skills and tasks such as facilitating student discussions and dealing with complex course design. They suggested that instructors should find a suitable way of how to incorporate MOOCs into their teaching scenarios more effectively and efficiently. Similarly, Dunn (2015) implemented a flipped learning approach with Coursera as shown in Fig. 9.2 and discussed that the role of the instructor changed to a coordinator, collaborator, time-manager, and mentor, and flipped learning can promote group activities and peer learning.

Based on the literature discussed above in this section, we identified the common benefits of integrating MOOCs in flipped learning. First of all, productive in-class time is achieved by making students more actively engaged in discussions, projects, and exercise practices. Students have more opportunities to interact with their peers and/or instructors. Secondly, the role of instructors changed from a knowledge-giver to a knowledge facilitator. Thirdly, MOOCs play an effective role in replacing and supplementing traditional lectures and promoting self-directed learning. However, it was also revealed that MOOCs lectures and contents cannot completely replace in-class lectures because students reported misaligned and irrelevant videos and

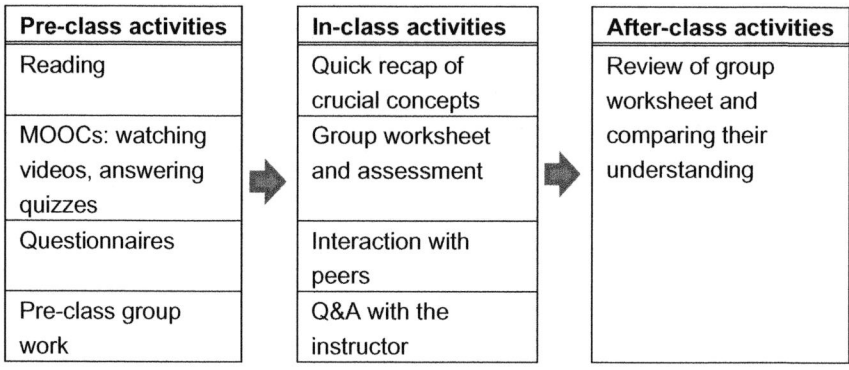

Fig. 9.2 Flipped learning approach with Coursera (Dunn, 2015)

assignments in MOOCs (e.g., Bruff et al., 2013; Ghadiri et al., 2013). In addition, students were not highly satisfied with MOOCs due to more efforts and time they should devote. In particular, Holotescu et al. (2014) emphasized that instructors are required with new course-redesign skills and pedagogical tasks as a facilitator. Therefore, it is crucial to consider how MOOC components can be integrated into traditional learning contexts more effectively and efficiently and how instructors can play a facilitator role during the in-class time to make flipped learning more successful.

9.3.3 Integration Approach III: Integrating MOOCs in Non-formal and Informal Learning

The final integration approach is to adopt MOOCs for non-formal or informal learning in higher education contexts. This approach reflects the original goal of OER and MOOCs, which is to benefit learners who would like to study with free, open, and flexible participation at their preferred pace and location. In addition, since many popular MOOCs are associated with world-class higher education (Alraimi, Zo, & Ciganek, 2014), such disruptive potentials, which mean not only to create innovative opportunities but also to have potential threats (Kaltencher, Huesig, Hess, & Dowling, 2013), can expand opportunities for non-formal and informal learning

OECD (2010) defines that informal learning is not structured or organized, whereas non-formal learning is associated with planned learning activities, but is not explicitly designed in terms of learning purposes, learning schedule, or learning supports. European Communities (2001) suggest that the differences between non-formal and informal learning lie in the structuredness in learning experiences and intention from learners' perspectives. Informal learning is more experienced-based learning, whereas non-formal learning is more intentional and structured. A common aspect of non-formal and informal learning is that learning does not necessarily lead to formal recognition such as degrees or certification. While some MOOC contents provide students with a structured syllabus, schedule, and certification, generally MOOCs do not force learners to such structured and certified learning experiences. Rather, MOOCs support learners to choose how, when, and in what ways they want to engage with flexible learning paths and goals. With the flexible nature of learning, MOOCs have attracted learners who have a variety of learning purposes and learning paths.

Table 9.6 summarizes previous studies related to the third integration approach. Earlier studies related to informal learning and non-formal learning through MOOCs focused on who studies, why and how learners study. For instance, Gillani and Eynon (2014) investigated the demographic characteristics of learners who were studying a Coursera-based MOOC. They found that the majority of learners were well-educated, young adults from developed countries, and had prior knowledge of the selected course. Among them, only 62.7% wanted to have a formal acknowledgment of their learning experiences. Similarly, Ho et al. (2015) investigated 68 courses from 2012 to 2014 through MOOCs by Harvard and MIT universities and found that 71% of leaners had a degree, 50% were younger than 30 years old, and 32% were from the USA. It was concluded that MOOCs might be utilized as a means for widening educational opportunities and for re-skilling and up-skilling purposes with a diverse range of goals (Sfiri, Pietkiewicz, & Jansen, 2016). Such diversity in learning goals led to diverse learner's participation behaviors such as no-shows, observers, drop-ins, passive participants, and active participants (Hill, 2013).

The absence of instructors and pre-determined structure in non-formal and informal learning settings requires learners to self-regulate own learning experiences (Hood, Littlejohn, & Milligan, 2015). Low completion rate is one of the main challenges that MOOCs faced (Jordan, 2014; Perna et al., 2014; Weller, 2014). Recently, researchers attempted to find factors that impact the completion of MOOCs and learner retention and to improve Self-Regulated Learning (SRL). For instance, Alraimi et al. (2014) found that perceived reputation and openness of MOOCs were stronger predictors for learner retention than perceived usefulness and enjoyment. On the other hand, Hone and Said (2016) focused on the factors related to MOOC features and user experiences that influenced learner retention in MOOCs and identified that perceived effectiveness of the MOOC contents affected learner retention. Another line of research into MOOC-integrated learning has focused on increasing the completion and retention rates by improving SRL strategies. Hood et al. (2015) found that learner's current contexts and learning purposes influenced their SRL in a MOOC about data science by Coursera. It was revealed that students who aimed to receive a Higher Education (HE) qualification had significantly higher SRL than those who were not studying for a HE qualification. Further, students with expertise in the data science area showed higher self-efficacy and meaningful learning approaches and strategies than those without expertise in the area.

Littlejohn, Hood, Milligan, and Mustain (2015) compared behaviors between learners with high and low self-reported SRL scores. They found that the intrinsic motivation and goals for high SRL-scored learners to develop knowledge and expertise in their workplace could lead to non-formal learning opportunities to select

Table 9.6 Summary of previous studies in the integration approach III

Reference	Methods	Subjects	Students	MOOCs platform and purpose	Major findings
Gillani and Eynon (2014)	– Case study – Pre and post surveys – Analysis of forum usage	– Business strategy	– 7,337	Platform: Coursera Research purpose: (1) To explore the MOOCs use and learner's activities (2) Demographic characteristics of students (3) Discussion patterns	– Majority of learners were well-educated, young adults from developed countries, and had prior knowledge on the selected course
Alraimi et al. (2014)	– Quantitative: Partial Least Squares (PLS)	– No information	– 316 • Coursera: 178 • edX: 104 • Udacity: 34	– Platform: Coursera, edX, Udacity – Research purpose: (1) To identify factors that enhance an individual intention to continue using MOOCs	– Perceived reputation and openness of MOOCs were stronger predictors for learner retention than perceived usefulness and enjoyment
Hone & Said (2016)	– Quantitative: Partial Least Squares (PLS)	(1) Management Information System (MIS) (2) Software skills	(1) 256 undergraduate (2) 245 postgraduate	– Platform: various MOOCs (Coursera, FutureLearn, Khan Academy, edX) – Research purpose: To explore the factors that influence MOOC completion and retention	– It was identified that the perceived effectiveness of the MOOC course contents affected learner retention

(continued)

Table 9.6 (continued)

Reference	Methods	Subjects	Students	MOOCs platform and purpose	Major findings
Hood et al. (2015)	– Statistical analysis: Pearson correlation, t-test, factor analysis	– Introduction to data science	– 788 from 79 countries	– Platform: Coursera – Research purpose: To measure SRL in adult learners in informal learning contexts	– Learner's current contexts and learning purposes influence their SRL
Littlejohn et al. (2015)	– Statistical analysis: factor correlations – Interview with 32 students from 16 countries via Skype	– Introduction to data science	– 788 from 79 countries	– Platform: Coursera – Research purpose: To compares the narrative descriptions of behavior between learners with self-reported high and low SRL scores	– Intrinsic motivation and goals for high SRL-scored learners to develop knowledge and expertise in their workplace could lead to non-formal learning opportunities to select activities and contents according to their specific needs

activities and contents according to their specific needs. They discussed that open, flexible, and non-linear approaches, which are different from traditional learning with a linear progression, promote SRL for highly intrinsically motivated learners. They also suggested that the completion rate of MOOCs might not be the indicator of MOOC quality and value, and new forms of evaluation criteria specific to MOOCs should be developed.

Overall, from the literature review on the third integration approach, it was found that a diverse range of students has utilized MOOCs with the purpose of informal or non-formal learning. The demographic profiles and learner behaviors in MOOCs shown in some case studies may imply that well-educated and young students consider MOOCs as a complement to traditional formal learning. However, there is still uncertainty about how MOOCs can be replacing or integrated into traditional classrooms due to the characteristics of massiveness and flexibility (Marcus-Quinn & Clancy, 2015). Such flexible open learning contexts and massive learners have led to diverse teaching and learning paths and models. Furthermore, as MOOC platforms are rapidly growing around the world, the diversity of learners, learning objective, and learning behaviors are also getting expanded.

Due to such features, most research related to informal or non-formal learning through MOOCs was conducted with a case study method. Recent literature tends to deal with the completion and SRL problems in MOOCs (Marcus-Quinn & Clancy, 2015). Littlejohn et al. (2015) found that one of the important purposes, why learners utilize MOOCs, is to enjoy open and flexible learning experiences. The perceived reputation and effectiveness of MOOC contents similar to the traditional learning contexts appear to make learners complete the course and increase retention (Alraimi et al. 2014; Hone & Said, 2016). Therefore, to promote informal and non-formal learning through MOOCs, open and flexible learning experiences should be strengthened with high-quality contents.

9.3.4 *Comparison Between Integration Approaches*

Some of the previous studies compared different integration approaches. Joseph and Nath (2013) conducted a pilot study to compare formal and informal learning with MOOCs. A key difference was found in the assignment completion rate that while all participants in the formal learning group submitted at least partial assignments, only 32.5% in the informal learning group submitted partial assignments. Furthermore, 71.4% in the formal learning group accomplished the course while 7.6% in the informal learning group did. However, the number of students who received distinction was about the same: 5.7% in the formal group and 3.0% in the informal group. Gutiérrez-Santiuste, Gámiz-Sánchez, and Gutiérrez-Pérez (2015) present comparative analyzes of two integration approaches: blended learning vs. non-formal learning. First, they compared sociological, psychological, technical, and cognitive barriers that students perceived during blended learning and non-formal learning with MOOCs (see Table 9.7). It was found that the highest barrier students faced in

Table 9.7 Satisfaction and dissatisfaction factors in MOOCs (Gutiérrez-Santiuste et al., 2015)

Planning	Instructional design, choice of topics, course organization, number of participants, course duration
Community	Social character, community and group work, sharing outside the platform
Contents	Content, resources
Technical	Technical/technological situations
Participation	Level of involvement and contributions to the course

non-formal learning was technical (53%), while students in blended learning encountered four barriers at the same level, namely 32 % in technical, 28 % in sociological, 20% in psychological and cognitive. Second, they compared satisfaction and dissatisfaction levels. Data indicate that 61.8 % of students were satisfied with blended learning, especially in terms of planning (30.9%), community (16.4%), and contents (7.3 %). On the other hand, 80.1 % expressed dissatisfaction, especially in terms of planning (24.1%), evaluation (17.8%), and contents and technical (9.4%).

Kursun (2016) evaluated the effect of credit on learners' achievement, perceived intrinsic and extrinsic goal orientations, and perceived course value by comparing credit-bearing vs. non-credit-bearing students. While the study did not specifically focus on the integration of MOOCs, the results and implications from the study are meaningful in that the credit recognition is an important factor that universities should consider when integrating MOOCs into their traditional higher education contexts. The study found a statistically significant difference between two groups, indicating that credits influenced learner achievement, goal orientations, and perceived course values. The credit-bearing group showed significantly higher achievement scores, perceived goal orientation, and course values than the non-credit-bearing group.

Overall, comparative studies show that there are significant differences in student participation, engagement, motivation, goal orientation, course values, satisfaction, and barriers. Such findings from the comparison studies provide universities with insights on how to integrate MOOCs into own contexts. In particular, it is noteworthy that students encounter technical obstacles such as inadequate infrastructure, connection, and transmission due to the bandwidth problem, and poor functioning in online learning environments regardless of integration approaches. Universities need to deal with technical barriers when considering the integration of MOOCs into traditional offline learning. For instance, MOOC platforms should be user-friendly designed with interfaces and functions to facilitate smooth online learning experiences. A small unit of video lectures can be also considered to deal with bandwidth problems.

9.4 Conclusion

In this chapter, we discussed how MOOCs can be integrated in higher education, for both formal and non-formal/informal learning experiences. The development of large-scale MOOCs offered by elite institutions has propelled MOOCs into the mainstream. MOOCs represent the democratization of education, by making education more accessible to a wide range of learners. However, this chapter problematizes that little frameworks are available to unpack the complex potential of integrating MOOCs in higher education. With that, the integration framework proposed in this chapter considers learners' purpose (e.g., for earning academic credits) and course structure (e.g., online vs. F2F). In this chapter, we mainly discussed three possible integration approaches: (a) integrating MOOCs in blended learning, (b) integrating MOOCs in flipped learning, and (c) integrating MOOCs in non-formal/informal learning. We then discussed some related research for the respective integration approaches to provide better understandings about how MOOCs can be integrated into various contexts of higher education.

The review of related literature revealed some limitations in the existing research studies. First, authors tend to use terms loosely, such as using blended learning and flipped learning in an interchangeable way while there are clear differences between the two approaches. Second, we found that there are few empirical studies conducted on this topic, and many of them adopted a case study approach. Methodologically, there is a need to conduct more empirical studies that investigate the potential and challenges of integrating MOOCs in higher education settings. Third, we suggest that higher education institutions may need to take cautious steps in offering MOOCs to fee-paying students for academic credits. Given that the initial goal of MOOCs was to reach out to a wider range of learners, including learners in disadvantaged areas and conditions, the increasing trend of offering MOOCs to fee-paying students who are already in formal higher education may indicate that MOOCs are failing in the initial philosophy on "openness". Indeed, it is true that such features of "openness" and "free" have led MOOCs to vivid arguments of the sustainability issues including dropout rates and cost. To make MOOC platforms more sustainable, both higher education institutions and MOOCs providers need to consider some possibilities of pricing strategies (e.g., cross-subsidy, third-party, freemium and non-monetary) in MOOC business models (Baker & Passmore, 2016). However, MOOCs providers should also consider the balance between the original goals of MOOCs and sustainable strategies. In this respect, we believe that this chapter provides some insights concerning how MOOCs can be integrated into higher education to provide meaningful learning experiences for a wide range of learners.

References

Abdelrahman, A. M. (2016). MOOCs integration in the formal education. *International Journal for Infonomics, 9*(3), 1210–1216.
Akgül, Y. (2018). Accessibility evaluation of MOOCs' websites of turkey. *Journal of Life Economics, 5*(4), 23–36.
Alraimi, K. M., Zo, H., & Ciganek, A. P. (2014). Understanding the MOOCs continuance: The role of openness and reputation. *Computers & Education, 80,* 28–38.
Atiaja, L., & Gueerero, R. (2016). MOOCs: Origin, characterization, principal problems and challenges in higher education. *Journal of e-learning and Knowledge Society, 12*(1), 65–76.

Baker, R. M., & Passmore, D. L. (2016). Value and pricing of MOOCs. *Education Sciences, 6*, 1–11. https://doi.org/10.3390/educsci6020014.

Belanger, V., & Thornton, J. (2013). *Bioelectricity: A quantitative approach - Duke University's first MOOC* (Report). Retrieved from http://dukespace.lib.duke.edu/dspace/bitstream/handle/10161/6216/Duke_Bioelectricity_MOOC_Fall2012.pdf.

Bergmann, J., & Sams, A. (2012) *Flip your classroom: reach every student in every class every day*, ISTE, ASCD. Retrieved from http://www.ascd.org/Publications/Books/Overview/Flip-Your-Classroom.aspx.

Bergmann, J., & Sams, A. (2014). *Flipped learning: Gateway to student engagement*. International Society for Technology in Education.

Bishop, J. L., & Verleger, M. A. (2013). *The flipped classroom: A survey of the research*. 120th ASEE annual conference & exposition, June 23–26.

Bralić, A., & Divjak, B. (2016). *Use of MOOCs in traditional classroom: blended learning approach*. 9th research workshop, best of EDEN 2016 (pp. 47–58).

Bralić, A., & Divjak, B. (2017). Integrating MOOCs in traditionally taught courses: achieving learning outcomes with blended learning. *International Journal of Educational Technology in Higher Education, 15*(2), 1–16.

Brown, M. (2018). Why invest in MOOCs? Strategic institutional drivers. In D. Jansen & L. Konings (Eds.), *The 2018 OpenupEd Trend Report on MOOCs* (pp. 6–9). Maastricht, NL: EADTU. Retrieved from https://tinyurl.com/2018OpenupEdtrendreport.

Bruff, D. O., Fisher, D. H., McEwen, K. E., & Smith, B. E. (2013). Wrapping a MOOC: Student perceptions of an experiment in blended learning. *Journal of Online Learning and Teaching, 9*(2), 187–199. Retrieved from https://my.vanderbilt.edu/douglasfisher/files/2013/06/JOLTPaperFinal6-9-2013.pdf.

Bryan, A., & Volchenkova, K. N. (2016). Blended learning: Definition, models, implications for higher education. *Educational Sciences, 8*(2), 24–30.

Cha, H. J., & Park, T. J. (2019). Applying and evaluating visualization design guidelines for a MOOC dashboard to facilitate self-regulated learning based on learning analytics. *KSII Transactions on Internet and Information Systems, 13*(6), 2799–2823.

Chamberlin, L., & Parish, T. (2011). MOOCs: Massive open online courses or massive and often obtuse courses? *ELearn, 2011*(8), 1.

Cornelius, S. (2019). Understanding learner engagement on a blended course including a MOOC. *Research in Learning Technology, 27*, 1–14.

Dunn, K. (2015). The challenges of launching a MOOC and reusing that material in a blended campus class. In *Proceeding of 2015 Canadian Engineering Education Association (CEEA15) Conference* (pp. 1–8).

European Commission. (2001). Making a European area of lifelong learning a reality (Communication from the commission). Brussels, 21.11.2001. COM(2001) 678 final. Retrieved from http://eur-lex.europa.eu/LexUriServ/LexUriServ.do?uri=COM:2001:0678:FIN:EN:PDF.

Flipped Learning Network. (2014). The four pillars of FLIP. Retrieved from https://www.flippedpl.ca/uploads/2/3/9/6/23960677/flip_handout_fnl_web__1_.pdf.

Ghadiri, K., Qayoumi, M.H., Junn, E., Hsu, P., & Sujitparapitaya, S. (2013). *The transformative potential of blended learning using MIT edX's 6.002x online MOOC content combined with student team-based learning in class*. Retrieved September 03, 2019 from https://www.edx.org/sites/default/files/upload/ed-tech-paper.pdf.

Gillani, N., & Eynon, R. (2014). Communication patterns in massively open online courses. *Internet and Higher Education, 23*, 18–26.

Graham, C. R. (2006). Blended learning systems: definition, current trends, and future directions. In *Handbook of Blended Learning: Global Perspectives, Local Designs*. San Francisco, CA: Pfeiffer Publishing.

Griffiths, R., Mulhern, C., Spies, R., & Chingos, M. (2015). Adopting MOOCs on campus: A collaborative effort to test MOOCs on campuses of the university system of Maryland. *Online Learning, 19*(2).

Gutiérrez-Santiuste, E., Gámiz-Sánchez, V. M., & Gutiérrez-Pérez, J. (2015). MOOC & B-learning: Students' barriers and satisfaction in formal and non-formal learning environments. *Journal of Interactive Online Learning, 13*(3), 88–111.

Halverson, A. C., & Collins, R. (2009). *Rethinking education in the age of technology*. New York: Teachers College, Columbia University.

Hill, P. (2013). *Emerging student patterns in MOOCs: A (revised) graphical view*. Retrieved from http://mfeldstein.com/emerging-student-patterns-in-moocs-a-revised-graphical-view/.

Ho, A. D., Chuang, I., Reich, J., Coleman, C., Whitehill, J., Northcutt, C., Williams, J. J., Hansen, J., Lopez, G., & Petersen, R. (2015). *HarvardX and MITx: Two years of open online courses* (HarvardX Working Paper No. 10). https://doi.org/10.2139/ssrn.2586847.

Holotescu, C., Cretu, V.I., Grosseck, G., & Antoanela, N. (2014). *Integrating MOOCs in blended courses*. The 10th international scientific conference e-learning and software for education, Bucharest, April 24–25, 2014.

Hone, K. S., & Said, G. R. (2016). Exploring the factors affecting MOOC retention: A survey study. *Computers & Education, 98,* 157–168.

Hood, N., Littlejohn, A., & Milligan, C. (2015). Context counts: How learners' contexts influence learning in a MOOC. *Computers & Education, 91,* 83–91.

Hung, C. Y., Sun, J. C. Y., & Liu, J. Y. (2018). Effects of flipped classrooms integrated with MOOCs and game-based learning on the learning motivation and outcomes of students from different backgrounds. *Interactive Learning Environments, 27*(8), 1028–1046. https://doi.org/10.1080/10494820.2018.1481103.

Hwang, G. J., & Lai, C. L. (2017). Facilitating and bridging out-of-class and in-class learning: An interactive e-Book-based flipped learning approach for math courses. *Journal of Educational Technology & Society, 20*(1). Retrieved from https://www.j-ets.net/ets/journals/20_1/17.pdf.

Iniesto, F., McAndrew, P., Minocha, S., & Coughlan, T. (2017). What are the expectations of disabled learners when participating in a MOOC? In *L@S '17 Proceedings of the Fourth (2017) ACM Conference on Learning* (pp. 225–228). New York, NY: ACM.

Jordan, K. (2014). Initial trends in enrolment and completion of massive open online courses. *The International Review of Research in Open and Distributed Learning, 15*(1). https://doi.org/10.19173/irrodl.v15i1.1651.

Joseph, A. I. M., & Nath, B. A. (2013). *Integration of Massive Open Online Education (MOOC) system with in-classroom interaction and assessment and accreditation: An extensive report from a pilot study*. Kolkata: Department of Computer Science, St. Xavier's College (Autonomous).

Kaltencker, N., Huesig, S., Hess, T., & Dowling, M. (2013). *The disruptive potential of software as a service: validation and application of an ex-ante methodology*. Thirty-fourth international conference on information systems, Milan, Italy.

Kirschner, P. A., Sweller, J., & Clark, R. E. (2006). Why minimal guidance during instruction does not work: An analysis of the failure of constructivist, discovery, problem-based, experiential, and inquiry-based teaching. *Educational Psychologist, 41*(2), 75–86.

Kuhn, D. (2007). Is direct instruction an answer to the right question? *Educational Psychologist, 42*(2), 109–113.

Kursun, E. (2016). Does formal credit work for MOOC-like learning environments? *International Review of Research in Open and Distributed Learning, 17*(3), 77–91.

Lapworth, A. (2018). Trends towards a sustainable MOOC platform. In D. Jansen, & L. Konings (Eds.), *The 2018 OpenupEd Trend Report on MOOCs* (pp. 6–9). Maastricht, NL: EADTU. Retrieved from https://tinyurl.com/2018OpenupEdtrendreport.

Littlejohn, A., Hood, N., Milligan, C., & Mustain, P. (2015). Learning in MOOCs: motivations and self-regulated learning in MOOCs. *Internet and Higher Education, 29,* 40–48.

Littlejohn, A., & Milligan, C. (2015). Designing MOOCs for professional learners: Tools and patterns to encourage self-regulated learning. *eLearning, 42*(4), 1–10.

Marcus-Quinn, A., & Clancy, I. (2015). Learning objects in MOOC: Good practice for learning object. In M. Anabela & P. Paula (Eds.), *Furthering higher education possibilities through Massive Open Online Courses* (pp. 150–164). Hershey, PA: IGI Global.

Morris, N. P. (2014). How digital technologies, blended learning and MOOCs will impact the future of higher education. *International Conference e-Learning, 2014, 401*–404.

National Research Council. (2012). *Discipline-based education research: Understanding and improving learning in undergraduate science and education.* Washington, DC, WA: National Academies Press.

OECD (2010). *Recognition of non-formal and informal learning.* Retrieved from http://www.oecd.org/education/skills-beyond-school/recognitionofnon-formalandinformallearning-home.htm.

Perna, L. W., Ruby, A., Boruch, R. F., Wang, N., Scull, J., & Ahmad, S. (2014). Moving through MOOCs: understanding the progression of users in massive open online courses. *Educational Researcher, 43*(9), 421–432.

Sandeen, C. (2013). Integrating MOOCs into traditional higher education: The emerging "MOOC 3.0" era. *Change: The Magazine of Higher Learning, 45*(6), 34–39.

Sfiri, A., Pietkiewicz, K., & Jansen, D. (2016). *Existing MOOC initiatives in higher education and business sector and the distribution of MOOC learners in EU28.* BizMOOC Discussion Paper. Retrieved from https://bizmooc.eu/papers/initiatives/?print=print.

Sharpe, R., Benfield, G., Roberts, G., & Francis, R. (2006). *The undergraduate experience of blended e-learning: a review of UK literature and practice.* York, UK: The Higher Education Academy.

Strayer, J. F. (2012). How learning in an inverted classroom influences cooperation, innovation and task orientation. *Learning Environments Research, 15*(2), 171–193.

Thai, N. T. T., De Wever, B., & Valcke, M. (2017). The impact of a flipped classroom design on learning performance in higher education: Looking for the best "blend" of lectures and guiding questions with feedback. *Computers & Education, 107,* 113–126.

Tucker, B. (2012). *The flipped classroom: Online instruction at home frees class time for learning, Education Next,* Winter 2012. Retrieved from http://www.msuedtechsandbox.com/MAETELy2-2015/wp-content/uploads/2015/07/the_flipped_classroom_article_2.pdf.

Weller, M. (2014). *Characteristics and completion rates of distributed and centralized MOOCs project details.* MOOC Research Initiative. Retrieved from http://www.moocresearch.com/wpcontent/uploads/2014/06/C9131_WELLER_MOOC-Research-Initiative-OU.pdf.

Hyunjin Cha is an Assistant Professor in the College of Hyangseol Nanum, SoonChunHyang University in Korea. She obtained a M.Sc. in Human-Computer Interaction with Ergonomics from University College London, and a Ph.D. in Educational Technology from Hanyang University, Seoul, Korea. Her current research areas include user-friendly teaching and learning environments and User Experiences (UX) in education as well as Universal design for learning. Previously, she worked for KERIS, Korea Education and Research Information Service, an affiliated organization of ministry of education in Korea. She has conducted several research projects on ICT in Education indicators with UNESCO Institute of Statistics (UIS) and ICT for Educational Development (ICT4ED).

Hyo-Jeong So is a Full Professor in the Department of Educational Technology, Ewha Womans University in Korea. Previously, she was with Pohang University of Science and Technology (POSTECH), Korea and National Institute of Education, Nanyang Technological University, Singapore. She received her Ph.D. degree from Instructional Systems Technology, Indiana University. Her main research interests include mobile learning, Computer-Supported Collaborative Learning (CSCL), and informal learning. She is particularly interested in examining how to integrate emerging technologies for teaching and learning from collaborative knowledge building perspectives. She has conducted several research projects on emerging technologies in education funded by Microsoft, Korean National Research Foundation, and IDRC, Canada. In addition, she has published several research papers in the international journals and working paper series with UNESCO.

Open Access This chapter is licensed under the terms of the Creative Commons Attribution 4.0 International License (http://creativecommons.org/licenses/by/4.0/), which permits use, sharing, adaptation, distribution and reproduction in any medium or format, as long as you give appropriate credit to the original author(s) and the source, provide a link to the Creative Commons license and indicate if changes were made.

The images or other third party material in this chapter are included in the chapter's Creative Commons license, unless indicated otherwise in a credit line to the material. If material is not included in the chapter's Creative Commons license and your intended use is not permitted by statutory regulation or exceeds the permitted use, you will need to obtain permission directly from the copyright holder.

Chapter 10
MOOCs and OER: Developments and Contributions for Open Education and Open Science

Maria-Soledad Ramirez-Montoya

Abstract The open educational movement has provided opportunities for the advancement of higher education. This chapter is framed in the development of 12 open mass courses (MOOCs) and more than 5000 open educational resources (OER) that were produced in a macro project focused on training for energy sustainability. The MOOCs integrated innovative strategies and emerging technologies (such as gamification, challenges, biometrics, virtual reality, augmented reality, virtual and remote laboratories) and the OER were produced with scalable and accessibility properties (such as reusability, atomicity, interoperability and durability). The question that guides the chapter is: What contributions can arise from formative instances such as MOOCs and OER for open education and open science? The project method was collaborative with multidisciplinary teams of energy, production and educational innovation, who designed and implemented 12 MOOCs through the MexicoX and EdX platforms, where more than 200,000 participants enrolled in the MOOCs. Similarly, the production of more than 5000 OER is available in an open-access repository. The results show contributions to open education in the areas of open innovation, open research and open science. Findings can contribute to academic communities (students, teachers, researchers, administrators), social communities, government, business and decision makers interested in learning environments and open educational practices.

Keywords MOOC · OER · Open education · Open innovation · Open research · Open science · Energy

10.1 Introduction

Advances in communication and technology have brought new possibilities for open education. The movement toward open education requires educators to expand and update their practice to keep up with new assigned responses (Littlejohn & Hood, 2017) and to expand the perspective of services and innovation that is required to become increasingly relevant (Shivdas & Sivakumar, 2016). However, it is important to recognize that there are still many opportunities in the open educational movement, ethical ideologies are not essential components of this movement, academics are required to develop a sense of cultures of digital participation and literacy, with the integration of technologies (Veletsianos & Kimmons, 2012). The open education movement has had ups and downs due to the initial interest in transparency, openness, lack of reuse of open educational resources, but has increased its interest in open mass courses (MOOCs) (Pirkkalainen, Pawlowski and Pappa, 2017).

Open educational resources (OER) have been an important engine in the open educational movement. Atkins, Seely and Hammond (2007) highlight UNESCO's definition when it defines them as resources for teaching, learning and research that reside in the public domain or that have been released under a licensing scheme that protects intellectual property and allows its use publicly and freely or the generation of derivative works by others. OER are identified as complete courses, course materials, modules, books, video, examinations, software and any other tool, material, or technique used to support access to knowledge. In this sense, MOOCs can be a type of OER when they are available openly and with open licensing.

MOOCs have been studied by multiple authors (Baggaley, 2013; Bartolomé & Steffens, 2015; Cabero, 2015; Fidalgo-Blanco, Sein-Echaluce, & García-Peñalvo, 2016; Zheng, Chen, & Burgos, 2018) defining them as mass dissemination courses, through online platforms for the achievement of desired learning, characterized by the use of open educational resources, in which there could be not a certificate of completion of them. This educational modality has been considered as a disruptive educational innovation that allows improving current educational practices in virtual learning contexts. Among the advantages of the MOOCs, one can enunciate the interactivity among the apprentices of the course that allows to generate learning networks, as well as a socialization of the same among the participants; the promotion and publicity that educational institutions can obtain with the dissemination and reach of MOOCs; as well as the need to propose new curricula, which grant flexibility and openness to innovative educational models such as mass open courses (Sánchez-Vera, León-Urrutia, & Davis, 2015).

However, despite the high expectations of MOOCs, as innovative and revolutionary educational models; there are criticisms and challenges that they face. Among the criticisms mentioned (Castaño, Maiz, & Garay, 2015; Teixes, 2015) is the lack of a pedagogical model that supports the teaching–learning process in this new work dynamic, a pedagogical model that is flexible, with contents or quality educational resources that focus on the student as the main actor of their learning, allowing to offer a more personalized and diversified teaching–learning process, which entails, in turn, to increase the motivation and decrease in the levels of desertion of the beating. Likewise, there is a lack of evaluation processes that address the needs and development of a MOOC course; the facilitation or delivery of the course is also considered a problem, due to the overcrowding that characterizes them, that is, the complicated monitoring of the performance of the registered participants.

For this reason, it has been considered to incorporate in MOOC, innovative educational strategies that help to face the aforementioned criticisms. One of them is gamification, which can be defined as a strategy that consists of the application of playful and game resources in an educational context (Apostol, Zaharescu, & Alexe, 2013, Gallego-Durán, et al., 2014). Several authors (Brull & Finlayson, 2016; Chang & Wei, 2016; Hamari et al., 2016; Hsin, Huang, & Soman, 2013) consider that gamification is a strategy that allows contributing to the promotion of motivation and interest of MOOC participants, as well as being an effective tool to generate the necessary commitment for the completion of the course and the improvement of the learnings.

In the potential of MOOCs, there are still technologies that could contribute to the design of these training and open education. One of them is the educational platform "T-Shaped" and the use of the "Internet of Things" to improve the accessibility, scalability and merits of online education (Jeffords et al., 2014). There are also several tools to work open knowledge: open platforms for course management, online tagging, blogs, visualization technologies and open access books, online exhibitions and institutional materials (Rojeski & Morse, 2016).

In the field of open education, we can find three strategic areas: open innovation, open research and open science.

Open innovation was born as a new paradigm of innovation at the beginning of the year 2000, which is opposed to closed innovation in which innovations only emerged within companies, since this consists in the free transfer of knowledge between different actors such as universities, companies and the government. It is defined as a new innovation model which is characterized by being dynamic and based on knowledge (Chesbrough, 2012). Open innovation is based on helping companies' internal innovation through the use of knowledge inputs and outputs, using technologies, in order to expand their market and become more competitive (Gassmann, Enkel, & Chesbrough, 2010; Ramírez-Montoya, 2018; Ramírez-Montoya & García-Peñalvo, 2018). It can be said that open innovation is a new model of innovation that consists in the generation and transfer of knowledge through collaborative networks within and outside organizations, with the aim of helping to improve the products and services they offer, that are more competitive.

Open research provides potential for new discoveries and solutions to global problems, so that they automatically extend beyond the limits of an individual research laboratory. By nature, they involve and lead to collaboration among researchers. This collaboration should be established at all possible levels: institutional, national and international (Hormia-Poutanen & Forsström, 2016). Concepts such as leadership, interorganizational learning and emphasizing the values of ethics, trust, creativity, honesty or initiative are integrated, which can be as important as—or even more than—the quantitative economic concepts traditional such as efficiency or return on investment (Martin-Rubio, Nogueira, & Llach-Pages, 2013).

Open science links research with academic communication: from publications and research data, to code, models and methods, as well as quality evaluation based on open peer review. It is the movement that aims to make scientific research and the dissemination of data accessible at all levels. It implies the publication in open (open access) and the publication and reuse of the data generated in the investigations (open research data). Participating in open science and sharing publications and research data stimulates scientific work, increases its citation and impact and contributes to the advancement of science (Aleixandre-Benavent et al., 2015). However, starting to implement open science may not be so easy for all interested parties. For example, what do research funders expect in terms of open access to publications and/or research data? Where and how to publish the research data? How to ensure that the results of the research are reproducible? (Schmidt et al., 2016).

The purpose of this chapter is to present what contributions can emanate from open training practices, such as MOOCs and OER for the field of open education, within the framework of a project aimed at training in energy sustainability. The Project comes from the 266632 Bi-National Laboratory on Smart Sustainable Energy Management and Technology Training, funded by the National Council of Science and Technology (CONACYT) and by the Energy Sustainability Fund of the Secretariat of Energy of Mexico (SENER) (Fig. 10.1).

The Binational Laboratory is made up of the Tecnologico de Monterrey, the National Technological Institute of Mexico, through the National Center for Technological Research and Development (CENIDET), the National Institute of Electricity and Clean Energies (INEEL), the Arizona State University and the Berkeley Energy and Climate Institute (BECI) of the University of California at Berkeley. Within the framework of the Binational Laboratory, joint work was established with the Federal Electricity Commission (CFE), which was key to the selection of open mass courses (MOOCs), which have led to the formation of more of 200,000 participants from more than 50 countries (data from the MexicoX and EdX platforms), where the following countries stand out by number of participants: Argentina, Bolivia, Brazil, Chile, Colombia, Ecuador, Spain, the United States, Guatemala, Honduras, Mexico, the Netherlands, Paraguay, Peru, the Dominican Republic and Venezuela. Figure 10.2 shows the MOOC topics and the suggested sequence for the participants.

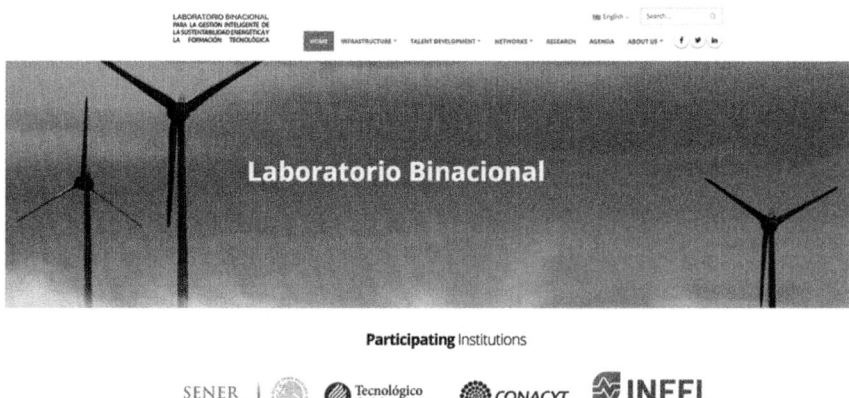

Fig. 10.1 Website portal of the project «Binational Laboratory for the Intelligent Management of Energy Sustainability and Technological Training» (https://energialab.tec.mx/en)

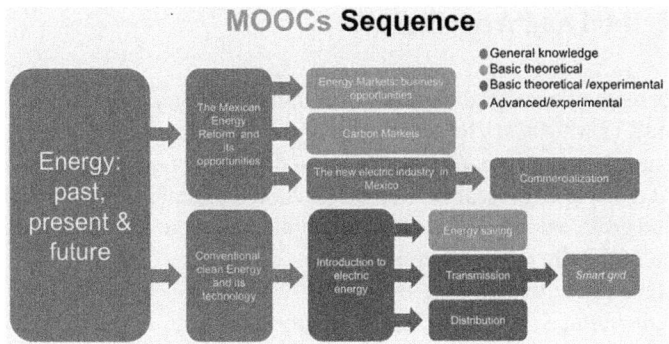

Fig. 10.2 MOOCs sequence of the binational laboratory project

Fig. 10.3 Learner's profile MOOCs

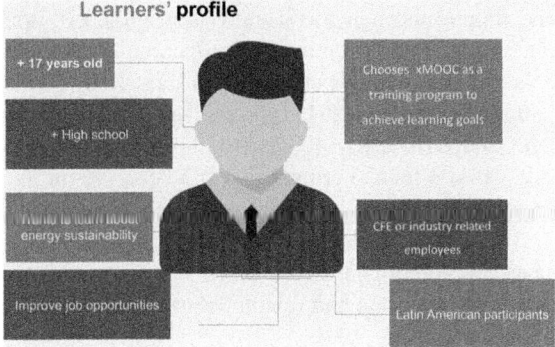

The MOOCs were designed considering a profile of participants who were interested in training programs for energy sustainability, online, older than 17 years of age and who had completed medium education (Fig. 10.3).

The question that guides the chapter is: What contributions can arise from formative instances such as MOOCs and OER for open education and open science? The method and activities are presented, how the courses were developed and linked results are analyzed open education in the areas of open innovation, open research and open science. The findings can contribute to academic communities (students, teachers, researchers, administrators), social communities, government, business and decision makers interested in learning environments and open educational practices.

10.2 Method and Activities

The project method was collaborative with multidisciplinary teams that designed and implemented 12 MOOCs. The production of the MOOCs and OER was developed through multidisciplinary teams: specialists in the areas of energy, educational technology and educational research, who have worked together in the development of MOOCs and OER, as well as in putting them into operation and educational research in each one of the formative experiences.

The collaborative work was a substantial element to achieve these designs and their implementations, where two research groups with strategic focus coordinated these actions: the Energy and Climate Change Group, the School of Engineering and Sciences and the Research and Innovation Group in Education, from the School of Humanities and Education, of Tecnologico de Monterrey. The activities were developed through four axes: experimentation with prototyping practices, discovery and linking through social innovation projects), open education (with open training instances and open innovation), collaboration (co-creation and networking) and research (analyzing open practices) (Fig. 10.4).

In its beginnings (2017), the courses were taught through the open platforms MexicoX and EdX. Currently (2019), the courses are taught only on the EdX platform. The website for the promotion of the courses on the EdX platform is presented in Fig. 10.5.

The gamification was a transversal integration in the 12 MOOCs of the project, as well as emerging technologies that had not previously been worked on in MOOCs (biometrics, virtual and remote laboratories, for example). The gamification board is reflected in Fig. 10.6.

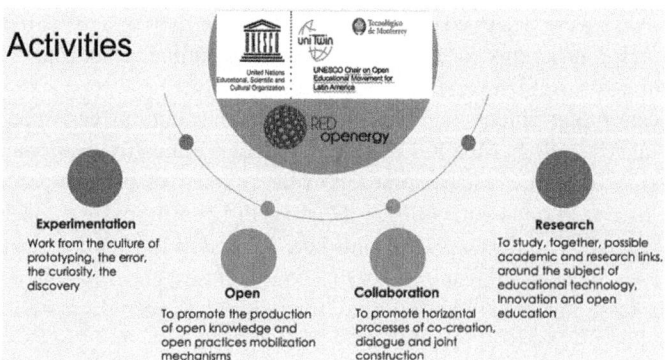

Fig. 10.4 Activities

Fig. 10.5 Promotion of MOOCs on EdX platform (https://www.edx.org/es/school/tecnologico-de-monterrey)

10.3 Results

10.3.1 Open Innovation Category

Open innovation is about ideas or solutions that present innovative applications of OER to create new opportunities or address existing challenges in open education (Open Education Consortium, 2019).

Three aspects are framed in this case: Interdisciplinary, collaborative and open innovation, in the project Energy Sustainability through MOOCs in the Latin American context. Outstanding innovation that brings a new approach to open education.

Fig. 10.6 Gamification in the MOOCs of the binational project

In the interdisciplinary, collaborative and open innovation project we work with new approaches to open education, integrating training solutions and applying OER through 12 MOOCs with innovative strategies, where we create new entrepreneurship opportunities for the challenge of energy sustainability (Molina-Gutiérrez et al., 2019).

We link the open innovation of the quad helix:

- Company (Federal Electricity Commission),
- Government (National Council of Science and Technology and Secretary of Energy of Mexico),
- Academy (Mexican institutions: Tecnologico de Monterrey, Tecnologico Nacional de Mexico, National Institute of Electricity and Clean Energies and international institutions: Arizona State University and University of California at Berkeley, as well as networks: research groups of strategic change approach Climate Change and Educational Innovation Research, Openergy Network and UNESCO Chairs/ICDE Open Educational Movement for Latin America) and
- Civil Society (more than 200,000 participants from more than 50 countries).

The objective is to support the formation of human resources specialized in energy sustainability, and develop human talent with the necessary capabilities to respond to the technological conditions prevailing in the energy value chain (Electric sector), through graduate programs, massive open online courses that will be available nationwide, and validate through competencies certification processes.

The collaborative and multidisciplinary construction was evidenced by the work of 23 members of the Energy and Climate Change Group; 36 members of the Research and Innovation in Education Group, the Openergy Network and the UNESCO-ICDE

10 MOOCs and OER: Developments and Contributions ...

Open Educational Movement for Latin America; and also 22 participants of the creative team of learning environments of the Tecnologico de Monterrey.

In educational innovation, contributions are made in the integration of new resources and strategies (biometrics, gamification, challenges, virtual and remote laboratories and open educational resources) in MOOCs (Table 10.1).

In open education, the contributions are given through training with 12 MOOCs that are implemented through the open platforms MexicoX and EdX. The MOOCs have had more than 200,000 participants, from more than 50 countries, with a terminal efficiency of 14% (exceeding the average of other MOOCs).

As a result, and contribution to open education, this project generates new approach to open innovation through the development of entrepreneurial talent and contributions to the knowledge of open educational innovation. It also generates new opportunities for products and services, such as educational innovations for environments with open technologies, services and strategies for open innovation, training models with technologies, new services for open innovation, new instruments for measuring open innovations, training services: workshops, diplomas, certificates and consultancies. With the project is contributed to open innovation through the transfer and linkage with Government, Companies, Institutions, NGOs and Civil Society (Ramírez-Montoya, 2019a).

10.3.2 Open Science Category

An open science initiative is when a practice in which different people can collaborate and contribute, where research data, lab notes and other research processes are freely and openly available. This may include public contributions through citizen science (Open Education Consortium, 2019).

The case Bi-National Laboratory on Smart Sustainable Energy Management and Technology Training emanates from two projects funded by the National Council of Science and Technology (CONACYT) of Mexico: "Bi-National Laboratory on Smart Sustainable Energy Management and Technology Training" and "Increase in the visibility of RITEC by improving the user experience and its interoperability with the National Repository".

The project highlights the excellent results of visibility and openness of science generated as a contribution of the two projects financed with public funds granted by CONACYT. These projects were aimed at supporting the national open access regulations indicated in the General Education Law and the Organic Law of CONACYT, Article 65:

> Open access means access through a digital platform and without subscription, registration or payment requirements, to research, educational, academic, scientific, technological and innovation materials, financed with public resources or that have used public infrastructure in its realization, without prejudice to the provisions on patents, protection of intellectual or industrial property, national security and copyright, among others, as well as information that, by reason of its nature or decision of the author, is confidential or reserved.

Table 10.1 Educational innovation elements

Innovation elements	Integration in MOOCs	Image in MOOCs
Gamification	• A question is presented to learners about the content they have studied • Badges are assigned to learners that solve the question based on how many opportunities and how long it took them to finish the exercise	
Virtual reality	• The use of this type of resources allows learners to interact with concepts and promotes active learning • The resources are selected on how they best support the learning experience	
Augmented reality	• The use of this type of resources allows learners to interact with concepts and promotes active learning • The resources are selected on how they best support the learning experience	
Remote lab	• Learners access the remote lab based at Tecnologico de Monterrey and complete several exercises to practice the concepts they have reviewed in the MOOC • There is a limited number or seats, so students have to make a reservation beforehand	
Biometrics	• MOOCs are delivered on MexicoX Platform, which is provided by the Mexican government • To this date the platform does not offer the use of biometrics, so this functionality will be tested using an external provider	
OER	• Anthology with OER	

The objective of the case presented here as a good practice was aimed at researchers, undergraduate and graduate students, as well as academics, business collaborators and civil society, participating in two projects, to incorporate the use of open access practices of the scientific and academic production management model of the Tecnologico de Monterrey, in order to support the open access policy of CONACYT aimed at increasing the social appropriation of scientific and technological knowledge (Ramírez-Montoya, Burgos Aguilar, González-Pérez, & Ceballos-Cancino, 2019).

The management model of scientific production generated by the academic community of Tecnologico de Monterrey, involves the production of open educational resources (OER), the selection of OER, the use of the Institutional Repository (RITEC) and the mobilization in open practices, such as mechanism to give visibility to academic and scientific production, as well as the consolidation of the digital identity of the Institution and its Researchers, aimed at strengthening the digital culture and open access to knowledge of our Institution and making it visible, in an open way, for the world.

Los OER were produced with scalable and accessibility properties (such as reusability, atomicity, interoperability and durability). The development of these OER took care of reusability (so that they could be reused in different educational contexts); interoperability (produced so that they were not limited to a single type of technological platform, but were easy to interact with and exchange with other technological uses), durability (the OER were produced under certain standards that guaranteed their documentation, classification and categorization; accessibility (so that they would guarantee their access and presentation); scalability (so that they could be part of modular components, to be expanded and serve a wide range of purposes in their use) and atomicity (with granularity so that they could be broken down into parts and thus generate educational entities by themselves that could be documented and identified).

Thus, from the scheme of open access practices, in the case presented here, we collaborated and built science with open instruments, open data, open innovation laboratories and open publications that are available in the institutional repository of the Tecnologico de Monterrey, with the open availability of more than 5000 OER. Of substantial importance was the collaboration of open networks (Openergy Network and the UNESCO Chairs/ICDE Open Educational Movement for Latin America) and the OpenergyLab laboratory. It is also important to connect with other open platforms such as OpenDOAR, La Referencia, Google, Remeri (Fig. 10.7).

As a result and contribution to open education, this project generates contributions to the open science through evidencing good practice of collaborative construction and visibility of knowledge, through more than 5000 OER available openly in the Ritec, built in the OpenergyLab, digitized postgraduate theses and OER produced in the binational laboratory. Open science was also contributed with a protocol for evaluating the user experience of a management model that involves visibility mechanisms of scientific production, thus contributing to incremental innovation with open systems to give visibility to knowledge and open science (Ramírez-Montoya, 2019b).

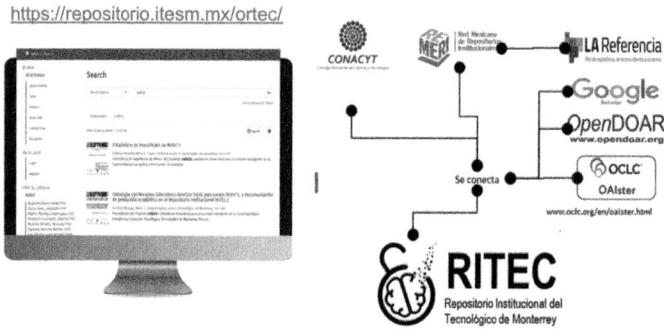

Fig. 10.7 Open science trough RITEC (https://repositorio.itesm.mx/ortec/)

10.3.3 Open Research Category

Open research is about research study or initiative about open education and/or related areas. A study or initiative that helps advance our understanding and demonstrate effectiveness related to challenges in discoverability, presentation, usability, accessibility or availability of OER (Open Education Consortium, 2019).

This open research initiative contemplates integrated studies of educational innovation in open mass courses and open repository systems. Research contributes to open education by analyzing the effectiveness of strategies, resources and learning in open environments, as well as the challenges of integrating educational innovation into technological systems, where open platforms and technologies have not yet reached their potential for accessibility, usability and availability of the OER (Ramírez-Montoya, 2019c).

The open research project: studies of educational innovation in the open movement highlights studies that are carried out by researchers, master students and students of two doctoral programs (Mexico and Spain) that participate in the Educational Innovation Research Group, in the Openergy Network and in the UNESCO/ICDE Open Educational Movement for Latin America Chairs.

The research activities are carried out in a network, with collaboration, open knowledge, experimentation and open education research. The results account for 5 graduate students of the Master's program, 3 Ph.D. graduates, 21 articles, 37 proceedings, 8 thesis and 3 books (production available in the open repository of the Tecnologico de Monterrey, link https://tiny.cc/Ritec-RedOpenergy). The focus of the research carried out revolves around the innovations of the MOOCs and the institutional repository where the knowledge generated is preserved and disseminated (Fig. 10.8).

This project contributes to open research with the development of talent, the scientific knowledge of educational innovation in open education, open publications, systematic mapping of literature and systematic reviews of literature. The knowledge generated supports the group of researchers to offer open education products

Fig. 10.8 Research mapping about project

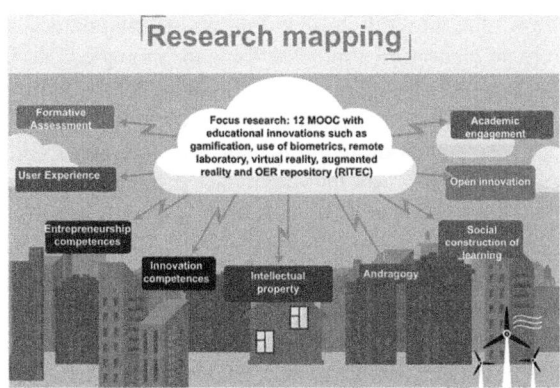

and services, such as educational innovations for open environments with technologies, services and strategies for open science, laboratory for social innovation and consultancy in educational research and open education.

The knowledge generated gives the possibility to open portfolios where knowledge is transferred, through some possibilities such as: training models with technologies, new services for open science, new instruments for measuring innovations OpenLabs, training services: workshops, diplomas, certificates and consultancies, research laboratory and open science in education and sustainable LivingLabs, among others. The transfer can be made to the sectors of the Government, the Companies, Institutions, NGOs and Society in general (Ramírez-Montoya, 2019d).

10.4 Discussion

Open innovation (which links the quadruple helix of the academic, governmental, social and economic sectors), is enriched by the integration of gamification, since it provides new opportunities for training institutions. This integration of gaming strategies promotes the motivation of the participants (Brull & Finlayson, 2016; Chang & Wei, 2016; Hamari et al., 2016; Hsin, Huang, & Soman, 2013) and institutional, national and international collaboration (Hormia-Poutanen & Forsström, 2016). The binational laboratory project was joined by the Federal Electricity Commission, the academy with several universities, civil society (with more than 200,000 participants) and the government (through funding agencies). In this way, open innovation, through MOOCs with gamification, enhances its possibilities for impact and innovation.

Emerging technologies are resources that reinforce the possibilities of open practices and the creativity of the designers is substantial to integrate them in environments where it seems that indexing is not possible. Although some authors have identified tools to work with open knowledge (Rojeski & Morse, 2016) there is still a lack of experimentation with new technologies to enrich open education. Table 10.1

shows the integration of virtual reality, augmented reality, biometrics, virtual and remote laboratories into MOOCs, technologies that had not previously been incorporated into MOOCs. Creativity and ingenuity with emerging technologies give new opportunities to establish open education practices.

Open education requires planning strategies to produce and disseminate knowledge, in such a way that its impact is transferable to different areas, beyond where they were generated. The authors agree when they state the need for dynamic and knowledge-based practices (Chesbrough, 2012) as well as the need to share publications and research data to contribute to the advancement of science (Aleixandre-Benavent et al., 2015). Figure 10.8 presents the map of collaborative research. Likewise, the project presents transference through the training of specialized talent in postgraduates and in the more than 200,000 MOOC participants, as well as in the more than 5000 OER that emanated from the MOOC pieces. Research and open science are presented as mobilizers to reach impact on society.

10.5 Conclusions

The open educational movement has an important impulse with the OER; in this impulse, it is possible to create opportunities for constructing educational practices with great reach. One of these reaches has been given through the MOOCs that can have a coverage in the formation and construction of very wide knowledge. The developments of OER and MOOC must take care of the properties of accessibility, scalability and above all of quality, both pedagogical and technological, with a view to achieving contributions of relevance to education.

The question that guided this writing was: What contributions can arise from formative instances such as MOOCs and OER for open education and open science? The results show contributions for open education in the areas:

- Open innovation (through the transfer OER and MOOCs and linkage with Government, Companies, Institutions, NGOs and Civil Society),
- Open research (with educational innovations for open environments with technologies, services and strategies for open science, laboratory for social innovation and consultancy in educational research) and
- Open science (with good practice of collaborative construction and visibility of knowledge, through more than 5000 OER available openly in the Ritec, built in the OpenergyLab, digitized postgraduate theses and OER produced in the binational laboratory, and also, contributed with a protocol for evaluating the user experience of a management model that involves visibility mechanisms of scientific production, thus contributing to incremental innovation with open systems to give visibility to knowledge and open science).

The findings can contribute to academic communities (students, teachers, researchers, administrators), social communities, government, business and decision makers interested in learning environments and open educational practices. The chapter is an invitation to continue analyzing the possibilities, impacts and challenges of integrating OER and MOOCs, as well as emerging technologies, especially in areas of the common good such as energy.

Acknowledgments We thank the multidisciplinary team that has worked on this project, their collaboration has been substantial in the transcendence of the achievements. Funding: This chapter is a product of the Project 266632 "Laboratorio Binacional para la Gestión Inteligente de la Sustentabilidad Energética y la Formación Tecnológica" ["Bi-National Laboratory on Smart Sustainable Energy Management and Technology Training"], funded by the CONACYT SENER Fund for Energy Sustainability (Agreement: S0019¬2014¬01).

Conflicts of Interest The author declares no conflict of interest.

References

Aleixandre-Benavent, R., Ferrer Sapena, A., Alonso-Arroyo, A., Vidal Infer, A., Lucas Domínguez, R., & González de Dios, J. (2015). Comunicación científica (XXVI). Cómo aumentar la difusión y el impacto de los trabajos pediátricos participando en la ciencia abierta. *Acta Pediatr Esp, 73*(8), 203–210. Retrieved from http://www.actapediatrica.com/images/pdf/Volumen-73—Numero-8—Septiembre-2015.pdf#page=33.
Apostol, S., Zaharescu, L., & Alexe, I. (2013). Gamification of learning and educational games. *Elearning & Software For Education, 2*, 67–72.
Atkins, D., Seely, J., & Hammond, A. (2007). *Report to the William and Flora Hewlett Foundation.* Retrieved from http://www.hewlett.org/oer.
Baggaley, J. (2013). MOOC rampant. *Distance Education, 34*(3), 368–378. https://doi.org/10.1080/01587919.2013.835768.
Bartolomé, A. R., & Steffens, K. (2015). ¿Son los MOOC una alternativa de aprendizaje? *Comunicar, 22*(44), 91–99. https://doi.org/10.3916/c44-2015-10.
Brull, S., & Finlayson, S. (2016). Importance of gamification in increasing learning. *The Journal of Continuing Education in Nursing, 47*(8), 372–375. https://doi.org/10.3928/0022012410160715-09.
Cabero, J. C. (2015). Visiones educativas sobre los MOOC. RIED. *Revista Iberoamericana de Educación a Distancia, 18*(2), 39–60. https://doi.org/10.5944/ried.18.2.13718.
Castaño, C., Maiz, I., & Garay, U. (2015). Diseño, motivación y rendimiento en un curso MOOC cooperativo. *Comunicar, 22*(44), 19–26. https://doi.org/10.3916/c44-2015-02.
Chang, J. W., & Wei, H. Y. (2016). Exploring engaging gamification mechanics in massive online open courses. *Journal of Educational Technology & Society, 19*(2), 177–203. Retrieved from http://www.jstor.org/stable/jeductechsoci.19.2.177.
Chesbrough, H. (2012). Open innovation: Where we've been and where we're going. *Research-Technology Management, 55*(4), 20–27. https://doi.org/10.5437/08956308x5504085.
Fidalgo-Blanco, Á., Sein-Echaluce, M. L., & García-Peñalvo, F. J. (2016). From massive access to cooperation: lessons learned and proven results of a hybrid xMOOC/cMOOC pedagogical approach to MOOCs. *International Journal of Educational Technology in Higher Education, 13*(1), 24. https://doi.org/10.1186/s41239-016-0024-z.
Gallego-Durán, F. J., Villagrá-Arnedo, C. J., Satorre Cuerda, R., Compañ, P., Molina-Carmona, R., & Llorens Largo, F. (2014). Panorámica: serious games, gamification y mucho más. *ReVisión, 7*(2), 13–23. Retrieved from http://hdl.handle.net/10045/37972.
Gassmann, O., Enkel, E., & Chesbrough, H. (2010). The future of open innovation. *R&d Management, 40*(3), 213–221. https://doi.org/10.1111/j.1467-9310.2010.00605.x.

Hamari, J., Shernoff, D. J., Rowe, E., Coller, B., Asbell-Clarke, J., & Edwards, T. (2016). Challenging games help students learn: An empirical study on engagement, flow and immersion in game-based learning. *Computers in Human Behavior, 54*, 170–179. https://doi.org/10.1016/j.chb.2015.07.045.

Hormia-Poutanen, K., & Forsström, P. L. (2016). Collaboration at International, National and Institutional Level–Vital in Fostering Open Science. *Liber Quarterly, 26*(1). Retrieved from https://www.liberquarterly.eu/articles/10.18352/lq.10157/.

Hsin, W., Huang, Y., & Soman, D. (2013). A practioner's guide to gamification of education. *Research Report Series Behavioural Economics in Action, 29*. Retrieved from https://pdfs.semanticscholar.org/c1df/e1970305f257b08a9f2b9844b346452eb869.pdf.

Jeffords, J., Kane, P., Moghaddam, Y., Rucinski, A., & Temesgen, Z. (2014). Exponentially disruptive innovation driven by service science and the Internet of Things as a Grand Challenge enabler in Education. In *2014 International Conference on Interactive Collaborative Learning (ICL)* (pp. 1021–1025). IEEE. https://doi.org/10.1109/icl.2014.7017922.

Littlejohn, A., & Hood, N. (2017). How educators build knowledge and expand their practice: The case of open education resources. *British Journal of Educational Technology, 48*(2), 499–510. https://doi.org/10.1111/bjet.12438.

Martin-Rubio, I., Nogueira, J. I., & Llach-Pages, J. (2013). Open innovation: Leadership and values. *Dyna, 88*(6), 679–684. https://doi.org/10.6036/5752.

Molina-Gutiérrez, A., Ramírez-Montoya, M. S., Mendoza Domínguez. A., Aldape, L. P., Farías, S. C., & González del Bosque, S. (2019). *Open innovation: energy sustainability training through MOOCs subproject* [Document]. Retrieved from http://hdl.handle.net/11285/633011.

Open Education Consortium (2019). Retrieved from https://www.oeconsortium.org/projects/open-education-awards-for-excellence/2019-winners-of-oe-awards/.

Pirkkalainen, H., Pawlowski, J. M., & Pappa, D. (2017). Educators' open educational collaboration online: The dilemma of emotional ownership. *Computers & Education, 106*, 119–136. https://doi.org/10.1016/j.compedu.2016.12.005.

Zheng, Q., Chen, L., & Burgos, D. (2018). Conclusions of construction and development of MOOCs in China. In *The development of MOOCs in China* (pp. 277–288). Springer, Singapore.

Ramírez-Montoya, M. S. (2018). Innovación abierta, interdisciplinaria y colaborativa para formar en sustentablidad energética a través de MOOCs e investigación educativa. *Education in the Knowledge Society (EKS), 19*, 11–30. https://doi.org/10.14201/eks20181941130. Retrieved from http://hdl.handle.net/11285/632776.

Ramírez-Montoya, M. S., & García-Peñalvo, F. J. (2018). Co-creation and open innovation: Systematic literature review. *Comunicar, 26*, 09–18. https://doi.org/10.3916/c54-2018-01. Retrieved from https://repositorio.itesm.mx/handle/11285/627964.

Ramírez-Montoya, M. S. (2019a). *Open innovation: Energy sustainability training through MOOCs subproject* [Video]. Retrieved from https://tiny.cc/OpenInnovation.

Ramírez-Montoya, M. S. (2019b). *Best practice in Open Science: The case Bi-National laboratory on smart sustainable energy management and technology training* [Video]. Retrieved from https://tiny.cc/OpenScience.

Ramírez-Montoya, M. S. (2019c). *Open Research: Studies of educational innovation in the open movement* [Document]. Retrieved from http://hdl.handle.net/11285/633012.

Ramírez-Montoya, M. S. (2019d). *Open Research: Studies of educational innovation in the open movement* [Video]. Retrieved from https://tiny.cc/OpenResearch.

Ramírez-Montoya, M. S., Burgos Aguilar, J. V., González-Pérez, L. I., & Ceballos-Cancino, H. G. (2019). *Best practice in Open Science: The case Bi-National laboratory on smart sustainable energy management and technology training* [Document]. Retrieved from http://hdl.handle.net/11285/633010.

Rojeski, M., & Morse, C. (2016). Keeping your options open: A review of open source and free technologies for instructional use in higher education. *Reference Services Review, 44*, 375–389. https://doi.org/10.1108/rsr-05-2016-0033.

Sánchez-Vera, M. M., León-Urrutia, M., & Davis, H. (2015). Desafíos en la creación, desarrollo e implementación de los MOOC: El curso de Web Science en la Universidad de Southampton. *Comunicar, 22*(44), 37–44. https://doi.org/10.3916/c44-2015-04.

Schmidt, B., Orth, A., Franck, G., Kuchma, I., Knoth, P., & Carvalho, J. (2016). Stepping up open science training for European research. *Publications, 4*(2), 16. https://doi.org/10.3390/publications4020016.

Shivdas, P. A., & Sivakumar, S. (2016). Innovation in services: A lancastrian approach to the field of e-learning. *Education and Information Technologies, 21*(6), 1913–1925. https://doi.org/10.1007/s10639-015-9427-z.

Teixes, F. (2015). *Gamificación: fundamentos y aplicaciones* (Vol. 7). España: Editorial UOC.

Veletsianos, G., & Kimmons, R. (2012). Assumptions and challenges of open scholarship. *The International Review of Research in Open and Distributed Learning, 13*(4), 166–189. https://doi.org/10.19173/irrodl.v13i4.1313.

Open Access This chapter is licensed under the terms of the Creative Commons Attribution 4.0 International License (http://creativecommons.org/licenses/by/4.0/), which permits use, sharing, adaptation, distribution and reproduction in any medium or format, as long as you give appropriate credit to the original author(s) and the source, provide a link to the Creative Commons license and indicate if changes were made.

The images or other third party material in this chapter are included in the chapter's Creative Commons license, unless indicated otherwise in a credit line to the material. If material is not included in the chapter's Creative Commons license and your intended use is not permitted by statutory regulation or exceeds the permitted use, you will need to obtain permission directly from the copyright holder.

Chapter 11
The Response of Higher Education Institutions to Global, Regional, and National Challenges

The Transformation Plan of the University of Bahrain 2016–2021 as a Case Study

Riyad Y. Hamzah

Abstract Higher education—as many other sectors—is challenged by the dynamics of the global and local socio-economic influencing our lives, economy, environment, and lifestyle. For instance, currently existing jobs and skills are expected to be replaced by super-fast artificial intelligent cloud-based employees. Traditional higher education system and institutions eagerly pursuing transformation to cope with the current and future demands in skills, teaching and learning, research, technology, funds amongst other demanding factors of our world. This paper showcase the University of Bahrain and present how the University is transforming to address the global, regional, and national challenges it is facing today. This Paper describes the key pillars and the key performance indicators of the Transformation Plan 2016–2021 of the University of Bahrain to respond to those challenges. The Transformation Plan is inspired by the Bahrain Economic Vision 2030. Furthermore, the Plan is aligned to the National Higher Education Strategy 2014–2024, and the National Research Strategy 2014–2024. The Transformation Plan also is in alignment with the national endeavors to achieve the United Nations Sustainable Development Goals 2030.

Keywords Higher education · University · Strategy · Challenges · Skills · Bahrain · GCC

11.1 Introduction

Higher Education Institutions (HEI) face numerous challenges in the 21st century as economics, environment, demographics, political, labor market, technological, as well as social and health issues, are rapidly changing. HEIs, therefore, need to be responsive to the opportunities and challenges set by these issues, which are shaping the higher education sector and the future of employment. Universities need

---

R. Y. Hamzah (✉)
University of Bahrain, Zallaq, Kingdom of Bahrain
e-mail: rhamzah@uob.edu.bh

© The Author(s) 2020
D. Burgos (ed.), *Radical Solutions and Open Science*, Lecture Notes in Educational Technology, https://doi.org/10.1007/978-981-15-4276-3_11

to have unique responses to these factors in order to maintain their competitiveness and quality of education. The competitiveness of institutes of higher education will depend upon their responsiveness to these variables of change.

The University of Bahrain, established in 1986, is the national flagship university of the Kingdom of Bahrain with an enrollment of more than twenty-eight thousand five hundred (28,500) students and over eight hundred (800) faculty members. It is comprised of nine different colleges offering ten doctoral degrees, twenty-six masters, and forty-seven bachelors programs, in addition to eight postgraduate and fourteen associate diplomas.

In 2016, the University of Bahrain launched a strategy plan designed to address the challenges of the 21st century, namely: Transformation Plan 2016–2021. The Plan was developed to incorporate the goals of the Bahrain Economic Vision 2030 (2008) of striving to develop an efficient and effective government, a robust knowledge-economy that benefits the people of the Kingdom, and a just and thriving society. It further integrates the themes of the National Higher Education Strategy 2014–2024 of enhancing the overall quality of higher education in Bahrain to:

- graduate job-ready students, professionally, and personally, and to enable them to fulfil their potential and contribute to society;
- aligning Bahrain's higher education sector to meet current and future regional and national priorities;
- improving the linkages between higher education, vocational and continuing education to provide equitable and strategic access;
- leveraging the newest trends in education technology to leap Bahrain's higher education sector;
- creating an entrepreneurship ecosystem for students in Bahrain; and
- leveraging research to enhance the overall competitiveness of Bahrain's economy.

The Plan also incorporates the objectives of the Bahrain's National Research Strategy, launched in 2014, to:

- participate in the establishment of a national research governance infrastructure;
- improve public awareness and understanding of research and innovation;
- address national research priorities, strengthen the university's research capacity; and
- strengthen the integration of the university programs with industry, international research institutions, and entities focused on Bahrain's economic and social priorities.

The Plan further is in alignment with the kingdom's endeavors to achieve the UN Sustainable Development Goals 2030 (UNESCO, 2017).

This Paper present the University of Bahrain as a case study to discuss the ways and means in which the University is addressing these challenges through its Transformation Plan. The Paper discusses the key pillars of the Plan, as well as the key performance indicators used to assess its progress towards its goals.

11.2 Transformation Plan

As new technologies emerge, universities must rethink the way learning and teaching is being conducted. Universities not only need to be reactive to the ever-changing external environment, but also become proactive pioneers to provide cutting-edge solutions addressing regional and global challenges. Today's educators must meet the needs of a new generation of learners aspiring to thrive and contribute in an increasingly interconnected complex world. This provides new challenges for academics, and demands that universities must constantly evolve and innovate to meet the changing needs of academia, employers, and millennial learners.

The traditional operations of universities are currently challenged as higher education institutions loose pace with dynamically changing demands. The rapidly-changing external environment led by technology is transforming learning, teaching, and research. Students and the wider society require year-round access to high quality programs and flexible modes of delivery. The regional economic context of the Gulf Cooperation Council (GCC) and challenges arising with the demands to develop and foster the private sector are also challenges that the University must respond to by focusing on producing a high quality and skilled human capital. Gaining international research impact is achieved by targeted and innovative approaches to research through international collaboration.

The impact of the University as the national university goes far wider than teaching and research. The graduates of the University are the number one choice of employers in Bahrain, the University is ranked in the top 500 globally for employer reputation according to the 2019 QS World University Rankings, and it has a flock of alumni who are leading nationally, regionally, and internationally.

Economic growth and community expectations drove the University of Bahrain to rethink its approach not just toward students but also to include faculty and staff members, industry, society and stakeholders in terms of brand, marketing, and international profile. The Transformation Plan aims to build a bridge to the future and provide a strategic roadmap to ensure that its graduates are sufficiently prepared and equipped to contribute to the social and economic growth of Bahrain by creating the next generation of leaders, influencers, entrepreneurs and innovators. The Transformation Plan has seven key pillars, which are as follows:

1. World-class Learning and Teaching: to transform learning and teaching philosophy to be responsive to changes in technology, labor market needs and the national and economic priorities.
2. Leading Edge Human Capital: to develop highly knowledgeable and skilled human capital by offering programs that will act as the catalyst for student success.
3. Research with National and Regional Impact: to concentrate on research that will contribute to national and regional priorities in areas such as renewable energy and water and food technologies.

4. A Dynamic, Innovative, and Entrepreneurial Environment: to become a competitive, efficient and entrepreneurial organization that thrives through developing an innovation culture through its people, policies and systems.
5. Local Engagement and International Reputation: to enhance local engagement and international reputation by becoming a driver for collaboration and partnerships.
6. Bahrain's Economic Diversification and Growth: to bridge the skills gap and place the university as the leading talent pool in the region.
7. A Transformative Environment: to transform the university to host a modern, inspiring and technology-led campus.

The Transformation Plan focuses on internationalization to: create global citizens, develop relations with industry in order to be more innovative and entrepreneurial, widen its academic specialties, promote lifelong learning, and produce research that has regional and international impact. The Plan focuses on a number of areas, including establishing a Unit for Teaching Excellence and Leadership to advance teaching methods, develop innovative pedagogy, and develop the teaching skills of faculty. Technology is employed not only to enhance learning and teaching, but also to create a smart campus populated with skilled and able professionals. Faculty and staff members alike are equipped with the critical digital skills, which has been enforced by the development of a Digital Literacy Certificate for all members.

11.3 Sustainable Development Goals and Innovation

The pressure of economic growth against failing oil prices and diminishing resources means that economies and organizations of the GCC need to be more dynamic, agile, and productive than ever before. The GCC region faces dwindling natural resources, stretched public funding, and increasing populations. The population is increasingly shifting to living in cities which consequently is putting excess strain on infrastructure of many cities. The population of the GCC has doubled over the past 20 years to reach 51 million in 2015. The GCC is one of the most highly urbanized parts of the world with 85% of its populations living in cities today, expected to rise to 90% by 2050 (PWC, 2017).

These issues are compounded by the environmental challenges that the GCC currently faces. The Middle East and North Africa (MENA) region as a whole currently faces significant environmental issues, water shortages, drought areas, air pollution, climate change, and rising energy consumption. The lack of access to sufficient clean water threatens in many ways mankind, and can lead to the spread of disease. Water scarcity and pollution threaten agriculture and food production. The Arab Forum for Environment and Development produced a report discussing these challenges to be faced by the region in the next ten years (AFED, 2017).

Considering these regional environmental issues, universities in the region need to comply with international and environmental requirements, including policies towards reducing the carbon footprint by moderating carbon emissions and energy consumption, controlling the waste generated, smarter use of air conditioning, promoting recycling as good practice, and introducing transport regulations on student and faculty car usage (endorsing public transport). Moving forward, it is critical that universities must take responsibility for their environmental footprints and aspire to integrate environmental management good practice into daily business. Higher education must aim for eco-friendly campuses by refurbishing, designing, and managing existing and future campuses.

In 2016, the University of Bahrain began to subscribe to the Green Metric ranking, ranked 307 globally in 2017 (Green Metric, 2017), in order to monitor its own progress and its key performance indicators towards becoming an environmentally friendly campus (Hamzah, Alnaser, & Alnaser, 2018).

As Bahrain's population increases, it is clear that technology is being used in the development of smart towns with energy efficient housing and roads designed to minimize traffic congestion through the use of interconnected traffic signals. The greatest potential savings are in energy consumption. Total household electricity spending in the MENA region is expected to reach approximately $250 billion by 2025. Technology such as connected thermostats and remotely controlled lighting could save around 10–15%, in addition to saving time through automated tasks.

Technology plays a significant role in innovation with the potential to address many of the regional challenges. Large investments in innovation, such as the partnership with Amazon Web Services, are testament to the growing importance of innovation on the business and national agendas of countries within the MENA region. Promptly, the University has established one of the first Amazon Academies in the region.

The rise of the Fourth Industrial Revolution has created talent mismatches, with 65% of employers and 59% of job seekers in the MENA region believing that a skills gap exists (Bayt.com, 2017). Clearly there is a disconnect between the requirements of new jobs driven by technology and the skill sets of graduates. The Fourth Industrial Revolution is disrupting the way work is being done, how public services are delivered and how economies are being shaped. We live in permanent disruption where the mantra is to innovate or become obsolete. According to the Future of Jobs and Skills in the Middle East and North Africa report, (World Economic Forum, 2017) the skills relevant in industry include complex problem solving, critical thinking, creativity, people management, coordinating with others, judgement and decision-making, service-oriented, negotiation, and cognitive flexibility. Numerous employer surveys suggest that the majority of students graduating from the education system lack these skills.

Graduates need to develop the relevant skills that allow them to compete in a competitive and dynamic job market, as one of the biggest challenges in the region is youth unemployment as a result of rapid change in labor market requirements. Universities must, therefore, revise how they operate, and investment in technology, teaching and career advice is critical to ensure skilled graduates and a productive labor market.

The Future of Jobs and Skills in the Middle East and North Africa analysis (World Economic Forum, 2017) found that, by 2020, 21% of core skills in the countries of the GCC will be different compared to skills that were needed in 2015. The report listed the top ten skills needed for 2020 and beyond. Heading this list are skills that universities do not typically prioritize, such as: problem-solving, creativity, teamwork, and people management. Therefore, a new way of delivering higher education is required, a paradigm shift.

Digital and related skills are predominately required by employers. The Transformation Plan adopts the premise that all students and teachers should have digital literacy as a minimum requirement. Teaching and learning should be repositioned to encourage inquiry-based learning and to encourage project participation. Assessment of students should focus on application of knowledge and skill development, not just passing exams. The University has responded by investing in upgrading teaching and curriculum development, in addition to re-designing student assessment, putting more emphasis on internships and industry engagement to shape learning experiences for students.

As some economic sectors shrink, others will grow, especially those powered by technology. The rise of digital labor markets will mean that graduates must not only have core digital skills but also must have entrepreneurial skills to become social marketers and have a range of communication and softs skills that sets them apart.

Universities are required to move to a multi-disciplinary approach or even transdisciplinary to allow students to explore creativity and nonlinear learning patterns that represent the digital age. Science, Technology, Engineering, and Mathematics (STEM) education is vital. In a world populated with super-fast and smart computers, however, STEM coupled with creativity can be considered as even more critical, STEAM (STEM + ARTS), the fusion of science and technology with creativity and liberal thinking.

Innovation led by technology can aid the region in addressing many of the sustainability challenges currently faced. It can enable countries to ensure that infrastructure meets the demands of society and consumers. It can potentially tighten standards on consumption, especially energy. It can help to make it easier setting up businesses and to incubate startups. Universities must not only embrace technology but also use it effectively to help create innovative solutions that will help to solve many of our sustainability issues. Here the role of technology transfer is vital. Taking academic research and using technology to commercialize is one way to deploy solutions on a wider and faster scale.

The impact of this is reflected in the 2017–18 Innovation Pillar from the World Economic Forum's Global Competitiveness Index which shows Bahrain's improvement in 7 out of 8 indicators, and driving this culture of innovation are the universities, significant improvements in innovation, capacity, quality of research institutes, and university/industry collaboration, as shown by the World Economic Forum Innovation pillar (World Economic Forum, 2018). As a result, Bahrain is emerging as a hub for Fintech entrepreneurship, powered by its skilled, labor market ready graduates, with large corporations such as Amazon Web Services and Huawei setting up their regional headquarters in Bahrain to enable them to tap into this rich dynamic potential.

The Transformation Plan has provided a real opportunity to examine the systems, architecture and infrastructure needed for universities to contribute to the economies, public services and societies of the Kingdom of Bahrain. As technology continues to change lives it is also redefining how universities can create a lasting impact with their students.

11.4 New Areas of Research and Innovation

The area of renewable energy is a critical issue for both the MENA region and globally. GCC countries have seen rapid economic diversification and have become major energy consumers in their own right. Regional electricity consumption is growing at almost 8% a year, meaning generating capacity has to be doubled every decade. Gulf countries will require 100 GW of additional power over the next 10 years to meet demand. Renewable energy offers Gulf countries a proven, home-grown path to reducing CO_2 emissions. GCC countries are in the top 14 per capita emitters of carbon dioxide in the world (PWC, 2017). Renewables offer a financially viable way to change that. Renewable energy in the Middle East is therefore offering real potential for large-scale development projects. Middle East economies are now beginning to turn to new, more sustainable means of meeting their nations' increasing consumption.

Faced with volatile oil prices and international demand, the move into alternative energies is only going to increase. As projects in the Gulf take off, demand for both investment and the best energy professionals is expected to be high, especially in solar energy, in which the region has an obvious advantage.

The University must be at the leading edge of this shift and also the drive to clean energy though research and expertise, which is extended to an array of renewable energy sources such as wind, solar, waste and geothermal.

Changes in the energy sector on a global basis, which include regulatory pressures for green generation, a push to harness energy in the most efficient way, supply constraints and the ever-growing demand by consumers for lower cost, are currently driving a rise in the development of new technologies with the ultimate aim of providing a regional and global clean energy network that is more robust and secure than ever before.

Innovative technologies such as smart meters and battery storage are becoming an everyday feature for the commercial and residential customer. From data analytics to virtual power plants, there are big changes taking place in the way energy is distributed and consumed. As the pace of change accelerates, governments, universities, and the private sector will be under pressure to spread their investment. The University, as the leading research institute in Bahrain and one of the regional leaders in the area of clean energy and water resources, has a critical role in supporting the government to achieve the national renewable and energy efficiency targets. The

University's ambition is to go beyond targets, and through sustainable partnerships, develop innovative solutions that have an impact on the environment, society, and the economy.

The key deliverables of current collaborations are:

- Capacity Building, through establishing University of Bahrain renewable energy labs, and preparing technicians and researchers.
- Research activities in the areas of energy and renewable energy, and water desalination and treatment.
- Training and workshops to disseminate the knowledge to society and those interested in the field of renewable energy from the private and public sectors.

11.5 Smart Future

One of the main components of the smart cities are the higher education institutions, and their role in human capital development and research and development to contribute to the advancement of ever smarter cities. The rise in smart cities or digital cities has been powered by certain trends, with around 68 per cent of the world's population expected to be urban residents by 2050 (UN DESA, 2018). The challenge to build more smart cities has become urgent. With the advent of digital technology and big data, changes are exponential, be it in public transportation, citizen services, or the way businesses are run.

Physical infrastructure from transportation systems to buildings, factories, and entire supply chains will sequentially be connected via the Internet. The Internet of Things means small computing devices are interweaved in the fabric of our environment. Services can be delivered through new platforms such as connected cars, smart homes, and connected public spaces, which ultimately leads to a better quality of life.

Smart cities will also require smart utilities. Sustainable energy consumption and 'green' energy production at home is becoming a new lifestyle. Today's hyperconnected consumer expects a reduced environmental footprint while still enjoying seamless services and ease of use, improving their quality of life through fully digitized processes that give them complete control over every aspect of their lives.

According to the International Data Corporation (IDC), 30 billion 'things' will be connected by 2020 (IDC, 2013). Everything from cars and appliances, to lights and temperature controls, will be connected in an interoperable network that will give consumers unprecedented control and choice over their use of their energy through the internet of things. The scale and pace of change is unrelenting. However, it's a challenge that academia must play a key part in and also move at speed to keep pace with rapid transformative change led by technology.

The University, through research, human capital developed, organizing Smart Cities Symposiums, and industry collaboration, is leading the drive for academia to understand the implications and opportunities for higher education. This can be achieved through the creation of research platforms, and extended collaborations.

Through collaborations and partnerships, the University also expects to create awareness about the future prospects of Smart Cities and serve as a platform to exchange ideas and learning through international case studies and best practice. The University is actively engaged in promoting a smarter Bahrain via its consultancy, and generating ideas and continuity, in the form of publications, and solving industry problems.

The University is preparing its graduate to work in current and future markets. Recently, the students participated in numerous local and global hackathons, competitions, projects, etc. Also in 2019, the Kingdom of Bahrain hosted Amazon Web Services Summit. The Summit included the first artificial intelligence hackathon, where 26 students from the University competed to provide solutions to real-world challenges. The focus in the participation in these kinds of competitions and hackathons is to develop digital skills for the students and improve their ability to innovate and invent.

11.6 Discussion and Conclusion

In 2016, the University of Bahrain embarked on challenging Transformation Plan. The Plan was developed to improve the impact of the University locally, regionally, and internationally. Corresponding, the University identified several key factors that will contribute to the successful implementation of the Transformation Plan, namely:

- **Transformed Governance**: in its pursue of excellence, the University need to modernized the decision-making and governance in the University. A review of its organizational structure was conducted to optimize and streamline processes.
- **Research Excellence**: the University focused not only to improve the number of publications and citation, but also on the impact of research locally, regionally, and internationally. The University established research partnership with international partners to build the national capacity in topics such as: renewable energy and water security. The result of this approach would lead to establishing the University of Bahrain as a flagship center of excellence in glocal research challenges and topics.
- **Promotion Reform**: academic promotion is linked to many aspects of institutional excellence. The University improved the planning, transparency of the process, and awareness of faculty members of the criteria. This resulted in improving the focus on individual faculty members and collectively improve the institutional output in areas related to promotion criteria.
- **Financial Sustainability**: the sustainability of the operations and services of the University is highly linked with its ability to self-generate income from a diverse set of sources. This is envisaged to gradually improve the funding projects, initiatives, activities, services, and academic programs when revenues are re-invested and systemically used.

In conclusion, the future of higher education institutions is highly linked to the socioeconomic dynamics. It is, therefore, necessary that higher education institutions develop challenging strategies that comprises objectives to support their pursuit of excellence and address the future challenges and needs of learners, labor market, society, and economy.

References

Arab Forum for Environment and Development. (2017). Arab environment in 10 years. Beirut, Lebanon. Retrieved from http://www.afedonline.org/webreport2017/afedreport2017.htm.
Bahrain Economic Vision 2030. (2008). From regional pioneer to global contender: our vision: the economic vision 2030 for Bahrain. Retrieved from https://www.bahrain.bh/wps/wcm/connect/38f53f2f-9ad6-423d-9c96-2dbf17810c94/Vision%2B2030%2BEnglish%2B%28low%2Bresolution%29.pdf?MOD=AJPERES.
Bahrain Higher Education Council. (2014a). National higher education strategy 2014–2024: putting higher education at the heart of the nation. Bahrain Higher Education Council. Retrieved from http://www.moedu.gov.bh/hec/UploadFiles/Bahrain%20Higher%20Education%20Strategy%20-%20Summary.pdf.
Bahrain Higher Education Council. (2014b). National research strategy 2014–2024: creating a smart Bahrain based on knowledge & innovation. Bahrain Higher Education Council. Retrieved from http://www.moedu.gov.bh/hec/UploadFiles/Bahrain%20National%20Research%20Strategy%20-%20Summary.pdf.
Green Metric. (2017). University rankings. Retrieved from http://greenmetric.ui.ac.id/overall-ranking-2017/.
Hamzah, R. Y., Alnaser, N. W., & Alnaser, W. E. (2018). Accelerating the transformation to a green university: University of Bahrain experience. In *E3S Web of Conferences* Vol. 48, p. 06002.
IDC. (2013). Worldwide internet of things (IoT) 2013–2020 forecast: Billions of things, trillions of dollars. (IDC #243661).
Bayt.com. (2017). Middle east skills report. Retrieved from https://www.bayt.com/en/research-report-34825/.
PWC. (2017). Middle East megatrends: transforming our region. Price Waterhouse Cooper. Retrieved from https://www.pwc.com/m1/en/issues/megatrends.html.
University of Bahrain. (2016). Bridge to the future transformation plan 2016–2021. University of Bahrain.
United Nations Department of Economic and Social Affairs (UN DESA). (2018). 68% of the world population projected to live in urban areas by 2050, says UN. Retrieved from https://www.un.org/development/desa/en/news/population/2018-revision-of-world-urbanization-prospects.html.
UNESCO. (2017). United Nation sustainable development goals (SDGs). Retrieved from https://www.un.org/sustainabledevelopment/sustainable-development-goals/.
World Economic Forum. (2017). The future of jobs and skills in the Middle East and North Africa. Switzerland. Retrieved from https://www.weforum.org/reports/the-future-of-jobs-and-skills-in-africa-preparing-the-region-for-the-fourth-industrial-revolution.
World Economic Forum. (2018). Global competitiveness report 2017–2018. Switzerland. Retrieved from http://www3.weforum.org/docs/GCR2017-2018/05FullReport/TheGlobalCompetitivenessReport2017%E2%80%932018.pdf.

Open Access This chapter is licensed under the terms of the Creative Commons Attribution 4.0 International License (http://creativecommons.org/licenses/by/4.0/), which permits use, sharing, adaptation, distribution and reproduction in any medium or format, as long as you give appropriate credit to the original author(s) and the source, provide a link to the Creative Commons license and indicate if changes were made.

The images or other third party material in this chapter are included in the chapter's Creative Commons license, unless indicated otherwise in a credit line to the material. If material is not included in the chapter's Creative Commons license and your intended use is not permitted by statutory regulation or exceeds the permitted use, you will need to obtain permission directly from the copyright holder.

Printed by Printforce, the Netherlands